WOMEN OF THE CATACOMBS

A volume in the NIU Series in

Slavic, East European, and Eurasian Studies
Edited by Christine D. Worobec

For a list of books in the series, visit our website at cornellpress.cornell.edu.

WOMEN OF THE CATACOMBS

Memoirs of the Underground
Orthodox Church in Stalin's Russia

Edited and Translated
by Wallace L. Daniel
Foreword by Roy R. Robson
Preface by Archpriest Aleksandr Men

NORTHERN ILLINOIS UNIVERSITY PRESS
AN IMPRINT OF CORNELL UNIVERSITY PRESS
Ithaca and London

Original Russian edition, *Katakomby XX veka: Vospominaniia* [Catacombs of the Twentieth Century: Memoirs]. Copyright © Fond imeni Aleksandra Menia, 2001

English-language translation, foreword, and editor's introduction copyright © 2021 by Cornell University

Illustrations courtesy of the Aleksandr Men Foundation

All rights reserved. Except for brief quotations in a review, this book, or parts thereof, must not be reproduced in any form without permission in writing from the publisher. For information, address Cornell University Press, Sage House, 512 East State Street, Ithaca, New York 14850. Visit our website at cornellpress.cornell.edu.

First published 2021 by Cornell University Press

Library of Congress Cataloging-in-Publication Data

Names: Daniel, Wallace L., editor, translator. | Robson, Roy R., writer of foreword. | Men', Aleksandr, 1935–1990, writer of preface. | Vasilevskaia, V. Ia. (Vera Iakovlevna). Katakomby XX veka.

Title: Women of the catacombs : memoirs of the underground Orthodox Church in Stalin's Russia / edited and translated by Wallace L. Daniel, foreword by Roy R. Robson, preface by Archpriest Aleksandr Men.

Description: Ithaca [New York] : Northern Illinois University Press, an imprint of Cornell University Press, 2021. | Series: NIU series in Slavic, East European, and Eurasian Studies | Translation of selections from Vera Iakovlevna Vasilevskaia's Katakomby XX veka. | Includes bibliographical references and index.

Identifiers: LCCN 2020016283 (print) | LCCN 2020016284 (ebook) | ISBN 9781501753657 (hardcover) | ISBN 9781501754401 (paperback) | ISBN 9781501754050 (ebook) | ISBN 9781501754067 (pdf)

Subjects: LCSH: Russkaia pravoslavnaia tserkov'—Soviet Union—Biography. | Christian martyrs—Soviet Union—Biography. | Persecution—Soviet Union—History. | Soviet Union—Church history.

Classification: LCC BX595 .W66 2021 (print) | LCC BX595 (ebook) | DDC 289.1092/52 [B]—dc23

LC record available at https://lccn.loc.gov/2020016283

LC ebook record available at https://lccn.loc.gov/2020016284

To my grandchildren—Sparrow, Eli, Jasper, and River—who represent the future, and to the Russian women who have kept alive memories of the catacomb church community

Contents

List of Illustrations   ix

Acknowledgments   xi

Note on Transliteration and Translation   xiii

Foreword by Roy R. Robson   xv

Editor's Introduction   xix

Original Preface to Katakomby XX veka: Vospominaniia *by* Archpriest Aleksandr Men   xxxiii

I. Fr. Serafim by Vera Iakovlevna Vasilevskaia   1

   Ante Lucem   1
   One Must Take up the Cross   11
   White Chrysanthemums   20
   The Grace of the Holy Spirit   24
   Holding on to Christ's Garments   35
   Go to Sarov   42
   In Ravaged Sarov   46
   It Will Be More Difficult   56
   The War   64
   The Last Days and the End   72

II. Fr. Pyotr Shipkov by Vera Iakovlevna Vasilevskaia   81

   In Zagorsk during the War   81
   On the End of the War. The Rebirth of the Church   86
   Fr. Pyotr in Exile (Letters)   88
   Return from Exile   91

Illness and the Final Days in the Life
of Fr. Pyotr   96
From the Letters of V. Ia. Vasilevskaia
to N. V. Trapani   99

III. My Journey by Elena Semenovna Men   101

Appendix: My Childhood and Youth
by Vera Iakovlevna Vasilevskaia   137

Notes   173

Index   199

Illustrations

1. Archimandrite Serafim (Batiukov) — xlii
2. Vera Vasilevskaia with her friend Zina in the 1920s — 3
3. The house in which Archimandrite Serafim served, in Sergiev Posad (Zagorsk) — 11
4. Icon of the Iverskaia Mother of God, before which Archimandrite Serafim prayed — 22
5. Hieromonk Ieraks (Bocharev), end of the 1920s — 32
6. Elena Tsuperfein (Men) and Vera Vasilevskaia, in the 1920s — 105
7. Elena Tsuperfein (Men), Veniamin, and Vera Vasilevskaia, September 14, 1924 — 106
8. Elena Tsuperfein (Men), beginning of the 1930s — 111
9. Elena Semenovna Men, June 27, 1938 — 119
10. Vladimir and Elena Men with their sons, 1939 — 121
11. V. S. Tsuperfein, V. Ia. Vasilevskaia, E. S. Men, A. V. Men, and Lenochka Tsuperfein, beginning of the 1950s — 133
12. Viktor Germanovich Rikman — 161
13. V. Ia. Vasilevskaia with her father, Iakov Veniaminovich, and her brother Veniamin — 164

Acknowledgments

I am grateful to Pavel Vol'fovich Men and Nataliia Fedorovna Grigorenko-Men—the brother and wife, respectively, of the deceased Orthodox priest Fr. Aleksandr Men—for permission to publish these memoirs. As a leader of the Aleksandr Men Foundation in Moscow, Pavel Vol'fovich has repeatedly made available to me the rich materials in the collection. His encouragement of my work has meant a great deal to me personally. Similarly, Nataliia Fedorovna has endeavored to keep alive the ecumenical spirit of her deceased husband. I am thankful for her support.

I owe a debt of gratitude to a great number of people, who assisted in the translation and accompanying materials of this book. I wish to thank Tanya (Mikhailova) Clark, managing editor of the *Journal of Church and State*. Ms. Clark read every page of my draft translation and worked with me in ensuring the accuracy of many difficult passages, using her native Russian language skills to capture the idiomatic expressions of Vera Vasilevskaia and Elena Men.

In addition, I thank the individuals, nearly all of them within the Orthodox tradition, who reviewed my translations of ecclesiastical terms, as well as their explanatory notes. These individuals, both in academia and in the Orthodox Church, willingly gave their time and expertise and made significant contributions to producing this book in the English language. They include Diana (Kovaleva) de Gratigny; Nataliia Illenzeer Munro; George Munro; The Rev. Fr. Theophan Buck of St. Innocent Orthodox Church; Grigorii Kliucharev of the Institute of Sociology, Russian Academy of Sciences; and Larisa Seago of the Keston Center for Religion, Politics, and Society at Baylor University. Jerome Gratigny of Mercer University provided important technological assistance.

The Keston Center and its accompanying archive contain a rich, expansive trove of original and secondary materials on the Russian Orthodox Church, the Soviet Union, and the social framework in which diverse religious groups struggled to maintain their integrity. Founded by Michael Bourdeaux in England and currently housed at Baylor University, the Keston Archive is a delightful place to do research. It has provided the background reading for my work, and I am thankful to Michael Bourdeaux for his leadership and to the archive's current staff: Tanya Clark, Janice Lozak, Larisa Seago, and the archive's director, Kathy Hillman, for making the archive's resources so readily available to me.

I am grateful to William D. Underwood, the president of Mercer University, for his support for my work. He has consistently encouraged international study and service, believing that the university must be connected to the world. I am thankful to members of the Faculty Writing Colloquium at Mercer—especially its leader, Deneen Senasi, for developing a lively, stimulating setting that I have found extremely beneficial to my work. Similarly, I thank colleagues in the Department of History for opportunities to discuss this project, and I particularly thank Robert Good for his comments on the introduction to this book. The translation and notes could not have been completed without the help of librarians at several institutions, who went out of their way to provide additional sources for this translation. I am grateful to Cecilia Williams, Janet Gillis, and Theresa Rhodes of Mercer University; Linda Daniel of Duke University; librarians at the University of North Carolina, Chapel Hill; and the late Ekaterina Iur'evna Genieva, director-general of the All-Russian Library of Foreign Literature in Moscow, who, many years ago, encouraged my work on Fr. Aleksandr Men, his family, and associates. She has remained a constant source of inspiration.

I cannot imagine a more highly skilled and committed publication staff than those at Cornell University Press. Amy Farranto, senior acquisitions editor, has believed in this book from the outset. In each stage of the writing, she has offered excellent advice, helped considerably with the book's organization, and has been a constant source of information and guidance. She is a consummate professional, with whom I have been privileged to work. I want to thank Christine Worobec, editor of the Slavic, East European, and Eurasian Series, who, several years ago, expressed interest in the women in this book and recognized their significance for the study of Russian history. The staff at Cornell University Press have been extraordinarily helpful, starting with Karen Laun and Brock Schnoke, and especially Carolyn Pouncy, who devoted careful attention to every part of the text. The anonymous readers of my original manuscript made many helpful criticisms and offered suggestions that significantly strengthened the entire presentation. I thank them.

I owe the largest debt of gratitude to my family and especially to my wife Karol Koger Daniel. In multiple ways, she has lived this book with me, tolerated my shortcomings, and encouraged me at every turn. Her steadfastness, grace, and good humor have meant more to me than I can adequately express in words.

Note on Transliteration and Translation

The following translation is from Vera Iakovlevna Vasilevskaia, *Katakomby XX veka: Vospominaniia* (Moscow: Fond imeni Aleksandra Menia, 2001). For the sake of coherence, and to keep the primary focus on the two memoirs that compose the heart of this volume, I have followed the organization of the original, with several notable exceptions. I have moved Elena Semenovna Men's memoir from the appendices and made it part 3 of the book. The memoir dealing with Vasilevskaia's childhood and youth I have inserted at the end of the volume as an appendix.

To keep the main focus on Vasilevskaia and Men, I have omitted from this translation the short reminiscences of catacomb leaders, written by five other Orthodox women, as well as additional materials (extracts from letters, court proceedings, and "Ten Songs" composed by Vera Vasilevskaia to the infant Aleksandr Men). Fr. Aleksandr Men's "Preface" concerns only Vasilevskaia's memoir, most likely because his mother's full memoir was originally included as part of the appendices.

I have used the standard Library of Congress system of transliteration throughout this book but have altered some Russian spellings of proper names. Well-known Russian surnames to an English-speaking public are given in their common spelling (for example, Tolstoi becomes Tolstoy, Dostoevskii is transliterated as Dostoevsky). In the text, Elena Men's family name is written in the English form as Men. In the case of published works in English, I have used the writer's spelling of names. In the text and notes, the names Elena Men and Aleksandr Men are used throughout, without the Russian soft sign. The exceptions are Russian language titles of books and articles, when the soft sign at the end of the family name is retained. I have used the *New Oxford Annotated Bible, with the Apocrypha*, 5th edition, for translations of biblical passages.

The writers translated here speak about their memories in the past. To maintain consistency within the text, I have used the past tense, even when the writers employ the present tense to describe earlier events. I have marked the notes in the original Russian text with the designation E. B. (editorial board), and incorporated them in the endnotes.

Foreword

Roy R. Robson

To be an Orthodox Christian in the Soviet Union of 1936 was to be an intentional Christian—also a Christian who lived in fear, sometimes hungry, often perplexed. Other Soviet citizens also felt fear, hunger, and bewilderment during the first twenty years of the Soviet experiment. What distinguished Christians from their Soviet peers also set them apart from Christians outside the Soviet Union. Always feeling vulnerable to attack by the state, Vera Iakovlevna Vasilevskaia, Elena Semenovna Men, and other Christians had to negotiate the smallest details of their Christian lives, knowing that they could be informed on, arrested, even imprisoned. This was not Christianity as a birthright, tradition, or cultural norm. Rather, this was Christianity with a clear purpose.

In her memoir, Vera Vasilevskaia often portrays her conversion to Christianity as something outside herself—a powerful force pulling her nearer to God. Readers of her memoir may disagree; we may describe her actions as a *podvig*, a spiritual feat often celebrated in the lives of Russian Orthodox saints. Growing up in a mostly secular Jewish family and working in an institute for disabled children in Moscow, it was Vasilevskaia's own decision to study Christianity and ultimately to be baptized. Along with her cousin and first cousin once removed (the future Fr. Aleksandr Men), Vasilevskaia risked estrangement from family when turning to Christianity. She courted disaster at work, where her superiors could fire her for Christian beliefs or actions. She even risked arrest simply for attending services at the little house church in Zagorsk, near the famous Trinity-Sergiev Lavra.

At that house, a church hiding in plain sight, believers endeavored to recreate the rhythms of Russian Orthodoxy in a hostile environment. Time cycled according to the specifics of the church calendar. They fasted and feasted so far as they could in the poverty of 1930s Soviet life. They celebrated long vigil ceremonies the night before a holiday, and Liturgy on the morning of the feast. Yet each of these actions was fraught, as authorities could easily interpret any religious activity as an anti-Soviet, counterrevolutionary act. "Before the beginning of the service," Vasilevskaia remembered, Fr. Serafim "sent someone out to ensure that the singing could not be heard on the street" (16). Even the arrival of a postal worker "could disturb the peace of the small house and its owner would have to hide" (57).

Elena Semenovna Men's memoir offers a more quotidian voice than her cousin. Yet her path was no less rocky than Vasilevskaia's, as the young Elena struggled with a growing passion for Christianity in a traditionally Jewish home, which added to the difficulty of being a believer in the first decades of Soviet rule. Indeed, Men provides more detailed insight than Vasilevskaia into the struggle to survive during the purges (when her husband was jailed) and during the Second World War, when she had to move from one house to the next in search of a room and food for her family. Time and again, Men saw the hand of God in her battle for survival: "On the way home, I again approached the [preserved mural of the] Crucifixion and saw a large bundle of beet leaves at the footboard of the Cross. I picked it up, clasped it in my arms, and carried it home, as a gift from Heaven" (127).

Vasilevskaia and Men's experience with Christianity departed from the norm in some important ways. They embraced Orthodoxy through a model called *starchestvo*—an emotionally intimate relationship between an elder and an acolyte. Vasilevskaia and Men both foreshadowed this path in the early pages of their memoirs, recounting trips to a resort at the former Optina Pustyn', the center of *starchestvo* in nineteenth-century Russia made famous by Dostoevsky in *The Brothers Karamazov*. *Starchestvo*—eldership—had flourished at Optina and other Russian monasteries in the late nineteenth century. In such places, a lower-ranking monk completely subjugated himself (or herself) to the advice of an elder, a spiritual discipline wherein the novice sought advice for all matters. Over time, disciples themselves might rise to the rank of elder. In a lay community such as Vasilevskaia's, however, the elder took on the role of spiritual father rather than monastic mentor. Although she lived in Moscow (about seventy-five kilometers from Zagorsk), Vasilevskaia traveled frequently to ask the advice of Fr. Serafim, her spiritual father, and receive his blessing. By following his directives, Vasilevskaia sought both spiritual freedom and health of her soul. Even at their first meeting, Vasilevskaia perceived great wisdom in the elder's words.

> Having prayed a little, Fr. Serafim asked "Why have you come to me?!" In the way he put this question, it seemed that he knew everything that had taken place with me, and at the same time he wished me to understand that I had not come here by my own will. . . . It seemed to me that the chains that had burdened me for many years had lifted. (12)

To the twenty-first-century ear, much of Fr. Serafim's advice might sound off-putting: instead of the Crimea, he told her to vacation in Sarov, home to the beloved St. Serafim Sarovskii. She was not to read poetry on vacation, as she preferred, but only to pray. She should not continue her studies and write a dissertation. And yet, rather than feeling his advice was too intrusive, Vasilevskaia believed that Fr. Serafim located her daily struggles in a broader spiritual context. While Vasilevskaia felt that she "had intuition," Fr. Serafim "had knowledge. I did not see and did not understand what was taking place in my soul, but he saw and understood everything."

As readers of this intimate memoir, we are left with a paradox that our authors never openly explore. On one hand, the authors bravely fought through every possible kind of adversity: persecution, war, poor health, self-doubt, even weather. Theirs was a heroic, intentional Christianity. Yet Vasilevskaia and Men saw life less as a spiritual feat than as a yearning for spiritual freedom through obedience and tradition, where "there is neither anxiety nor agitation, the future doesn't frighten, and for the present, I give thanks to God" (89).

Editor's Introduction

> The world without the sacred is not just disenchanted but deprived of some kind of depth—that is, of the sense that what we encounter is already part of a complex of interrelation before it is part of our world of perception.
>
> —Rowan Williams, *Dostoevsky*

The catacomb church in the Soviet Union came into existence in the late 1920s and played a significant part in Russian national life for nearly fifty years. Adherents of the Orthodox faith often referred to the catacomb church as "the light shining in the dark."[1] The memoirs presented here offer an intimate portrayal of life inside the "catacombs" of the Russian Orthodox Church from the late 1920s through the 1940s.[2] Vera Iakovlevna Vasilevskaia and Elena Semenovna Men were cousins, the latter the mother of the famous Orthodox priest Fr. Aleksandr Men. They were young women when they elected to follow their chosen pathway, and despite the obstacles, they never veered from it.

In translating their stories into English, I have attempted, as much as possible, to retain the spirit of the writers. A literal, word-for-word translation would not have been true to this spirit, nor would it have resulted in the readable, clear, and meaningful text that these writers deserve. My intent was to convey the passion, the humility, and the dedication of the writers to what the twentieth-century theologian Paul Tillich termed "the courage to be." These women were Russian Orthodox Christians and their words and the spirit in which they wrote were anchored in that tradition. Their writings exhibit the depth and beauty of this tradition, without the political distortions that later analysts often attributed to Russian Orthodoxy.

How did Russian Orthodoxy remain a viable, alternative presence in the Soviet state, when all political, educational, and cultural institutions for three-quarters of a century attempted to indoctrinate Soviet citizens with an atheistic and materialist perspective? Historians have offered multiple responses to that question. One explanation focuses on classical Russian literature, poetry, and drama, in which eternal spiritual values never lost their presence.[3] Another emphasizes the inability of Soviet ideology to provide convincing answers to the meaning of life—and death.[4] Still another pays tribute to Soviet grandmothers—those "ambassadors of the spirit"—who inculcated certain religious values in the children they nurtured.⁵ Yet there is an additional explanation for Orthodoxy's survival. It relates to the emergence and endurance of the catacombs, that segment of the Russian Orthodox Church that Western scholars have either given cursory attention to or ignored.⁶

The Historical Context

In 1921, at the end of the Civil War and their consolidation of power, the Bolsheviks faced only one national institution capable of challenging their political and moral authority. The Russian Orthodox Church represented a major holdover from the tsarist regime, but its significance went far beyond its attachment to the previous political and social order. The Orthodox Church epitomized Russia's national identity, and to millions of Russians who remained strongly devoted, the Church provided meaning to their lives. Its rituals, ceremonies, and teachings were central parts of their view of the world. In coming to power, the Bolsheviks were committed to sweeping all of this away. They aimed to develop a new society, to transform old attitudes into modern, secular ways of thought, and to replace what they deemed to be magic and superstition with scientific understanding and forward-looking ideals. In 1922, Vladimir Il'ich Lenin declared a never-ending "struggle against the governing religious obscurantism."⁷ The following text provides a brief overview of a response to that pronouncement and the violent campaign that led to the birth of the catacomb church.

Western European history contains many examples of illegal churches that refused to pledge allegiance to the state. The French Revolution offered an immediate precedent for the Church's conflict with the state in Russia. In France, Catholic priests declined to support the religious policies of the revolutionary government, which required the Church's subordination.⁸ Hostile to the revolution and resentful of the new government's attacks on church tradition, a significant segment of the Catholic clergy went into opposition and either hid or fled the country. Although Napoleon Bonaparte and subsequent French governments attempted to heal the breach with the Church, parts of the clergy never accepted the state's overtures. Their dissension provoked a political crisis that festered for more than a century and forced many of the clergy to operate solely in the private sphere.

In Russia, the first secret religious societies came into existence shortly after the October Revolution, when groups of religious believers went into opposition to the Bolsheviks' accession to power. These groups formed in response to Patriarch Tikhon's appeal to believers in January 1918, in which he pronounced an anathema on the Bolshevik government and called on archpriests and priests to create immediately "spiritual unions, which they should invite the faithful to join."[9]

In 1922, the Soviet government pursued two different strategies aimed at weakening the Orthodox Church and countering religious belief. In the spring of 1922, severe hunger enveloped much of the lower Volga territories, the Urals, Ukraine, and Kazakhstan. Already suffering from crop failures of the previous year, the ravages of the Civil War, and drought, nearly twenty-two million people fell into poverty and as many as one million people died from starvation.[10] The Central Committee of the Communist Party issued orders for churches and local people to turn over their valuables to aid the starving peasants. Many of them complied, but they resisted when it came to consecrated items used in church services.[11] The government used this occasion to solve two problems: to ransack and despoil places of worship in the search for church valuables, and to arrest and, in many cases, execute recalcitrant clergy.[12] The government's actions crippled the Church in these regions but also led to widespread resentment among local people directed at the valuables campaign and the policies promoting it.

The second strategy concerned an effort to divide the Orthodox Church from within. At precisely the same time as the seizure of valuables, a group of reformers emerged within the Church. Known collectively as Renovationists, they enjoyed the government's endorsement to challenge the Church's leadership. They represented a wide range of individuals, from self-promoting careerists to genuine idealists, but they were united by the belief that the Church needed to support the social goals of communism.[13]

In May 1922, under the pretext of the Church's resistance to the seizure of valuables and with Bolshevik backing, the Renovationists initiated a coup against the church leadership. To aid in the seizure of power, the state security police (GPU) arrested Patriarch Tikhon, charging him with counterrevolutionary activity for his protests against the government's appropriation of church valuables.[14] A Petrograd priest, Vladimir Dmitrievich Krasnitskii, was the leader of a particularly active faction among the Renovationists named the Living Church.[15] In the spring and summer of 1922, Krasnitskii and the Living Church served as willing instruments of the Soviet government, which allowed this faction of the Orthodox Church to take control of the large majority of Orthodox churches and appoint their own pastors. Clergy and laypersons who opposed these actions were arrested by the GPU. Local people, however, refused to accept these arrangements or the newly appointed pastors and refused to enter the churches staffed by them.

According to the historian Mikhail Shkarovskii, the first use of the term "catacombs," signifying opposition to the government and its policies, took place in the spring of 1922, in reaction to the valuables' campaign as well as to the Renovationists' attempt to compromise Patriarch Tikhon.[16] In protest, in several districts of the country, Orthodox priests who were dismissed from their churches held services secretly.[17] After the return of their churches, the need for secrecy came to an end, only to reappear on a much larger scale a few years later.

In 1925, Patriarch Tikhon died, leaving the Church in a severe leadership crisis. In 1927, serving as provisional head of the Church and guardian of the patriarchal throne, Metropolitan Sergii (Stragorodskii), made a fateful decision that would shape the future of the Orthodox Church for the next generation and beyond. Faced with the choice of making an alliance with Soviet power or taking the beleaguered Church underground, he chose the former. The final draft of his statement addressed to "The Clergy and Faithful of the Patriarchate of Moscow," signed on June 16/29, 1927, pledged the Church's collaboration with the Bolshevik regime in the following famous words: "We want to be Orthodox and, at the same time, to recognize the Soviet Union as our civil motherland, the joys and successes of which are our joys and our successes and the misfortunes of which are our misfortunes."[18] The Soviet government required all members of the clergy to sign the declaration of loyalty. Priests who refused lost their positions in the Church and frequently faced arrest. As the Orthodox scholar Nikita Struve has noted, Sergii's letter, promising to make the Russian Orthodox Church an "active ally of the Soviet Government," was certain to provoke an immediate controversy and induce a "new schism in the Church."[19]

In the late 1920s and the 1930s, following Metropolitan Sergii's declaration of loyalty to the Soviet government, catacomb churches emerged in large numbers. Throughout the country, from the western provinces to Siberia, an unofficial network of illegal organizations came into being around self-sacrificing priests and nuns who, in extremely meager circumstances, continued to fulfill what they believed to be a holy mission: to safeguard the sacred traditions of the Russian Orthodox Church. Facing the antireligious policies of the Soviet government, some priests, monks, and nuns refused to take the oath of allegiance the government required and went into hiding. There, concealed in the homes of Orthodox believers or in other secret locations, they tried to recreate a setting where they could carry on religious services. Normally, to avoid discovery, these settings had to be small in size and limited in the number of people who participated. Although it is difficult to establish the precise number of the catacomb organizations, the network they established continued to thrive, notwithstanding the extremely difficult challenges they confronted. They created an alternative culture not only to the Stalinist state but also to the official Orthodox Church.

Members of the catacomb church formed only a small segment of Orthodox believers in the Soviet Union. As a whole, the Orthodox Church represented a vast institution composed of many different perspectives and allegiances. In their responses to Metropolitan Sergii's declaration, the same variety characterized priests and their flock. In Iaroslavl', for example, Metropolitan Agafangel, an elderly and highly respected pastor, led a group of high-ranking priests who advocated total separation from Metropolitan Sergii. After negotiations with Sergii, they recognized his authority, but their alliance with him always remained shaky.[20] In Leningrad (St. Petersburg), Metropolitan Iosif (Petrovykh) owed his appointment to Sergii, and although Leningrad remained his diocese, the Soviet government forced him to live in the historical city of Pskov. In mid-September 1927, claiming that Metropolitan Iosif was unable to administer his Leningrad diocese, Sergii transferred him to the Black Sea port of Odessa, in Ukraine. Charging Sergii with abuse of power, Metropolitan Iosif would become the leader of his "most uncompromising opponents," and a major target of the security police.[21] In Tambov province, at the end of the 1920s and in the early 1930s, an oppositional group formed, asserting its antipathy not only to Metropolitan Sergii but to the entire Soviet order. Calling themselves True-Orthodox Christians (Istinno-pravoslavnye khristiane, IPKh) and largely composed of peasants, members of these village catacombs refused to take any part in the "sins of the godless," and they interpreted the red five-pointed star as the physical emblem of the Antichrist. By the early 1930s, the IPKh had spread throughout the southern provinces.[22]

The historian Irina Osipova is one of Russia's preeminent scholars of the catacombs. Her major book on this topic underscores the dangers and the constant threat that priests and the laity faced in trying to put their faith into practice.[23] The government kept close watch over all of these movements, and in the late 1920s, its policies toward the Church took a sharp turn. In December 1928, having gathered information from local informants, including the names of oppositional priests, the government conducted a large-scale operation against the most active priests and monks, and throughout the following year it continued the campaign. At the end of 1929, the number of condemned clergy reached more than five thousand individuals, mostly in Leningrad, Moscow, Iaroslavl', and Voronezh. In 1930, the security police targeted the followers of Metropolitan Iosif and groups of the IPKh. In Leningrad, the police had discovered a "Church-Administrative Center," led by

Metropolitan Iosif, which developed connections with bishops in Ukraine, the Black Sea region, the southern provinces, and the North Caucasus. The bishops and their associates were accused of being in opposition to Metropolitan Sergii; more than thirteen thousand priests were arrested, more than twice the number in the previous year. Beginning in the fall of 1931 until the early spring of 1932, police operations expanded even further, aimed at liquidating "branches" of opposition in the central region, around Voronezh, and in the Don River and Kuban River regions, as well as in Leningrad, Moscow, Novgorod, and Pskov. More than nineteen thousand priests were arrested, far exceeding the number of the previous year. In the seven-year period from 1928 to 1934, the police arrested 51,625 clergymen. These priests and monks, among the "most irreconcilable and firm in their faith," Osipova writes, were "rubbed out."[24]

How did the catacombs manage to survive, given the tight restrictions placed on the population by the political establishment and the security police in the late 1920s and especially the 1930s and 1940s, when most of the action in this book took place? As the reader will see, these restrictions, so often found in popular literature, were not as all-engulfing and stifling as perhaps imagined. Whole layers of activity functioned beneath the veneer of official life. The protagonists in this book constructed their own ways of being, although they remained constantly aware of the hazardous external conditions around them. They were careful neither to overstep certain political boundaries nor to assume the longevity of the catacomb community in which they participated. The priests who served this community also could take little for granted, whether they lived in the back rooms of a house on the outskirts of the city, occupied a cramped, one-room attic apartment, or worked as a bookkeeper in the city and traveled in the early morning darkness to the house where they served. It was a precarious life, and priests and participants in the catacombs often did not last long before they were arrested, but they created a lively and purposeful world, as the catacomb community in Zagorsk would bear vivid witness.

The Catacombs in Zagorsk

In the ancient city of Zagorsk (Sergiev Posad), a short distance (70 km) to the northeast of Moscow, one of the most distinctive of the *katakomby* came into being. The location is significant. It was the setting of one of Russia's greatest monasteries, the Trinity-Sergiev Lavra, one of the holiest sites in the country. The monastery was founded in 1337–1340 by St. Sergiis of Radonezh, who as a boy went with his brother into the forest, looking for an ideal place to follow a spiritual existence. They built a small chapel in honor of the Holy Trinity. Sergii played a significant role in Moscow's emergence from Tatar control and the unification of Russia under Moscow's preeminence.

The great nineteenth-century historian V. O. Kliuchevskii attributed to Sergii the reawakening of Russia's moral consciousness. During the most difficult periods in Russian history, "when the country was plunged into the deepest despair," Kliuchevskii wrote, Sergii inspired "in the people an inherent feeling of moral strength."[25] Beginning in the fifteenth century, monks in the Trinity-Sergiev Lavra considered the monastery to be under the Mother of God's protection. Icon painters portrayed Sergii as having powers of intercession with God on behalf of Russia, and a cult of Sergii developed in the minds of both the elite and commoners. In times of national danger, he represented the saint to whom Russians turned for deliverance from peril.[26]

On the outskirts of Zagorsk stood an old, unpainted, and nondescript house, its window shades generally lowered, as if to project an image that either an elderly couple lived there or the owners had gone away. The setting, too, was deliberate. The unexceptional appearance, the inhabitants hoped, would attract neither the attention of the police nor curious onlookers on the street. But inside the house, another world existed. On entering, the visitor passed through a large outer room before encountering an inner space roughly designed as the interior of a small Orthodox church. Icons covered the walls, and an altar occupied a place at the front. Beyond this space, after entering through another door, a person came upon the small living quarters of the house's occupants and the catacomb priest. This set of rooms was located at the very back, concealed as much as possible from untrustworthy company.

In this house and in another house nearby lived a priest and a nun who play a large part in this book. Both of them fostered catacomb communities that sustained many individuals through some difficult times. Both were deeply steeped in Orthodox tradition, but they also had wide interests, never turning their backs on the world and the cares of others. Both had a wonderful sense of humor, yet simultaneously displayed little tolerance for disrespectful behavior toward what they viewed as sacred. Both the priest and the nun had a significant influence on the religious upbringing of Fr. Aleksandr Men, arguably Russia's most outstanding Orthodox priest in the second half of the twentieth century.

The priest was Fr. Serafim (Sergei Mikhailovich Batiukov, 1878–1942). Born and raised in Moscow, Batiukov's early formal education did not prepare him to enter the priesthood. After receiving a technical education in Moscow's Commercial School, he worked for several years as a bookkeeper, then in the management office of a large manufacturing company in the city, and after that, in the Library of the Rumiantsev Museum. While working at these jobs, he often traveled to the famous hermitage at Optina Pustyn', where he began a long spiritual relationship with the Optina elder Nektarius (1856–1928). Increasingly, he felt his true calling was to the priesthood, and for years he read deeply in the writings of the church fathers. After he attended lectures at the Moscow Theological Academy and intensively prepared himself for his vocation, in 1919 he was consecrated by Patriarch Tikhon as a priest in the Orthodox Church.[27]

Beginning in 1920, he served in one of Moscow's most dynamic parishes, the Church of the Sacred Martyrs Cyril and John, located in the heart of the city. In 1922, he took the name of Serafim, after St. Serafim of Sarov, one of the most revered saints in the Russian Orthodox Church (1758–1833, canonized in 1903). In the same year and again in 1924, he took trips to two places that, as the reader will see, would remain deeply lodged in his memory: the Diveevo Monastery and the nearby wilderness location where St. Serafim had lived and served.[28] Although he suffered arrest in April 1925 and was imprisoned for four months, he returned to his church. Fr. Serafim never compromised his values and commitment to his calling. He refused to sign the required pledge of allegiance to the Soviet government, which led, in the summer of 1928, to his discharge from the official Church. He avoided arrest by moving from place to place and hiding from the police, before settling in Zagorsk in 1930. He was first concealed from the police in the home of Sergei Fudel' and his wife.[29] Shortly afterward, he moved into the home of Kseniia Ivanovna Grishanova, a former Diveevo nun, who hid him in a small room in the back of her house.

The nun, Mother Mariia (1879–1961), had little formal education, but she had a reputation as a devoted, outward-looking, and pragmatic servant of the Church. Like Fr. Serafim, her life took multiple turns before she arrived in Zagorsk. She became a nun at an early age and, like Fr. Serafim, was deeply influenced by the Optina Pystyn' elders, from whom she learned the importance of reaching out to the world, helping one's neighbors, and trying to alleviate human suffering. For many years, she served in a women's monastery in the Saratov region, on the right bank of the Volga River.[30] She developed a large following of people who came to her for spiritual advice and personal guidance, and some of them continued to travel to Zagorsk after she moved there. Short in stature but large in the impact she made on those who sought out her help, Mother Mariia, as a fellow nun depicted her, was a person of "deep wisdom," which she exemplified in the counsel she willingly gave to people in need.³¹ She was "full of humor, of life, of the humor of the common people, rich and robust."³²

After the death of Fr. Serafim in 1942, Mother Mariia became the spiritual guide of the young Aleksandr Men, and she had, by his own testimony, a formative influence on him. Her method of teaching and approach to Christianity mirrored those of the elders of the Optina Pustyn' Monastery. She neither forced the young Aleksandr Men to learn nor required him to attend religious services, but instead spoke to his imagination and his sense of wonder. In the persons of Mother Mariia and Fr. Serafim, Men encountered the "living continuation" of the dialogue with the world that characterized the elders at Optina Pustyn'.³³ Even after its closure by the Soviet government in 1924 and the death of its elders, the influence of Optina Pustyn' transcended the monastery's official termination. It remained alive in the catacomb church in Zagorsk.

The Optina Pustyn' Monastery occupied a unique place in the history of Russia. The monastery was founded in the sixteenth century, near the central Russian town of Kozel'sk. The name of *Pustynia*, or desert, refers to the desert communities, "places of silence," where monasticism originated.³⁴ But at Optina Pustyn', in addition to contemplation, the elders there reached out to the world. Under the guidance of several remarkable leaders, beginning with the elder Leonid (Nagolkin, 1768–1841) and continuing under Fr. Makarii (1788–1860), who served as director from 1836 to 1860, the monastery moved away from its patronage by the court and focus on the elite and developed a new model of monastic life that looked out on society as a whole. The monastery operated outside the Church's institutional framework and became renowned for relating to people on a personal level.³⁵

Under Fr. Makarii and especially under his successor, Fr. Amvrosii (1812–1891), Optina Pustyn' developed a network of devoted followers. Fr. Amvrosii had an outstanding ability to relate to people and to see into their inner being, listen to their problems, and offer them counsel, whether they were a poor student, an uneducated peasant, or a government official. All people were equal, and all required the best spiritual assistance that he could provide. Some of Russia's most renowned cultural figures of the nineteenth century traveled to Optina Pustyn' to seek out these elders, including Pyotr Kireevskii, Nikolai Gogol, Ivan Turgenev, Pyotr Tchaikovsky, Fedor Dostoevsky, Leo Tolstoy, and Vladimir Solov'ev. Fr. Amvrosii spent most of each day talking with people. The Optina Pustyn' elders provided a bridge over the deep cultural divide separating the Church from Russian society.³⁶

Elders occupied a unique position within Russian Orthodoxy. They could be either monks or priests, and as Irina Paert has shown in her important study, their status did not arise from within the institutional church but "from below," from disciples who found in them wisdom and special guidance for their lives.[37] Elders first emerged in the ascetic communities of early Christianity and in Russia in the thirteenth and fourteenth centuries, but their widespread reputation came much later. They did not comprise a uniform group; some followed an ascetic life. At Optina Pustyn', they were known as "healers of the spirit," who "helped people with kind advice" and whose spiritual wisdom enabled them to transform their lives.[38] Elders played an especially important role in times marked by the closure of churches and when the state attempted to superimpose its ideology over the entire society.[39]

In Optina Pustyn', the elders demonstrated an all-embracing love of humanity and a compassion for every person they encountered. *The Brothers Karamazov* brilliantly portrays the distinctive form of Orthodoxy the elders practiced, and through the life of Father Zosima in the novel, Dostoevsky brought to it widespread popular attention. In 1878, soon after the death of his three-year old son Alexei (Alyosha), Dostoevsky and Vladimir Solov'ev traveled to the monastery, where the former had several meetings with Elder Amvrosii. As Dostoevsky's wife, Anna, recounted, the trip made a profound impression on him, resulting in the images of the monastery he conveyed in his novel.[40] Although Dostoevsky normally did not base the characters in his novel on any one individual, the theology of the Optina elders was imprinted on several parts of the story: in the love for all of creation; in the icon hidden in every human being, whose task it was to uncover it; in the importance of self-discovery; and the need for reconciliation between all segments of the world.[41]

In his study of the great writer, Rowan Williams writes, "The basic polarity in Dostoevsky's moral world is not between good people and bad people but between those who acknowledge their iconic dimension and those who struggle to resist and extinguish it."[42] At Optina Pustyn', the elder's central role was to help the individual discover this iconic dimension and, putting aside one's own selfish desires, find the road a person should follow. "There is no higher virtue," according to Amvrosii, "than love and no worse vice and passion than hatred."[43] This hatred and division between human beings, this exaltation of the self above other human beings, had become main features of the modern world, whose dangers Dostoevsky explored in the chapter "The Mysterious Visitor."[44] The Orthodox tradition that Fr. Serafim later upheld in the catacomb church in Zagorsk emphasized this need for unity, for brotherhood, and for seeing all human beings, as well as the earth, as interconnected parts of a single organism.

It was this belief in the organic unity of creation that Fr. Serafim, Mother Mariia, and others who served in the catacomb church in Zagorsk passed on from the Optina elders to their spiritual children. It was a conviction that lay at the core of their teachings. They rejected the view that the world had to be interpreted through narrow, rigid categories; they did not see Christianity as an ideology. In their thoughts and actions, they remained open to all kinds of possibilities. They were never authoritarian in dealing with participants in their community, and although "obedience" was a vital part of Mother Mariia's requirements of the women who lived with her, she was neither harsh nor tyrannical. The generosity exhibited at Optina Pustyn', the welcoming attitudes to visitors, and the interest elders displayed toward all kinds of subjects characterized the catacomb church in Zagorsk. Despite the dangerous conditions under which Fr. Serafim and the others lived, their humility, compassion toward people in need, and lack of hypocrisy and bigotry distinguished these servitors of the catacomb church and deeply influenced the perspectives of their followers.[45]

In one other significant way, the catacomb leaders in Zagorsk transmitted to their community the theological lessons of the Optina elders. At Optina Pystyn', the elders did not view creation as completed, fixed, and, therefore, immutable. They viewed the Divine Creator as being in continual dialogue with the world.[46] Recalling Fr. Serafim and Mother Mariia, Fr. Aleksandr Men saw them as a "living continuation of that dialogue," which he considered one of the defining themes of Orthodox Christianity.[47] Dialogue with other opposing views contributed to the overcoming of violence and offered the potential for mutual understanding. Moreover, dialogue with different faiths and traditions offered a pathway to reconciliation and to finding the connections that united all human beings. By opening itself up to diverse points of view, dialogue expanded the Church's capacity for imagination and wonder. Key elements of Fr. Aleksandr's worldview originated in the teachings of the catacomb church in Zagorsk.

The Authors and Their Purposes

On the surface, Vera Iakovlevna Vasilevskaia and Elena Semenovna Men were very different people. Vasilevskaia was born in 1902 (d. 1975) in Moscow and lived all her life in Russia's capital city, the daughter of a military family whose forebears had long ago settled in the city. She had reached adolescence at the time of the Russian Revolution and the beginning of the Bolshevik political order. Born in 1908 (d. 1978), Men, whose maiden name was Elena Tsuperfein, spent her early years in Switzerland, where she was born, the daughter of parents who had gone abroad to study chemistry at the University of Bern. In 1914, the family returned home to Khar'kov for a visit, when the First World War interrupted their lives and their plans; they would not leave Russia again. Still a child at the time of the revolution, Men's formative experiences would be much different from Vasilevskaia's.

The two women had dissimilar family circumstances, education, and temperament. Yet despite their differences, they had important similarities. They were cousins and shared the same Jewish family heritage. Both were tender people, sympathetic to the needs of others, and open-spirited in demeanor. Their theological views of the world did not consist of abstractions but beliefs that they incorporated into their lives. Fr. Viktor Grigorenko, the nephew of Fr. Aleksandr Men's wife, Nataliia Fedorovna Grigorenko, knew both women. As a child, Fr. Viktor and his brother Misha lived for some time in Elena Men's apartment in Moscow. He vividly recalls how she took care of them during some difficult times. He remembers her reading a great deal, how she constantly tried to expand her knowledge, and how prayer, too, formed an essential part of her daily activities.[48]

He knew Vasilevskaia less well, although she often visited her cousin's home. He and his brother called her "Grandmother Vera." Like her cousin, she directed a lot of their attention outward to other people, particularly those in need. "They would gather the last things they had and share it with people who had little. They sent many of their belongings to those in exile. They constantly helped others, and he attributed these qualities to the teachings of the catacomb church."[49]

Pavel Vol'fovich Men, the younger brother of Fr. Aleksandr Men, remembers Vera Vasilevskaia, whom he called "Auntie," as a highly cultured person who "opened the door for Aleksandr into the world of philosophy and culture."[50] He remembers her as an extremely reserved person, as someone "difficult to talk to," but who, nevertheless, was "an incredibly kind person." She lived in an apartment of only nine meters, yet after the war she "took in this old woman, who was destitute, had lost her flat, and had nowhere to go. The woman, Mariia Markova, was a stranger, but "Auntie took her in as one of her own."[51]

Pavel Men speaks extremely warmly of his mother, Elena Men. Despite the difficult conditions they faced, especially during the war, she never lost hope. "It was miserable in those days," he said, "and Mother sometimes had to exchange clothes and other stuff for a piece of bread or a potato, and both my mother and aunt worked hard to help us stay alive."[52] The hope, confidence, and capacity to endure in times of hardship Elena Men instilled in her children.

Vera Iakovlevna began writing her story in 1939 and worked on it for the next two decades, completing it in 1959. The precise dates of Elena Men's "Moi put'" (My Journey) are uncertain, but it is likely that she wrote the large part of it during the same years.

The Catacombs adheres to several large themes. The first is biographical and deals with the particular circumstances in the life of Fr. Serafim. This first part of the book is rich in its concrete details about Fr. Serafim's personhood, activities, and, most of all, relationships with his parishioners. Fr. Serafim served in Zagorsk during an extremely turbulent period: Stalin's terror, the assault on the clergy, and the coming of the Second World War. He presents a different picture from the stereotype found in much of the literature about the typical Orthodox priest's personal distance from parishioners. Deeply involved in the lives of people gathered around him, he was invariably encouraging and warm-spirited in relationships with them.

Vasilevskaia's story includes discussions of two other catacomb priests, both of whom had distinguished church service before their refusal to pledge loyalty to the Soviet government. Fr. Pyotr Shipkov became Vasilevskaia's spiritual father after Fr. Serafim's death; with German troops near Zagorsk and threatening the city's survival, he played an extraordinary role in the lives of both Vasilevskaia and Men. The second priest, Fr. Ieraks (Bocharev), became Vasilevskaia's spiritual father following the arrest of Fr. Pyotr.

But this book is about more than the Church. A second theme concerns the stories of Vera Vasilevskaia and Elena Men, who seamlessly weave their own journeys into the framework of a community that functioned apart from the state in the Stalin era. In the process, they offer a larger view of the catacomb community—its personalities, circumstances, and activities—than we have previously had. Living in tumultuous times, politically and socially, the two women searched for a solid anchor that would give them hope and a sense of well-being. They were not compliant persons who bent with the prevailing political winds. In different ways, each was a rebel. The women struggled against the social norms of their times and looked for their own meaning, which they found in the natural world, in poetry, in their work, and eventually in Orthodoxy.

The personal accounts of Vasilevskaia and Men stand in contrast to the views found in many Soviet autobiographies. These autobiographies, emanating from the Stalin years, reveal an attempt to align one's own inner thoughts with the goals of the Soviet state.[53] Aligning oneself with the goals of the state allowed a person to overcome fear. Vasilevskaia and Men did not follow this pathway but rather moved in an opposite direction. They did not suppress their inner feelings but revealed them openly. They made little effort to coordinate their personal desires with external aims and objectives; they directed much of their attention toward the discovery of their own internal calling, a quest that gives their stories a distinctive quality.

The third theme of the book concerns the larger political, social, and religious setting in which the protagonists lived. The reader gets a more intimate picture of the political and social framework of the early twentieth century and later Stalinist times than found in many textbook accounts. Here the descriptions and analyses are intensely personal and evocative. Vasilevskaia and Men offer descriptions of the school system in late tsarist Russia and later, in the 1920s, of educational practices, their classmates, and their teachers, some of whom had a lifelong influence. The writings of both women are transparent about their struggles. They give the reader a firsthand view of family life, society, and religious quest in Russia during the revolutionary years, the 1920s, the Second World War, and the late 1940s.

As Fr. Aleksandr Men noted in his preface, Vera Vasilevskaia and Elena Men never intended their stories to be published officially. They wrote for the "desk drawer," with the intention of keeping a personal record, recording their experiences with catacomb priests and the community, most likely thinking that, at some future point, their accounts would be circulated among Orthodox believers. They aimed to provide testimony to the ideals the leaders of the catacomb church preserved, hoping to keep these ideals alive in the face of severe political repression. Writing about the late 1920s, 1930s, and 1940s, the decades when they were most active, these women understood they not only served the present but safeguarded Orthodox beliefs and values for the future. As one of the members of the catacombs wrote, citing former Patriarch Tikhon, "He said that the person who understands, who knows the Truth, must stand in opposition, because what is unique to us is the capacity to witness to the Truth."[54] The lives of Vera Vasilevskaia and Elena Men illustrated this way of living.

Original Preface to *Katakomby XX veka: Vospominaniia*

Archpriest Aleksandr Men

"The Catacomb Church" ... One often encounters mention of it in the pages devoted to the new history of Russian Orthodoxy. Most often, these citations do not exceed two-three words or conjectures. This is not surprising, since there does not exist a complete collection of documents and eyewitness accounts, even about those phenomena and events in the life of the Church during this period, which took place in plain view of everyone. It is even more difficult to collect information about that which, by its very name, tells the story about the existence of "the underground church."

Several accounts deny the reality of the "catacomb church," while others disseminate extremely inauthentic information about it. Did it exist in reality, and if so, what was it like? In order to answer these questions, it is necessary briefly to touch on the history of the church division, which emerged in the period between the two world wars.

Since the seventeenth century, the epoch of the Old Believers' schism, the Church in Russia hardly lived through such a stormy period, full of dramatic events, as it did in the first half of our century. The prerevolutionary years of the twentieth century were not peaceful, and attempts were made to free the Church from the guardianship of the government. Although a sizable part of the clergy and laypeople was accustomed to the existing (synodal) situation, more and more persistently voices were raised, calling for the renaissance and renovation of church life. Desperately waiting for change, many priests developed very radical views, and some came out almost as "leftists."[55]

The appeal to the Orthodox Church of leading representatives of the intelligentsia (S. Bulgakov, N. Berdiaev, P. Florenskii, S. Frank, V. Ern, V. Sventsitskii, and many others) contributed to the enlivening of discussion about troubling questions, related, in part, to reexamining the relationship of the Church to the government and to social life.

Because of the government's opposition, an All-Russian Sobor that aspired to become the voice of the Church and define its future road could not meet before the revolution.[56] Therefore, the Sobor could open only in 1917, after the collapse of the monarchy, when the country had already entered a period of war and revolution. The resolutions of the Sobor were not realized in practice. A new epoch of Russian history had begun.

The October events of 1917 immediately brought the Church into conflict with the new Bolshevik government. This happened for two reasons. On one hand, a significant part of the church leadership, still closely connected with the former governing structure, was not prepared for such a transformation. On the other hand, the government openly proclaimed its goal to eradicate completely "religious prejudices." In the very first year of the revolution, the Bolsheviks created a plan to close all churches and forbid the sacrament of the Eucharist. Although the government did not carry out this plan in full, the onslaught rained down on the Church and exceeded in its power everything that history had known from the time of the Roman emperors and the French Revolution. Elected by the Sobor, Patriarch Tikhon, who courageously defended the Church, was arrested in 1922, and shortly thereafter the so-called Renovationist Schism took place.[57] Its initiators, promising believers to introduce long-awaited church reforms, had as its main objective to place the church in the same relationship to the government that had existed before the revolution.[58]

The Renovationist movement's "sobor" passed a series of fairly unsuccessful and inopportune innovations, but its main goal entailed the proclamation of its political platform. Among other things, the documents of the "sobor" declared capitalism a mortal sin but revolution—an accomplishment of evangelical desires.[59]

Having the support and assistance of the government organs, the unauthorized Higher Ecclesiastical Administration (VTsU) seized the majority of churches, both in large cities and in the provinces. Nevertheless, public recognition of the so-called Living Church was not achieved. After Patriarch Tikhon was released from prison—which came about through the pressure of world public opinion—those church leaders who remained loyal to the patriarch rallied once again. This created confusion in the ranks of the Renovationists. Furthermore, a struggle between different factions began to tear their movement apart. Each day, the relationship of many believers to "the Red Church" (the Renovationists) became all the more suspicious and hostile.

After his release from prison, Patriarch Tikhon tried to make peace with the government but without making any compromises that might undermine church life. His death in 1925, however, awakened in the governing authorities hope that a compromise with the Church finally could be reached. But the church leaders appointed by the patriarch resolutely continued his line. As a result, the office of patriarch remained vacant for a long time.[60]

In the West, at the end of the 1920s, a broad campaign developed for the defense of Christianity in Russia, which was given the name of "spiritual crusade" (*dukhovnyi krestovyi pokhod*). The campaign offered a response to mass repressions, which a majority of our bishops and a large number of priests and active laypeople who had remained loyal to Patriarch Tikhon had suffered. Churches and monasteries were being closed; even, earlier, religious schools were shut down; many thousands of religious believers—priests, monks, laypeople, both men and women—filled prisons, labor camps, and distant places of exile. The persecutions were officially masked (truthfully, not especially carefully) under the slogan "the struggle with counterrevolution."

During this time, Metropolitan Sergii (Stragorodskii), fulfilling his responsibilities as keeper of the patriarchal seat (*mestobliustitel'*, patriarchal *locum tenens*, interim patriarch) spoke out, both in a declaration and interview, in which, for tactical reasons, he denied the existence of religious oppression in Russia.[61]

Wanting to secure the "legalization" of the Church within the framework of the Soviet order, he made a series of concessions, making possible control over the life of the Church.[62] These concessions met with a negative response from many of his colleagues and laypeople. Soviet historians acknowledge that Metropolitan Sergii attempted to "gain the initiative" from the Renovationists, having made the patriarchal Church completely loyal [to the Soviet government].[63]

Opponents of the metropolitan's course of action maintained that his action did not help the Church, because the governing power did not change its principal relationship to the Orthodox faith, and by no means did the government intend to become reconciled with the existence of the Church. At most, what the government (temporarily) could agree upon was the creation of an obedient marionette hierarchy, which would lead believers until the government could completely eradicate the influence of religion in the country. Supporters of the "Sergievskaia line" in the Church argued that, in the present complex situation, the path of compromise was the only possibility. Leaders of the Moscow patriarchate have maintained this point of view to the present.[64]

Not enough time has passed yet for an objective historical evaluation of the affair of Metropolitan Sergii, who became patriarch in 1943.[65] It should be recognized, however, that he and his successors managed to ascend above the Renovationists and achieve an elementary stabilization in the Church's situation in the country.

The Second World War played an enormous role in the transformation of the Church's status, during which the patriarchate (as did also the

Renovationists) took a patriotic position. Stalin valued the role of the Church as a means of strengthening the people's spirit, and he showed sympathy for it. Between the two courses, he preferred the Sergievskaia line as more traditional, corresponding more than the other one to the perspectives of believers and corresponding more also to his own great power tastes.[66] He liquidated the Renovationists and, in 1945, decided to summon the Church Sobor to elect a patriarch. With his agreement, thousands of churches were opened, and religious schools were revived. In many believers, hopes were then awakened that the time of oppression had passed. Further events, however, revealed that small concessions coming from the government were followed with large concessions required from the church hierarchy; sometimes concessions made to the Church bore no results. This became especially clear during the Khrushchev period, when, in spite of the well-known loosening of social life, the government subjected the Church to new pressures (the mass closing of churches and religious schools and the strengthening of antireligious propaganda began again).[67]

But let us return to the 1920s. A series of representatives of the bishops and clergy, disagreeing with the policy of Metropolitan Sergii, did not follow him. Referring to the permission granted them by Patriarch Tikhon, in time of need, to form temporary independent associations (*avtokefalii*) of bishops,[68] many of them formed independent groups (mainly in Moscow and Leningrad). From the point of view of the government, these independent groups represented a dangerous church opposition. The majority of unruly hierarchs were arrested, but from exile and from the camps, they continued to lead their priests and "flock." Those who remained in freedom went into an illegal status and secretly celebrated the liturgy in private homes. Thus emerged the phenomenon subsequently given the name "Catacomb Church."[69]

In the Moscow region (*oblast'*), to the Catacomb Church belonged Archimandrite Serafim (Batiukov); Fr. Pyotr Shipkov,[70] who in the past had served as secretary to Patriarch Tikhon; Ieromonakh Ieraks (Bocharev);[71] the priests Vladimir Bogdanov, Vladimir Krivolutskii,[72] Konstantin Vsekhsviatskii, Aleksei Gabriianik,[73] and Dmitrii Kriuchkov;[74] and others. The majority of them considered Bishop Afanasii (Sakharov) as their bishop.[75] In 1945, the Catacomb Church de facto ceased its existence. On one hand, the government hunted down and arrested almost all members of the priesthood; on the other hand, after the Sobor in 1943 and the election of Patriarch Aleksii, Bishop Afanasii distributed a letter to believers, in which he acknowledged the legality of the new first priest (the patriarch) and called for unity with the patriarchal Church. According to some undocumented rumors, in the deep provinces, separate individuals and even groups still remain who refuse to have any relations with the patriarchate, but, if this is true, their influence is insignificant.

Representatives of the Catacomb Church had as their goal to preserve the purity of the spirit of Orthodoxy, carrying it through the years of church struggle, repression, maneuvers, and compromises. They included prominent servants of Christ who had enormous influence on people searching for a genuine church life. Unfortunately, few memoirs, documents, and testimonies about them have been preserved. An exception is Bishop Afanasii, whose compiled materials and biographies have been partially collected and published.[76] Below, we will introduce memoirs about several priests of the Catacomb Church, among which one of the best is the memories of Archimandrite Serafim (the former confessor of Bishop Afanasii).

Fr. Serafim (in the world, Sergei Mikhailovich Batiukov)[77] was born in 1880 in Moscow. In his early years, he felt called to service in the Church, although he became a priest only later in his life. Having received a technical education, Sergei Mikhailovich worked in one of the enterprises in the capital city. At the same time, he began to visit the Optina Pustyn' Monastery, attended lectures at the Moscow Theological Academy, and studied theology and sacred literature. He was a multifaceted, gifted person, with wide interests, and completely devoted to the Church.

Like two other leading activists in the Russian Church, Fr. Sergii Bulgakov and Archbishop Luk Voino-Iasenetskii, he was ordained during the most difficult time for the Church.[78] In 1919 and for several months afterward, he served in the Church of the Resurrection in Sokol'niki, together with Fr. Ivan Kedrov, the Father Superior of the Church and the founder of the "Sokol'niki" community.[79]

Before that, church officials proposed that Fr. Sergii become head priest in the Church of the Resurrection of Christ, which existed by the conservatory. But Sergii took pity and gave his spot to the young priest Fr. Dmitrii Delektorskii, who would have been doomed to death if he had been sent to serve in the countryside.[80]

In 1920, Patriarch Tikhon summoned Fr. Sergii and appointed him to the Church of the Sacred Martyrs Cyril and John on Solianka Street. In 1922, he took monastic orders with the name of Serafim, and, at the end of 1926, the Church elevated him to the rank of archimandrite. According to rumors, his superiors prepared him for service in the church hierarchy.

Shortly thereafter, Fr. Serafim was arrested on the charge of concealing church valuables. This was a time when the majority of religious people and laypeople suffered while protecting their sacred objects. Subsequently, the case against Fr. Serafim was dismissed, since it turned out that some Serbians had removed the valuables (they were found in the courtyard of the Church of the Sacred Martyrs Cyril and John).

The archimandrite [Fr. Sergii] had a negative reaction to the declaration [1927] of Metropolitan Sergii. In July 1928, he left the church and went into illegal status. Fr. Ieraks (in the world Ivan Matveevich Bocharev), who served there from 1929 to 1932, also took the same pathway. From this time on, all religious people who refused to accept the declaration of Metropolitan Sergii were arrested (if they did not manage to hide themselves), and their churches were closed.

Only by a miracle did Fr. Serafim escape arrest. For some time, he lived secretly in various places, and in the end settled in Sergiev Posad (renamed Zagorsk) at the home of two sisters, nuns from Diveevo.[81]

There, in a small room, an altar was placed before the icon of the Iverskaia Mother of God, and there the liturgy was celebrated.[82] Here many religious people conducted the worship service. In the interval between his arrests, Bishop Afanasii, in whose jurisdiction Fr. Serafim served, also frequented the house.[83] In this unremarkable house on the outskirts of town, the spiritual children of the archimandrite, seeking advice and comfort, gathered from everywhere. During the years of denunciations and incessant arrests (until 1943), it is remarkable that this church center remained intact for so long.

In his pastoral activity, Fr. Serafim, like the Fathers Mechev,[84] was guided by the advice of the Optina Elder Nektarius,[85] who in that time had already left the destroyed Optina Pustyn' Monastery. In addition, Elder Zosima (in the Zakhariia *skit*), who came to Moscow from the closed Trinity-Sergiev Lavra, served as Fr. Serafim's mentor.

Fr. Serafim was a true adherent of traditional eldership. He always had a deeply individualized approach to people. As pastor, he conversed separately with each person, and his advice was conveyed only to the given person (he often even forbade transferring it to others). He saw his main calling as a shepherd, a nourisher of souls, and "a protector of the purity of Orthodoxy."

Among the like-minded thinkers gathered around Fr. Serafim was the outstanding above-mentioned Fr. Pyotr Shipkov (1881–1959). Consecrated in 1921, he went into the "catacombs" approximately at the same time as Fr. Serafim. Fr. Pyotr worked as a bookkeeper in Zagorsk and conducted his services in private homes. He was a person of inexhaustible life-giving joy and of some unusual spiritual light. Years of hard experience (cumulatively, he was imprisoned for nearly thirty years) did not place the stamp of bitterness and hardness on him. He was fated to live a long time after Fr. Serafim, who died in 1942, and, following his exile, to finish his days as the head priest in the cathedral in the city of Borovsk.

Fr. Ieraks lived in Bolshevo, outside Moscow, in the home of one of his spiritual daughters.[86] The owner of the house had to hide from her relatives [the fact] that a church was located in her attic and a priest lived there. Fr. Ieraks was arrested in this home in 1943. Subsequently, like Fr. Pyotr, the authorities rehabilitated and freed him. The labor camp experience and exile severely damaged his health, so that he could no longer serve. Fr. Ieraks died in Vladimir, while a pensioner of the patriarchate.

Although the following memoirs were not intended for publication and are distinguished by their intimately personal character, they retain their significance as an historical document and spiritual witness. Because the images of "catacomb" priests are depicted through the prism of the internal biography of the author, we see in these images the elders' guidance in all its concreteness and depth. The memoirs show how intently Fr. Serafim and Fr. Pyotr devoted themselves to the smallest movements of the souls under their guidance, how they engaged with everyone who came to them, suffered with them, supported them, and helped them with advice and prayer. We learn about their relationship to very different circumstances and life's problems, and this, if you will, better than any chronicle, offers new generations a view of the spirit of the Catacomb Church and its pastors.

The author of the writings, Vera Iakovlevna Vasilevskaia, was a research scientist, a specialist in pedagogy and mental and physical disabilities. She graduated from the Philosophy Faculty of Moscow University and the Institute of Foreign Languages. To her belongs a series of works, some of which are published. The main one of them is *Ponimanie uchebnogo materiala uchashchimisia vspomogatel'noi shkoly* (Moscow: AN SSSR, 1960). To her also belongs translations of books: E. Kheisserman, *Potentsial'nye vozhmozhnosti psikhicheskogo razvitiia normal'nogo i nenormal'nogo rebenka* (Moscow: Nauka, 1964); K. De Griunval'd, "Kogda Rossiia imela svoikh sviatykh" (unpublished); and Frantsisk Sal'skii, *Vvedenie v blagochestivuiu zhizn'* (Brussels: Zhizn' s Bogom, 1967). She began writing her memoirs nearly twenty years ago and completed them in 1959.[87]

WOMEN OF THE CATACOMBS

FIGURE 1. Archimandrite Serafim (Batiukov)

Part I

Fr. Serafim

> In remembrance of my mama
> —Vera Iakovlevna Vasilevskaia
>
> For though you might have ten thousand guardians in Christ,
> you do not have many fathers.
> Indeed, in Christ Jesus I became your father through the gospel.
> —1 Corinthians 4:15

Ante Lucem[1]

"God's ways are inscrutable." The more this feeling and consciousness penetrate a person, the more difficult it is to manage the past, and the more difficult it is to share one's memories, understanding that we factually see and understand reality so little, and we get to know even one's personal life and fate only "as conjecture through a mirror."

The meeting with Fr. Serafim, personal contact with him, my baptism and, subsequently, his guidance of my life, for me are the very most authentic and greatest miracle and, at the same time, the very most irrefutable, central reality of my existence.

Fr. Serafim's visible guidance began in 1935 and ended in 1942 with his death. But in reality, it began in 1920: that is, it continued for more than twenty years. Invisibly, undoubtedly, it continues also now, since that spiritual connection, created during baptism, when he literally "accepted my soul into his," cannot be dissolved at the end of earthly existence.

The religious feeling was born in my soul very early. It arose not in isolation but emerged as a free set of feeling, during the first attempts to reflect on my life. It arose together with the sense of history, the consciousness that one belonged to a people who "revealed" God to humanity. People lived in the darkness of paganism, when in Israel, the Unified True God "was revealed." Other people discovered the rotation of the earth, electricity, the law of gravity, and many other things, but the revelation given to the Jewish people was the most important. The thought of this filled the childhood soul with a feeling of a large moral responsibility.

I always had a deep spiritual connection with my mother. I trusted her with everything that developed in my soul, although much was uncertain, unclear to me, and in her I always found a response and support. My mother was one of those people about whom Meister Eckhart said, "They live and act among everyday things, but give such an aura that they stand precisely in the highest celestial circle, extremely close to eternity."

Nothing in the material world attracted her; she never wanted anything for herself, and she loved those close to her with a special spiritual, selfless love. She carried in herself all the troubles and burdens of life, but not for one minute did she give way to earthly vanity. Her connection with us, her children, had some kind of special spirit: "If you had not been born, I would have always yearned for you," my mama once said to me, when I was still a little girl. And when I had grown so much that Mama could dress me in my black dress, she said quietly, in an almost joyful voice, "Well, here is my young girl already grown, and I can soon die." Nothing in our childhood seemed to Mama too small or unnecessary. Sometimes I asked Mama, "Perhaps it is not necessary to tell you this; perhaps it will not be interesting to you." Mama unfailingly replied, "Everything that interests you, interests me also." We lived a single interior life. Once I fell seriously ill. When it was diagnosed, Mama came to my room and, with a smile, said, "Do not be afraid of anything, we will be sick together."

I remember how, having told Mama about some bad behavior, I asked, "Will you forgive me this time?" "Not only this time, but always," Mama firmly answered. This promise of permanent forgiveness was stronger than the most terrible danger.

"What happiness it is to be with you," I would say to Mama, when we were alone. With a sad smile, Mama would answer, "May God give you great happiness." In her heart, anxiety had been creeping in, and once she said to me, "I am afraid that you will be a very solitary person."

In reality, I sensed that even then, when in 1918 I entered the university and met people close to me in spirit, who shared my religious searches. These were the last years of the philosophy faculty of the old order. We listened to the lectures of I. A. Il'in,[2] and G. I. Chelpanov,[3] and came together in religious-philosophical meetings, in which we discussed all the troubling questions of the spiritual life and the Gospels. Students came to the lectures

FIGURE 2. Vera Vasilevskaia with her friend Zina in the 1920s.

of Il'in in such numbers that the auditorium could not contain all of them. Among them were many *maroseiki*, "the spiritual children of Fr. Aleksei Mechev."[4] Although I was close to several of them, I always felt myself a stranger and distant from their lives. In 1920, after the death of my mother, my world fell to pieces and lost not only its attractiveness but also its reality. The occupations of philosophy and psychology, although deeply engaging, did not give me the nourishment for which my soul called out.

Soon afterward, I went to work in a kindergarten, while continuing my studies in the university. In contact with children, I felt the possibility of a more interdependent understanding than with adults. "Why do I feel so good with children?" I once asked, many years later at Fr. Serafim's. "This is because," Fr. Serafim explained to me, "your soul is at peace."

Among the children (in the preschool colony, as it was called then), I immediately felt differently than among grownups. The children seemed to grasp my most secret thoughts and emotions, which I was not willing to share with anyone. One evening, when my heart felt especially heavy, one of the older boys (so chipper and sprightly during the day) called out to me, saying, "Come sit with us; we are scared." My personal fear and melancholy, as it were, disappeared. From that time on, every evening I sat with the children and watched them until they fell into a peaceful sleep.

I will never forget these evenings! To remember the contents of our conversations is almost impossible: the children talked about home, about moves to new places, about guns and machine guns, about the winter, about the stars; they told fairy tales. This was not a conversation of an educator with pupils. In spite of the difference in age, we were equal, equal before the sunset, before the advancing night, before the terrible world around us, before God, whose presence they felt more clearly than I. I was not able to answer many of their questions, but they always answered mine. Several girls knew the prayers by memory and sometimes read them aloud. I did not know the prayers and listened to them, holding my breath. They were said with special power from the mouths of children, and to me they brought a mysterious joy.

During the day, on our walks, we said little. We listened to what the birds, the flowers and the trees, the forests and the ravines said to us.

I remember that once I returned from a walk and sat down on the porch of the home. In my hands, I had a large cornflower blue bouquet; I pressed it to my face, and for a minute I was lost in thought. A small, black-eyed boy ran up to me, one of the very naughtiest of the children and, turning to me, asked, "Do you know who is better than everything?" I did not know what to say. "God," he said. "You know what God can make?" the boy again asked, and, not receiving an answer, added, "Create a human being! . . ."

Sundays were always especially melancholy for me, but I never could account for the cause of this melancholy. On one Sunday morning, I walked out into the field: it was quiet; in the distance a church bell rang. "Everyone has Sunday, but you do not have Sunday," unexpectedly said one of the little boys who came up alongside me.

"Why do they always know everything?" I thought.

In the kindergarten, I became acquainted with Tonia Z.,[5] through whom I subsequently learned of Fr. Serafim, who fourteen years later became my godfather. Apparently, the Lord led me to this kindergarten.

I was eighteen years old, Tonia nineteen. Like me, she had recently lost her beloved mother. Like me, she felt herself a stranger among the others and found comfort and consolation in her relationship with children. Tonia worked with a younger group (of three-four years old), and I with middle-aged children (five-six years old). We both loved the nighttime duties. How good it was to protect the sleep of children. A sleeping child seemed to be conversing with the angels. How much unlimited trust and serenity was in his pose, in his smile! It was as though they did not suspect the existence of evil—these "children of the terrible years of Russia," who had already been through a lot.[6]

During these summer nights, both of us did not want to sleep, and we had nighttime duties together. I told Tonia about my mama; she told me about hers. I knew that Tonia lived an entirely special life, distinctively different from all those around her. In her, I sensed a large stable light, which illuminated her soul and life and transcended the boundaries of her personality. I did not know how and decided not to ask about this; she did not know how and could not talk about it. Only one time, when we were both sad, Tonia said, "There are people with whom one can talk, as with Mama." These words deeply imprinted themselves in my heart, but I decided not to ask about them. This was a mystery, whose disclosure could only take place at some time when we were alone.

I grew closer and closer to Tonia, and we understood each other without speaking. That world, in which Tonia lived, increasingly attracted me, but to attempt to penetrate it seemed impossible, as it is impossible to enter someone's garden, no matter how wonderful it is, if you are not invited in. Tonia told me what she found possible, but she did not always call things by their names and often used allegories. She did this with an extraordinary sensitivity and tender treatment of the soul of another [human being], and I deeply valued this. Subsequently, she acknowledged to me that she was afraid to disturb the "finest weaving" (*tonchaishee pletenie*), as she called this internal work which flowed, undoubtedly, under direct guidance from above.

One time Tonia told me about a dream. "I dreamed," she said, "that I was walking in a meadow, sown with wonderful flowers. I wanted to collect a large bouquet of these beautiful flowers and present them to you. My heart is full of joy: you see, such flowers can be found nowhere! The bouquet grows in my arms, and I want even earlier to give it to you. Suddenly, I notice that you are standing on the other bank of the river. I extend the bouquet to you, but you are not able to take it. The river is deep, and there is no bridge . . . 'I cannot give you the flowers'—with sadness, I say. But you, you do hear, you do sense their fragrance!"

Did I feel it? I felt it everywhere; the whole world was changing and coming alive for me, as the forest comes alive in the rays of the rising sun.

A cold wind rises before the daybreak, twittering anxiously in the predawn mist . . .

The soul of man aches until the Morning Star begins to shine in the heart.

"Sadness before dawn"—that is what poets called this condition of the soul . . .

Tonia left from P. each Sunday. I knew that she was where there were "people, with whom it is possible to talk, like with Mama."

Once, during our nighttime duty, Tonia said, "I talked about you. They remember you there." "Thank you," I said. She said little to me, but she always asked me to speak my mind. "Then, it will also be easier for me," she persuaded me. "You see, I can ask about anything." But I could not speak. Something was slowly ripening in my soul. I had no words.

Only when we departed at the end of the summer, I gave Tonia a book in memory, having written in it my favorite quatrain of Victor Hugo "At the Foot of the Cross" (U podnozh'ia Kresta):

> You are everything, who in tears trust yourself to God,
> Because tears He sheds.
> You, who in sorrow come to Him,
> He gives healing.
> You, who know only fear, come to Him,
> He sends you a smile,
> You, whose life only lies in ashes, come to Him,
> He eternally lives.

That winter we hardly met. I was loaded down with work and my studies in the university. Tonia, with household problems (her family remained in her care) and with sicknesses.

The following summer we again met in "the children's colony," but this time we worked in different kindergartens. On one occasion, Tonia invited me to her room on a free day, and I stayed the night. The circumstances of her room produced an indelible impression in me. I especially remember a picture, *The Blessing of the Children*. When I had already gone to bed, I saw that Tonia went up to the icons, crossed herself, and read a short prayer. This prayer, it seemed, pierced me all the way through; I felt this strength of faith with all my soul, which is possible only in Christianity. I never had thought that God was so near!

This year I conducted nighttime duty alone, but the Gospels were always with me, which I read at night, while protecting the sleep of the children.

Life conveyed many impressions and worries. But in everything—in sadness and joy, in nature and life, in science and art—to one thing only my heart aspired, an opening to a world to which, in my soul, I was irrepressibly drawn. In miraculous ways, the Lord was sending me always and everywhere impressions, meetings, and circumstances, which strengthened me on this path. I wished for someone with whom to share my feelings. Not having the opportunity to meet with Tonia, who lived now out of town, I began to write letters to her.

I did not immediately receive answers to my letters, but when they finally began to come regularly, the powerful feeling and depth of thought with which they were written affected me. It was difficult to fathom that an inexperienced and young woman wrote them. I knew that often, for a long time, she did not respond to the letters, because she needed "to seek advice," and for a long time, I did not know who the real author of these letters was. Later I learned that Fr. Serafim wrote them, and Tonia only recopied them, as if they had come from her.

Years passed. One day, when we ran across each other, Tonia said to me, "Do you know what they told me about you? They told me: 'She has made it halfway.'"

It means that I was not alone during all these years, but someone unknown, with surprising attention and love, "like Mama," watched over all these movements of my soul.

In 1931, I become ill with typhus and pneumonia. After the illness, they gave me a voucher to go to a vacation resort—in Optina Pustyn'.[7] Here I found myself in a wonderfully wholesome atmosphere, within the walls of the small, secluded monastery, among the Optina forests. At the time, I knew about Optina only from Dostoevsky. The fact that this was a resort with a multitude of vacationers did not disturb or distract me. The silence of the ancient forest, the alley leading up to the monastery, the flowerbed at the entrance, the houses of the monastery, and the monastic walls captivated me; all of them spoke about one thing, and everything else was becoming unimportant, almost unreal. For entire days, I wandered through the woods, and, early in the morning and, in the evening, before sunset, I went into a large empty church, where a craft workshop was located. When there were no workers, emptiness and quietness prevailed, and only the swallows bustled about under the roof. All the walls and the internal ceilings of the church were painted in marvelous pale-rose tones, which, it seemed, were taken directly from the colors of the sunset. I found it impossible to tear myself away from these wonderful pictures. Mostly, I remembered Christmas and the road to Emmaus.

Upon arrival, I communicated my impressions to Tonia. She was somewhat surprised by my enthusiastic mood after I returned from Optina. "Yes," she said, "for you this is good, but I could not live there now . . . in a resort; it would be hard for me."

In the spring of the following year, my sister Lenochka[8] married, and, in the summer, went away with her husband to the south. I was going through a difficult period of life, but I did not share my feelings with anyone. Unexpectedly, I received a letter, which contained the following lines that clearly did not belong to Tonia, since they did not sound like the advice of a friend: "That Lenochka married must not serve as an example to you, because this is not your road." This was the answer of a person who saw a long way into the future and to whom was given the strength and the power to show the way.

Once, I wrote Tonia how excruciatingly in my youth I wanted to have a child, and I finished with the sad conclusion, as it seemed to me, "Most likely, I do not deserve it." "You think that you do not deserve it," came the answer. In one of his subsequent letters, Fr. Serafim wrote, "I understand your wish to have and to raise a child as a wish to keep the Christ Child in your heart." Such words seemed strange to me. Once, in a letter, I wrote that for me Christ was the only Beacon in the darkness of life. To this, Fr. Serafim answered, "There will come a time, when Christ will not be a Beacon, but the Helmsman, directing all your life." The following year, I went away on a trip to Lake Seliger.[9] I wanted to go with tourists, take part in excursions, and try to "be as everyone else," no different from those around me, as many advised me at that time. The group bonded very well. I did not suspect what would again take place in a sacred place (Nilus Pustyn').[10] Despite my effort not to separate myself from the group, on the following day, my sidekick asked me a surprising question: "You, apparently, love solitude, don't you?"

All around was such beauty that it was difficult to tear myself away from this sight. The favorite place of my stay was a small watchtower on which it was possible to climb up, and from there peacefully view the surroundings. On all sides were unfolded innumerable picturesque lakes, with their quaint inlands and inlets. On one side of the islands, the white walls of a former monastery rose up, and a tall white bell tower stood out on it.[11]

After a thunderstorm, when the air was especially transparent and clear and one could see all the surroundings as far as the horizon, I climbed up on my favorite watchtower, in order better to feel the beauty of God's world, and I began to write a letter. I wanted, as much as possible, to convey in words everything I saw and that filled my soul in these quiet moments, with nothing clouding my contemplation of nature around the lake's countryside.

Once, on the eve of an excursion to the source of the Volga, I fell asleep and had a miraculous dream. In a white church, a service was underway, they were singing the Symbol of Faith.[12] I tried to listen attentively to this harmonious singing, which came from there, from above, from the white church, and it seemed that I forgot about everything in the world. Suddenly, from below, from the lake, resounded other sounds: there were boats, filled with people, and music blared, with the sharp dissonant sounds of the "Internationale." My head began to whirl, and I lost consciousness. The dream was cut short. It was dawn. It was necessary to rise and to go on an excursion.

We walked for a long time along a beautiful forested road. In the depth of the forest, I came across a chapel; I left my traveling companions and went up to it. On the walls of the chapel, I saw in full the written Symbol of Faith, which I had only just listened to in my dream. I never thought that a dream could so vividly resonate with reality.

On another day, having returned to the base, I received a letter from Tonia, dictated by Fr. Serafim. As I learned later, it was written in two copies: one was sent to Moscow to my home address, the other to the base on Lake Seliger. This letter was an answer to what I had written on the watchtower. It began with these words: "Without God's will nothing happens. Think to what places the Lord leads you. Not so long ago you breathed the wholesome air of Optina Pustyn', and now you find yourself on Lake Seliger, in the place of the heroic deeds of Nilus Stolobenskii" (subsequently, Fr. Serafim named Nilus Stolobenskii my divine protector). Fr. Serafim analyzed my letter in detail, taking from it a whole series of quotations. In my letter, were the words, "Why do the swallows so move me, especially when they hover over their nest?"—"The grace of God touches you. The angels hover over your soul; do not drive them away," came the answer.

Fr. Serafim also referenced a fragment from my letter, where I had described the flowers of the forests and the fields and which depicted the harmony of colors and aromas, as though each of them aspired to bring everything into the full completion that the Creator, in an upsurge of love and sacrifice, endowed them. This is the complete love, about which the apostle Paul speaks in the Epistles and in Corinthians, the love that "does not insist on its own way" (1 Corinthians 13:5). Fr. Serafim compared this letter, written in the seclusion of the watchtower on Lake Seliger, with the feelings that the Great Martyr Barbara experienced, living among the pagans and becoming conscious of the true God through nature.[13] For him, this letter conveyed direct instruction that, for me, the time to accept baptism had come.

All this came unexpectedly. When I wrote my letter, I did not think at all about the Church and baptism. I did not immediately respond to the letter, only when I returned to Moscow. I did not understand what Fr. Serafim wrote. "Why is it absolutely necessary to unite with the Church?" I was perplexed. "Is it really not possible, without this, to profess Christ with my life and death?"

In a following letter, he answered my question. "Do you think that by not accepting Christ, you can confess Him?"

I had little understanding of these words at the time, and they seemed cruel.

The question of baptism seemed to me to be unnecessary, almost vain. Answering these thoughts, Fr. Serafim wrote, "You speak about vanity, not noticing, by alleging the opposite, into what narrow pride you are falling."

It was difficult for me to comprehend his words.

In the winter, Lenocha was due to give birth. Tonia came to tell me that if neither of us was prepared for our own baptism, then it would be good to baptize Lenochka's baby first, after the birth. Both of us joyfully accepted her proposal. Thus the question about the baptism of Alik was decided long before his birth, with the guidance and blessing of Fr. Serafim. Shortly before the birth, I received a letter, which instructed me to convey to Lenochka the wish that her upcoming trials would go peacefully and the hope that she would have God's compassion and the Protection of the Virgin Mary of God.

After the birth of Alik, Fr. Serafim sent me a letter, in which he offered instruction to Lenochka that, while feeding the baby, she should recite three times "The Lord's Prayer," three times "The Theotokos," and one time "The Creed."[14] Thus he considered it necessary to begin Alik's spiritual education from his very birth.

Our grandmother and other relatives insisted on performing the Old Testament rites over the infant, but Lenochka protested. We had to ask Tonia to make a special trip to Fr. Serafim and ask him what to do. Referring to the words of the apostle Paul, Fr. Serafim gave his blessing for us to concede this matter.[15]

The baptism of Alik and Lenochka was scheduled for September 3 (1935). I went to the station to see off all three of them. A strange feeling came over me: anxiety and uncertainty, combined with a sense of joy, about that which had become necessary and almost inevitable. I did not know where they were going and did not ask anything about it. At the station, I said to Tonia, "I neither know anything nor anyone, but I trust you in everything." "May you have peace," she answered, "but if you wish, come with us." This I could not do! . . .

After the baptism, Sister began more often to go to the church, and still more often in the evening, she left Alik with me.[16] It seemed to me that he always understood everything. Sometimes Alik took off his cross, put it on me, and smiled. Several times Tonia invited me to travel to Zagorsk. "By delaying, you are only tormenting yourself," she said, but I could not resolve to go. Lenochka often went to Zagorsk. Listening to her stories, I thought, "No, I cannot do it." "They do not require anything from you," Tonia said. "They will find the approach that you need." "And I will not be put in the position of a difficult child?" I asked (I was then already working in the Institute of Mental and Physical Disabilities). "Precisely so," Tonia responded. The degree to which I really was a "difficult child," I learned later, when Fr. Serafim related to Lenochka that, after he wrote every letter to me, he lay ill for several hours because of the strain this required of him.

One Must Take up the Cross

And so, the winter went on. Letters came more rarely. In my soul, a kind of heaviness resided that I wanted to convey on paper, yet it seemed almost indifferent to me whether or not someone read what I had written. Once, having written some letter, I reluctantly put it in the mailbox, and I was surprised when, in answer to the letter, I read these words: "Your last letter reads as if it exhibits repentance for your entire past life—that is, precisely what is necessary before entering into Orthodoxy." When I wrote my letter, I did not suspect that it contained forgiveness.

Once, Tonia proposed that I agree to go, under the pretense that I needed to talk about Lenochka. "So that you will feel better," she said.

Finally, we decided the question about the trip to Zagorsk. We settled on January 29. But on the day of the departure, an unexpected event arose. At night, Lenochka felt bad, and there was no one who could stay with her and the baby. Only now did I feel the extent to which desire and necessity

FIGURE 3. The house in which Archimandrite Serafim served, in Sergiev Posad (Zagorsk).

combined for me to go on this trip, and how it was impossible to refuse. At this point, I received unexpected help. At that moment, when it was impossible to ponder any longer, a young woman whom we did not know rang at the door and offered her services as a household worker. We immediately liked Katia and left her with Lenochka, and I could leave in peace. Later we told her everything, and she herself committed to Fr. Serafim.

I went to the station directly from work. It was crowded in the train car, and we stood the entire way. We arrived in Zagorsk at night. The temperature was below freezing; stars filled the sky. In the darkness, we walked silently. One time only did Tonia ask, "Where do you think you are going?" "I do not know, and I am trying not to think," I said.

"Think that you are going to talk about Lenochka, and it will be easier for you," said Tonia sympathetically.

The pathway led us to a small house, on which the shutters were tightly shut. It seemed that everyone was asleep or had left a long time ago. Tonia rang four times, as agreed. They quickly opened the door for us. In the small house, it was light, warm, and cozy. In everything, I felt myself a piece of some particularly harmonious life. Everyone was affectionate and welcoming, as that feeling of awkwardness, common in an unaccustomed circumstance, gave way to a certainty that everything was entirely simple and could not be otherwise. Fr. Serafim beckoned us to come into his room and simply, as to a child, explained to me how to receive a blessing, about which I had no idea. Then everyone went into the dining room. At supper, the conversation was about ordinary things: about Moscow, about the trip, about Lenochka. The time grew late, and everyone went to lie down to sleep. Fr. Serafim and I were left—just the two of us. He asked me to go with him into the small kitchen, enclosed on all sides and covered with icons, and had such a festive appearance, as had everything else in the home.

We sat at the table. Having prayed a little, Fr. Serafim asked, "Why have you come to me?!" In the way that he put this question, it seemed that he knew everything that had taken place with me, and at the same time he wished me to understand that I had not come here by my own will. "For me it was very difficult," I answered, feeling that all normal human conditions here were irrelevant. However, when he asked me to tell him about myself, I asked, "You will excuse me, if what I will be saying may be unpleasant to you?"—"I am a priest," Fr. Serafim briefly responded.

It seemed to me that the chains that had burdened me for many years had lifted. I spoke for a long time, told him everything that seemed essential at this given moment. When I finished, Fr. Serafim looked at me with a special attentiveness and said, "You are tired. You are very tired." "From what?" I was surprised. "From a conscientious attitude to life," came the answer.

Then he began to speak himself, and I was astounded that he knew about separate details of my life, things I had not told him: the characteristics of my parents, their relationships, and many other things. "Your mama," said Fr. Serafim, "lived almost a Christian life . . . Almost a Christian life," he repeated, as if to strengthen the significance of these words. "However, I wouldn't have proposed to her that which I propose to you . . . To you it remains only to take up the cross . . . This is not necessary for anything else, but for the settling of your soul. Do you understand me?" This question Fr. Serafim constantly asked during his conversations, and how many times did I subsequently answer it negatively, as I strived to grasp his thought as best I could, and he repeatedly and patiently made clear his thought for me, as in my childhood Mama for the tenth time tried to explain to me a difficult math problem.

Many questions troubled me about the Church's situation at the time, about its necessarily clandestine nature, about the false position in which I had put myself in relation to the people around me. Even in order to come here, I had needed to deceive the people who were closest to me. Fr. Serafim sympathized with everything I said. "You do not know at what a time you came to me!" he said, as though wishing again to underscore that not everything lay open to me and that it was not my will at work here. "Here are the catacombs," he said, referring to everything that surrounded us. "I am here not because I wish some kind of evil on anyone or wish to struggle with someone. I am here only in order to preserve the purity of Orthodoxy."

Fr. Serafim talked about many things. Several times during our conversation, he posed the question: "Do you love the apostle Paul?"

The apostle Paul was "my" apostle; he gave me the key to understanding the Gospels—how could I not love him?

Meanwhile, it began to get light.

"You came to me at night, like Nikodim," said Fr. Serafim thoughtfully, "and I put before you the question: Do you wish to accept baptism?"[17]

"Right now, for me this question is beyond my strength," I answered, "entirely beyond my strength."

Fr. Serafim asked me to kneel, and when I did this, he pressed my head to his heart, so that I could hear each beat.

We went into another room. The day had set in. Fr. Serafim led me to the window and said, "Remember the way here. You will come to me again; there is no need to ask anyone."

He gave me a blue crystal egg for me to keep in memory of this occasion; then he blessed me, and I left for home.

The letters no longer came by mail, but he sent them personally through Tonia.

At the beginning of Lent, I received a long letter from Fr. Serafim. It differed significantly in content from his previous letters. It was written in especially simple, warm, and concrete language. Fr. Serafim wrote about what prayers to recite daily, in the morning and evening, how to conduct oneself during Lent, and he offered many other practical instructions that related to everyday life and were especially encouraging. He already considered us his [children] and cared about us, as an attentive mother, who tried to anticipate the movements of her child—external and internal.

The advice of Fr. Serafim that uplifted me most called for me each morning, while leaving for work, to ask a blessing. Once, in a conversation with Tonia, I asked whether it was permissible to make the sign of the cross before being baptized. Fr. Serafim also did not forget this question. "Not only is it possible, but it is necessary," he answered. By such means, spiritual aspirations shifted from something in isolation to something that became part of the organic unity of life, and the organic unity of life was being restored in all its dimensions.

Shortly before the beginning of Lent, Grandmother began to develop gangrene in her leg. Over the course of three months, she did not rise from her bed, and she suffered severely. Relatives took turns watching over her at night. Grandmother was already at a very advanced age, and her body could not fight the sickness. She was dying. Throughout her life, she remained an extremely energetic, cheerful, and sociable person. But now she gradually withdrew from everything: she refused her favorite dishes that were brought to her, did not want to listen to the reading of letters sent to her from her children and grandchildren, and did not allow even Alik (the long-anticipated grandson) to be brought in to her. She no longer needed anything.

When I spent nights by her bed, it seemed to me that I existed on the boundary of two worlds. I sensed this boundary, and at that point, I did not want to let go of this feeling, which I had not known until now. When the entire house slept, and the dying woman looked at me, seemingly unaware of anything, and with her "understanding" look, this did not frighten me. On the contrary, a kind of mysterious peace filled my heart, and when I went to work in the morning, no one could imagine that I had spent a sleepless night.

Like this, Lent progressed. Like this, I prepared to meet Passover—the holiday of the victory over death. How pleased I was when, not long before

Passover, Tonia brought me a large candle of green color (the symbol of hope) from Fr. Serafim, with an invitation to both of us to come to him for the Easter service.

Only one thing troubled me: I did not want Grandmother to die in my absence. But not to accept Fr. Serafim's proposal was almost impossible. Easter night corresponded with my watch night, but I succeeded in prevailing upon my aunt to stay in my place. I said that I was spending the night at Tonia's house.

In Zagorsk, we arrived late. As it had the previous time, the outside of the small house in which Fr. Serafim lived appeared deserted and unoccupied. Inside, however, it was full of people who had gathered in this small house, enclosed on all sides, to celebrate the sacred holiday with Fr. Serafim, as they had celebrated it before in the church.

Fr. Serafim occupied himself with arranging the altar and the iconostasis. The small room required conversion into a church, where the Easter service would take place.

When everything was ready, everyone moved into the large room, leaving Fr. Serafim alone.

I did not know anyone among those present, except for the owner of the house. After a short time passed, Fr. Serafim summoned me to him. "You should feel as though you are among your very closest people," he said, convinced that I understood everything exactly as he wished, and then he simply added, "Now go, sit in that room, and I will begin to hear their confessions." Probably, the others had been forewarned, since no one asked me any questions, and I soon began to feel that all these people, having come here on this Easter night, really appeared to be people close to me, to whom I was connected in the very deepest sense, yet to me the threads were unclear. I would not have been able to appreciate this, if it had not been a direct order of Fr. Serafim: he freed me from my customary shyness; he allowed me to feel good. Listening to the utterances of the people around me and partly participating in them, I began to understand the foundational distinctiveness of life "in the Church": life "under the guidance" from this internally disorderly, chaotic existence, which all these people had led and in which, up to now, I had spent my life. Two fundamental understandings defined the distinctive characteristics of this new model of life for me: "blessedness" and "obedience." Not being able to comprehend fully, in the deepest sense, what they comprised, since such understanding required the long experience of spiritual life, all the same I appreciated them as the only pathway. With all the conditions of his life, his words, actions, and behavior, Fr. Serafim taught everyone with whom he came into contact how to enter more deeply into this pathway with the heart and mind and, simultaneously, to assimilate its practices. In many ways, this pathway was diametrically opposed to what the family, society, and literature had taught (not only after the revolution, but also before it).

Among those present were two people, Natasha and Serezha Pankratov. They were both spiritual children of Fr. Serafim, but before then they had not known each other. They were now husband and wife. Personal feeling had not united them, but the blessing of Fr. Serafim had done so, and personal feeling came afterward. At the foundation of their unity lay not passion, not a crush, on which secular writers place such high regard, but the love of God and the desire to lead a Christian life. During the ceremony, Serezha stood beside me, and particularly nicely, like a child, he prayed.

Later Serezha was killed at the front in the war, and when I remember him now, he appears before me as he was on that Easter night . . .

Fr. Serafim heard the confession of each person individually.

Before the beginning of the divine service, he sent someone out to ensure that the singing could not be heard on the street.

The Easter service began, and the small house was converted into a radiant church, in which one incomparable feeling united everyone—the joy of the Resurrection. They carried out the Procession of the Cross inside the house, in the entrance hall and the corridors. Fr. Serafim distributed icons to everyone for participation in the religious procession. He gave me the Icon of the Three Hierarchs, as I later learned from Tonia, because at that time, when the icon was in my hands, not once did I dare glance at it.[18]

After the liturgy, everyone sat down at the Easter table and lively conversations began about how many parts to divide the *solianka*, and who and where people celebrated Easter now.[19] Fr. Serafim commanded the attention of everyone and said that all around, even in the immediate neighborhood of the house, no one had any idea of what took place here. Time passed. I did not want to leave, but I began to worry that, if I lingered, Grandmother might die in my absence. Noticing my anxiety and turning to me but in such a way that everyone could hear, Fr. Serafim said, "Be at peace, nothing will happen. Mary, Mother of God, will not permit it. You came to glorify Her Son, and She will protect your entire home."

In the summer of 1936, Sister lived in a dacha in Tarasovka.[20] Sometimes in the evenings, she and Katia read the evening prayers together, and then I joined them. Nevertheless, for me it was necessary to have solitude, since it was essential, in the end, to think over everything and make a final decision. I went to a remote village not far away from Kaliazin.[21] There I lived in complete solitude, and for entire days, I walked alone among the fields and woods.

Rumors swirled about the inevitability of war. I was afraid that war would find me defenseless, and remembering the words of Fr. Serafim, I thought, "What if something happens? I have to take up the cross! . . ."

In freedom, I decided to write letters, in which I clarified to myself everything that troubled me, prevented me from crossing over the abyss, and separated me from the desired goal. I chose for myself a spot on the edge of the forest, not far from the marsh, over which wild ducks clamored. I went there to write, and no one disrupted my solitude.

I attempted to draw together all the negatives coming from childhood about the image of the Orthodox Church, about what it had been in the past, as its officials had represented it, about the numerous compromises, the hypocrisy, the antisemitism, and much more, which erected perhaps external, but difficult surmountable obstacles for everyone who found themselves on the outside of the Church but wanted to get closer. I wrote about those oppressive and frightening historical associations, which to me evoked the Jewish words "Avodo Zarah"—"foreign worship."

Deeply sympathetic, Fr. Serafim accepted everything. "I understand your fear before the words 'foreign worship,'" he wrote. He also agreed that the external history of the Church, to a significant degree, presented "a chain of compromises," and added, "continuing into the present time." Further, he wrote about the Church, whose head is Christ Himself and Mary, Mother of God, and to which belonged the assembly of martyrs and saints. "To such a Church I, with all my deficiencies, also belong," Fr. Serafim concluded his letter.

In my last letter, written in Kaliazin, I attempted to sum up everything. Nevertheless, the result surprised me. I had to acknowledge that, personally, there was nothing really to decide, that the question of my baptism had been decided and predetermined long ago—when, even I did not know. Perhaps I had to think about the time. Even this, apparently, was not in my power. The traveler sees the lights in front of him. He goes toward them. Where are they, far or near? He cannot say. He may be deceiving himself . . .

When I returned to Moscow, Tonia came to tell me that Fr. Serafim would be at her dacha and wanted to receive me there. I went to Bolshevo.[22] But when he sent [someone] to summon me, I suddenly felt that I could not go. Some kind of inexplicable power simply took hold of me. "I will not go; I am not in the right state of mind," I said.

At this time, Katia came to Bolshevo. She asked and even demanded that Fr. Serafim receive her, but he refused, saying, "It does not reside in my soul to receive her." "You see how surprising it can be: one person is motivated to come, but she is not received; another they summon, and she does not come," Tonia said.

With great difficulty, I overcame my resistance, after Tonia said to me that Fr. Serafim had remained today especially for me, and it would be totally inappropriate not to go to him. Finally, I went up the stairs. Fr. Serafim was alone in the room. The window to the garden was open, however, and a white curtain hung over it; therefore, what took place in the room was not visible from the outside.

Tenderly, Fr. Serafim talked with me, "And you say to the Savior: here I come to You, like a loose woman." These words so struck me that I unwillingly covered my face with my hands, and in an instant, such goodness and light came into my soul. I attempted, nevertheless, to continue my "oppositional proofs," but I soon fell silent, as they now seemed irrelevant. In the garden, a nightingale sang.[23] "Well, now we are sitting here together," said Fr. Serafim. "It is as though we have disagreements," he repeated, as though wishing to show that it only seemed like it, but in reality, no kind of disagreement existed. "And a nightingale, do you hear how it is singing?" he concluded.

Still more loudly in the garden resounded the song of a nightingale, and everything in it was understandable, everything was harmonious, and there were no "disagreements."

It seemed to me that my soul split into parts. "Forgive me," I finally said. "I have taken so much of your time." "I am suffering together with you," Fr. Serafim answered.

I arrived home late at night. On the street, I met my brother. He was very worried and had searched for me everywhere. I said that I had been talking with Tonia and, therefore, had stayed longer than usual.

After this day, we did not see Fr. Serafim again for a long time. Each time, in his letters, he explained to me the real significance and meaning of my personal thoughts and feelings.

In one of my letters, full of conflicting feelings, I cited the verses of Tiutchev: "The soul is prepared, like Mary,/To the feet of Christ forever cling"—and finished it with this question: Am I ready? Should I begin to get ready?

In a series of examples, Fr. Serafim, tried to show me what that preparation consisted of.

In essence, that was what our correspondence was about: I had "kind of," he had "truly." I had "intuition," he had "knowledge." I did not see and did not understand what was taking place in my soul, but he saw and understood everything.

I wrote to Fr. Serafim about the incontrovertible impression the words of T. K. made on me.[24] "A Christian is one who loves only the one Christ and no one and nothing more." Fr. Serafim answered, "You would understand these words still better, if you recalled the parable about the mite of the poor widow."

Once I conveyed in my letter the verses of Baratynskii:[25] "And for Your strict paradise / Give my heart strength!"

In response, the elder wrote, "The poet's words you are citing I receive as the breath of prayer."

Finally, on October 30, 1936, Tonia and I planned a new trip together to Zagorsk (at the time we worked five days and on the sixth rested; this was a free day). Tonia came to me on the evening of the twenty-ninth, in order to spend the night at my place. The twenty-ninth was my papa's birthday. Relatives gathered around the table. I said that I felt bad, and I did not go out to visit them.

"For Jews it is a temptation, and for Greeks it is madness," wrote the apostle Paul. Everything in my soul came from the Greeks, and the Jews again rose up against the call of grace. I cried the entire evening.

In silence, Tonia sat beside me, as they sit alongside the very sick. Only one time she said, "Everyone must go through suffering."

Early in the morning, we went to Zagorsk.

"Well, have you made a decision?" Fr. Serafim asked.

"No," I answered.

"And you will not," calmly said Fr. Serafim.

Then I began to talk about the many things that remained unclear to me, the many questions I could not answer, and, unexpectedly to me, I concluded with the words: "Here (that is, in Christianity) for me it is not a worldview but a calling . . ." "That is the best!" rejoiced Fr. Serafim. "That's what's necessary. A worldview comes gradually. From where might you have developed it now? That is impossible."

Then he began to talk about how the baptism would take place. "I understand you," he said. "For you this is an operation, but an operation without risk." On the contrary, it seemed to me that the risk was immeasurably large: either new horizons opened up behind that boundary, or something fatal and incorrigible would happen . . . "I believe, Lord, help my unbelief . . ."

November 5 was Tonia's birthday. On this day, she had to be in Moscow in the church (the only church to which Fr. Serafim then permitted his spiritual children to go was a Greek residence on Petrovka Street). Sister also intended to go there. I asked her to find Tonia and give my note to her. The note had the following content: "The second half of the pathway is close to the end. It has been a long and difficult struggle. Much is difficult and painful now, but vacillations do not exist any longer. How good to succumb, when the victor—is Christ!"

Very quickly, Tonia sent my letter to Zagorsk and, after several days, she came to say that, on the fifteenth, my sister must go to Zagorsk to get the necessary instructions (I was at work), and the day of baptism was set for November 18.

On the fifteenth, Lenochka traveled to Zagorsk, and I just went to the opening of an exhibition of Rembrandt's paintings, in order to ask forgiveness for everything that had taken place in my life until now. For me, this was both sad and joyous, and I gradually became calm. The paintings of Rembrandt helped me do this.

On the seventeenth, I had to go to Zagorsk straight from the institute. Tonia met me at the station.

It was difficult to work that day. Children from a German home for children came for a consultation. I had to talk with them in German. It was difficult for me to gather my thoughts, and I could hardly await the hour when it was possible, finally, to go to the station.

White Chrysanthemums

Tonia and I met in a darkened train car. Seeing me, she was very happy. "I was afraid that you would not come," she acknowledged to me . . . I did not have clear thoughts and feelings; it was as if all the powers of my soul froze in the expectation of that unknown trust that had to come to completion. Now the only thing remaining was resignation. Not my will, but the will of God was in everything, and this understanding was combined with the feeling of unlimited trust in what was needed to fulfill that will . . .

On this evening, the small house of Fr. Serafim had an especially festive appearance. Large white chrysanthemums filled the room in which the divine service usually took place.

Meeting us, Fr. Serafim joyfully said that the chrysanthemums he received had arrived precisely for this day. "The people, who brought them from the south, did not know for what celebration these flowers were intended," he said. Chrysanthemums are flowers for which, from early childhood, for some reason, I have had a special tenderness. While in the Crimea, when I was six years old, I always kissed them at night when leaving the garden. Certain bonds extend through all our life, through the sky and the earth everywhere, and, in a mysterious way, make contact with us.

The dinner was meatless. Serving at the table, a nun, the owner of the home, asked Fr. Serafim whether to pour oil onto his plate. "It is not necessary," he said. "And for Verochka," he said, "perhaps, it is also not necessary."

On this evening, Fr. Serafim wished that not one nonessential person be admitted and asked that no one come for a visit. Accidentally, a spiritual daughter, M. G., dropped in because of some urgent matter and so fervently implored Fr. Serafim to permit her to stay that he yielded. Her presence turned out to be fortuitous, since she took part in the singing.

Fr. Serafim divided the divine service into two parts: the preparatory part would take place in the evening, and the performance of the sacrament itself would take place at four o'clock in the morning.

Fr. Serafim then said I needed to make my confession. My confession was short. I did not know how to make confession, and I had already answered the simple questions put to me. Fr. Serafim mentioned sins, unknown or forgotten by me, and gave me absolution.

"How do you feel?" asked Tonia, when the evening service had almost concluded. "Good," I answered. "Thank God," Tonia said, as if some kind of weight fell from her.

Everyone lay down to sleep. I immediately fell asleep, so lightly and peacefully I felt in my soul. Fr. Serafim did not sleep, and when I awakened during the night, through the wall I heard often repeated the words:

"God, cleanse me of sin! . . ."

I felt serenity during this night, like an infant, but the difficulty he took on himself did not resemble the baptism of an infant. Undoubtedly, he felt all the weight of my sins "free and unfree," "known and unknown," that lay heavily on my soul from my previous life, from the chaos that still ruled in my soul, and from the struggle between hostile powers that could come to an end only by an act of grace, summoned up by him.

They awakened me at four o'clock in the morning.

Before beginning the service, Fr. Serafim asked me to call out the names of people whom I wished to remember in the liturgy. "They will take part in absentia," he said.

The divine service Fr. Serafim decided to perform that day was unusual. He united the service performed at my baptism with the service dedicated to the martyrs of Faith, Hope, Love, and their Mother Sophia.[26]

This added a special meaning to the entire service. For the first time, I heard the wonderful troparion [hymn]: "Your Lamb Faith calls out to you, O Jesus, in a loud voice: I love You, my Bridegroom, and in seeking You, I endure suffering . . ."

A deep connection between this and the baptismal service was revealed in the words: "In baptism I was crucified, so that I might reign in you."

Fr. Serafim did everything calmly and simply, but with such an internal power that seemed almost impossible to imagine in a person. In everything, even to the smallest detail, it was necessary to fulfill his will, as he fulfilled the will of God.

Nothing was conventional. The internal and the external flowed together. Thus the leaves on the trees grow out, thus come life and death, thus comes together each action of God on heaven and on earth . . .

FIGURE 4. Icon of the Iverskaia Mother of God, before which Archimandrite Serafim prayed.

Fr. Serafim asked me to get on my knees, lay the cruciform hands on my breast, and read aloud the Symbol of Faith.

After the performance of the sacrament of baptism, Fr. Serafim himself brought me the new clothes that they had prepared for me and held them out before the icon of the Holy Mother, then allowed me to venerate the icon and, only after this, permitted me to dress.

By these actions, Fr. Serafim visibly showed me that, from this moment, the whole world before me was sanctified, and everything that I see and have I receive anew as a gift of grace, as the love of the Holy Mother.

After this, as I put on the dress of a light-blue color, Fr. Serafim brought in two crosses. "You wished to have a wooden cross," he said (I wrote about this desire in a letter to Tonia four years ago). "This is a very good wish. Earlier still, I kept this cross for you (Fr. Serafim took out an ancient silver cross); it was located at the altar in our church on Solianka. The wooden cross (with these words, he took out a small wooden cross depicting the Crucifixion), you will wear. Although your baptism has to be kept secret, the cross may be fastened with a pin. And the other one, for the time being, conceals it."

Fr. Serafim placed the cross on me, on the top of my dress, and I wore it up to my departure.

I was not prepared for the receiving of the Sacred Mystery, as I also had not prepared for confession.[27] In the moment when it was necessary to go up to the Chalice, I was so lost that Fr. Serafim said to Tonia that she should take me by the arm.

When everything was completed, Fr. Serafim addressed those present with several words. He wished that they would remember well this day and everything they had witnessed.

"Her soul came to Christ, which for such a long time it had aspired to do," he said. Tears were in his eyes . . .

Meanwhile, Lenochka had arrived. After blessing her, Fr. Serafim said, "I congratulate you with your natural sister. You are from the same stem, and no one can be closer to you."

Before my departure, Fr. Serafim gave me three large chrysanthemums.

"In this moment of your baptism," he said, "the soul of your mama appeared before me."

While taking leave of me, Fr. Serafim led me to the window, from which could be seen the cupola of the Trinity-Sergiev Lavra (at that time it was closed), and said, "St. Sergii has received you."[28]

With these words, he not only showed that internal deep connection which henceforth existed between St. Sergii and me, but also that everything performed by him was carried out with the help and blessing of St. Sergii.

The Grace of the Holy Spirit

Correspondence with Fr. Serafim became rare, but my trips to Zagorsk [became] more regular although, because of the conditions of those times, not frequent. His guidance more and more involved all my life, externally and internally, and it became impossible to accomplish anything without his blessing.

"There are holy people," Fr. Serafim once said, "and there are people who are not holy but are 'righteous.'" "Only God can judge holiness. Righteousness serves as a guiding star for many people; surrounding such a person, it helps them swim across the sea of life without losing the necessary direction." I wished to bring everything to Fr. Serafim so that he might check my actions, thoughts, feelings, and spiritual movements.

Often it turned out that what seemed helpful to you was not helpful, that what seemed a mistake was necessary.

On one of my first trips to Fr. Serafim after my baptism, I told him that for twenty-two years I had kept a diary, in which I recorded all the important stages and events of my internal life. I thought that Fr. Serafim would find this diary interesting and would approve this activity both now and in the future. But Fr. Serafim related to it completely otherwise. "Before, it was a time of searching, and not a period of fulfillment," he said. "Now you must bring everything here." With these words, he showed me the icon of the Holy Mother.

"And what should I do with these diaries that I possess?" I asked. Fr. Serafim proposed that I destroy them. Of course, I carried this out the very same evening.

Fr. Serafim asked whether I had at home some kind of representation of Mary, Mother of God, or the Savior. I had the Madonna of an Italian artist. In this painting, the artist portrayed Mary, Mother of God, worshipping the Christ Child to whom she had given birth. The painting was depicted in pale blue tones, and I loved it very much. I had bought a second reproduction in a small bookstore on Nevskii Prospect fifteen years ago, when I traveled to Leningrad for a psycho-nephrology conference; each morning before the sessions began, I went into the Kazan' Cathedral, where the Crucifixion was placed against the background of Jerusalem, which I found impressive.[29]

Fr. Serafim did not approve of this Madonna, and I had to relinquish this image, but he requested that I bring the Leningrad reproduction to him. In it, the Savior was represented walking in a wheat field, in the company of His disciples.[30]

Fr. Serafim blessed it, gave it back to me, and said, "For fifteen years you have had this ordinary postcard, and now it is living." He also gave me a photograph of the Tenderness Icon, which had a special place of honor in the church on Solianka, photographs of which all his spiritual children kept.[31] I kept it in my room, but for a long time, I could not get used to it, so sad, it seemed to me then, to see Mary, Mother of God, without the Christ Child. Tonia soon brought me icons of St. Sergii and St. Serafim. Earlier I had often seen them at her place. When she left for Sarov, before my baptism, several times I accompanied her to the train station. During one of these trips, while taking leave of me, Tonia said, "You will be with me everywhere where I feel good."

Growing accustomed to the icon took place gradually, although in my soul lived the unforgettable memory of seeing once an icon of the Savior in the room of a friend during my university years, when we studied together for the Greek exam and when, in this representation, the living presence of the Image almost immediately opened up to me.

At that time, the majority of my acquaintances were not believers. Once, I asked Fr. Serafim how to act when a person (not a believer) shared his experiences with me, told me what was worrying him, and I did not know what to do, how to help him. "During the time he talks to you," said Fr. Serafim, "recite to yourself 'Lord have mercy upon us,' and the Lord will hear your confession."

At the beginning of Lent, I wrote a letter to Fr. Serafim, in which I expressed the thought that now was the time for me to enter the beginning class of a spiritual life. I kept his answer to the letter, and I could convey it not by memory but verbatim. Here was his letter, dated March 25, 1937:

> In the First Epistle, chapter 4, the Apostle John the Theologian clearly and definitively warned that a person not believe each thing [every spirit], but experience the spirits, in order to recognize the Spirit of God and the spirit of fallacy.[32] The Sacred Apostle thus defined: Every spirit, who confesses that Jesus Christ is come in the flesh, is from God.[33] Every spirit that does not confess that Jesus Christ is come in the flesh is not God: and this is that spirit of the antichrist. In reality, a person personifies life with his spirit, and therefore help or harm to a person and from a person is defined by this spirit, which he carries in himself and which he breathes; this is not only important, but also essential for a person, in order that he knows what spirit acts in him and what is the direction of his will. When the apostles, assaulted by Samaria's rejection of their Teacher and Sovereign, addressed Jesus Christ with a request to permit them a prayer for fire to come down from heaven, in order to address the shortcomings of the Samaritans, the Lord, stopping them, said, "You do not know what kind of spirit

you are of." In reality, only the day of Pentecost, the day of the procession of the Holy Spirit, permitted them, and, in that time, neither the heart nor the mind comprehended them.

In a similar way, neither an individual person nor all of humanity combined is in a position to comprehend together with the so-called culture of that sense of life, to whom the Lord summons and directs, if a person does not comprehend the fullness of the Holy Spirit, of that which the Holy Orthodox Church confesses with all its mysteries. The acquisition of the Holy Spirit! It not only opens the mystery of the human soul, which was inactive before, but gives one the strength to comprehend it.

Let us turn to the past. What took place with you? From where came the blessed movement represented in your last letter? Those wise in the blessed experiences say: The only condition of the spirit, through which gives a person all one's spiritual gifts, is humility. What does humility represent? We say, This is the continual prayer, faith, hope, and love of the trembling soul, given by your life to the Lord. "Your Lamb . . . calls out to You, O Jesus, in a loud voice: I love You, my Bridegroom, and in seeking You I endure suffering. In baptism, I was crucified so that I might reign in You, and I died so that I might live within You. Accept me as a pure sacrifice for I have offered myself in love. Through Your prayers, save our souls, since You are merciful." Humility is the door, opening up the heart and giving it the means to a spiritual existence. Humility gives the heart graceful rest, to the mind it gives peace, to one's thoughts—concreteness. Humility is strength, encompassing the heart, separating it from all that is earthly, giving it understanding about the existence of eternal life, which cannot enter the heart of the carnal person. Humility gives the mind its original purity. It begins to see clearly the difference between good and evil in everything. And to each spiritual situation and movement it knows their name, as the primordial Adam named the animals according to the characteristics he perceived in them. With humility, silence proposes to be imprinted on everything that is in each person, and, in this silence, the spirit of human beings, submitting to the Lord in prayer, hears his prophesies. Until the sensation of humility resides in one's heart, there cannot be a pure prayer. The God of continually present memory hinders the scattering of our thoughts, absorbing from our mind its vain cares. Only when all our life is wholly directed toward God, when a person becomes able to see and to trust in God in everything, then in all important extenuating circumstances of life, both in the very smallest—and in everything—to submit to His will, without which there cannot be either memories of God or the continual purity of prayer. Even more harmful to memories of God, and thus also to prayer, are feelings and passions. Therefore, it is necessary, rigorously and constantly, to heed the heart and its movement, firmly resisting passions that drive the spirit into impenetrable darkness. Every passion is a suffering of the soul, a sickness, and demands quick medical treatment. Depression itself and other forms of coldness of the heart toward spiritual activity are the essence of sickness. Similar to a person who was sick with fever, after the lapse of the sickness, for a long time still remains weak, sluggish, incapable of action—thus also the soul, sick with passion, is indifferent, weak, powerless, unfeeling, and incapable of spiritual activity. These are spiritual passions. To equip oneself against them, to struggle against them, and to conquer them is the primary task. It is essential to labor diligently in this struggle with spiritual passions. Prayer reveals the passions in us that live in our heart. The passion that is impeding our prayer is also the one that we must urgently struggle against, and prayer itself will help us in this struggle; with prayer, the same passions are eradicated. The lamp with which the maidens can meet the Bridegroom is the Holy Spirit, which enlightens the soul, [which] dwelling there, purifies it, making it Christ-like, and transforms all the characteristics of the soul according to the great [divine] Prototype. Christ recognizes such a soul as His bride, recognizes in her His likeness. If she is not enlightened by this lamp of the Holy Spirit, then she will be in darkness, and, in this darkness, moves the enemy of God, who fills the spirit with various passions and likens her to himself. Christ does not recognize Himself in such a soul and separates it from His contact. In order that the lamp is not extinguished, it is constantly essential to add fuel to it, and the fuel is constant prayer, without which the lamp cannot light the way.

Then, for the first time, I read the Great Canon of St. Andrew of Crete.[34] It seemed to me very difficult and incomprehensible.

Having come to Fr. Serafim, sadly, I said to him that I did not understand the canon, and I did not like it. "Don't be embarrassed," said Fr. Serafim, "I expected this." "Not only did I not like it, but it provoked some kind of protest," I indecisively added. "And this must be, and do not be embarrassed by this," Fr. Serafim answered.

In reality, subsequently, this canon became for me intimate and beloved.

I so wanted to submit to the guidance of Fr. Serafim not only by my will but also by my feeling and thought. Therefore, I laboriously endured those times when I could not agree with what Fr. Serafim said; at the time, such instances were many. I attempted to understand and assimilate his thought, but candor was most important of all.

One time Fr. Serafim directly said to me: "If you don't agree with me, then for what reason do you object?" "I am here not to object," I responded. "No, no, it is unavoidably necessary to disagree," said Fr. Serafim. "Otherwise, you will not have clarity. Besides, there are many questions in which each person may have his own opinion, and this impedes nothing. For example, I like green, and you—blue," he joked.

Fr. Serafim's incredible understanding of someone's heart was not only because of his spiritual sensitivity to the incredulous comprehension of someone else's heart, but it was also his spiritual gift.

Once, in the evening, preparing to go to Zagorsk to see Fr. Serafim, I was unsettled. The constant need to conceal and to deceive lay heavily upon me, as well as the fear that this next trip might end unpleasantly, not only for me but also for him. Before my departure, in order to calm myself, I randomly opened the Gospels and read the following words: "Peace I leave with you; my peace I give to you. I do not give to you as the world gives." (John 14:27).

When I came to Fr. Serafim, he opened the Gospels and read me these very same lines. Then I told him about everything. "You see!" he said, allowing me to understand that this "confluence" was not accidental.

Visiting the church from time to time before my baptism, I picked up only separate fragments of the service. When I heard the songs "Christ Is Risen" or "Lord, Have Mercy," I wished it would never end. Gradually, the Great Doxology, "O Gladsome Light," and others began to stand out as small islands.[35] The words of "Holy God" produced an especially strong impression on me, which I read once in a chapel in Hunters' Row, returning late in the evening on foot from the university.[36]

Sometimes, coming to the church and having incorporated some especially startling, new to me, moment contained, for example, in the words "Alleluia, O Give Thanks unto the Lord," or in the individual hymns of Lent, I left the church, because I could not take anymore, and sometimes walked the streets for a long time.

Here everything was different. Having come to Fr. Serafim, I felt that the whole world remained somewhere on the periphery. During the divine service, in addition to me, only two or three other people were often present. Fr. Serafim stood very close, and the entire divine service, from beginning to the end, took place in front of me. In this unusual situation, Fr. Serafim served in the same way that he served in a large church overflowing with people.

This striking incongruity between the divine service and the external situation in which the service took place underscored with extraordinary sharpness the deep, objective, cosmic significance of the liturgy, which had to be performed independently of how many people attended, as the surf of the waves of the sea cannot be suspended because there are no witnesses.

Sometimes everything taking place seemed to me of such significance that I ceased to understand why I was here, what right did I have to be present here.

In performing the divine service in the catacombs, Fr. Serafim fulfilled a great historical mission: "he preserved the purity of Orthodoxy." This conviction gave a special coloring to all of his activity: he was not banished—he left by himself; he did not hold out but created; he worked not only for this narrow group of people, who were with him in these conditions, but for the Church, for the future.

But not for one minute did he forget also the living people. Standing near Fr. Serafim during the service, I knew that he felt my state of mind in each moment and tried to help me. The knowledge that he understood everything calmed me and did not allow me to make a mistake. At the time, I was afraid to make some kind of movement by my own accord, since it always seemed to me that I did not do what was necessary. I knew that several people appraised my conduct as coldness. They did not understand that my feelings were still constrained, that I made every external manifestation of feeling with great effort and in a way that may have appeared impermissible.

Once, when everyone bowed during the reading of the prayer "Lord and Master . . ." and I attempted to follow their example, Fr. Serafim came up to me and quietly said, "To bow to the ground is not necessary." These words not only freed me from constraint, but they allowed me to appreciate clearly the great internal meaning of the earthly bow.

Fr. Serafim very much wanted me to be present for the traditional liturgy. To do this was very difficult, since it was impossible for me to travel to Zagorsk on a workday. Finally, one morning I somehow managed to free myself, and I traveled to Zagorsk on the eve and spent the night. The divine service had to begin before sunrise. When I went into Fr. Serafim's room, the "hours" had already begun. The words of the psalms and prayers animated the small house, so that it seemed that the very air, furnishings, and walls participated in the divine service.

The sounds lifted above, encircled the icon of Mary, Mother of God, and filled everything with them.

During these blessed minutes, with all the power of his soul, with all the intensity of the faith and love available to a person, Fr. Serafim prayed for himself, for us, and for the whole world: "O Lord, You sent Your most Holy Spirit upon Your Apostles at the third hour. Take Him not from us, O Good One, but renew Him in us, who pray to You."

Now, after many years, when in church in the days of Lent, the priest proclaims the third hour, it seems to me that I hear the voice of our elder.

After the end of the divine service, I needed to hurry to work.

"I am happy that you had the opportunity to be present for the Liturgy of the Pre-Sanctified Gifts," Fr. Serafim said to me.[37]

During this year, Fr. Serafim gave Lenochka his blessing for her to live in the dacha in Losinka.[38]

Losinka was so close to Moscow that they decided that she would live in the dacha for a half-year, which, because of the living conditions, was very desirable. Fr. Serafim wished for them to live specifically there, since on the second floor of this house lived the monk Ieraks, one of his closest spiritual children and assistants. Fr. Ieraks lived in the same situation as Fr. Serafim, but in circumstances more complex than his. Those who lived with him left for work, and among those living below, several must not know that a living person remained in the house; therefore, Fr. Ieraks had to do everything—even move about—entirely noiselessly, and only under the cover of night could he leave the house. Such a life, as I understood, required enormous effort, but Fr. Ieraks bore everything meekly and patiently, trusting in God's will and his spiritual father, who blessed him in this feat. He always appeared pleasant and joyous. Above were two rooms: one of them was his living quarters, and in the other room, with a balcony, Fr. Ieraks daily conducted the divine service. Spending whole days alone, Fr. Ieraks worried a great deal about the grandeur of his small church, which was always so clean, light, and adorned with flowers that inaudibly climbing the narrow wooden staircase and entering there, one immediately felt oneself in another world, where a quiet joy reigned, as on the Holiday of the Annunciation.[39] The tender flowering of the fruit trees outside the window merged with the interior furnishing of the room. Hostile elements of the world, it seemed, could not gain admittance here.

Having settled Lenochka in this dacha, Fr. Serafim undoubtedly wished to give us the opportunity to attend the divine service more frequently, since to travel often to Zagorsk was impossible. In addition, the arrival of an outsider family could ostensibly attract attention away from Fr. Ieraks. Lenochka did not miss one service, and I could attend very rarely, but, in Passion Week, I managed to come every evening. Only after these days passed did I remember that I was almost isolated from everyone and that I had completely stopped devoting attention to the people who needed it. "Really, is it possible that the desire to attend the service has made me so egotistical?" I thought, frightened. When I talked to Fr. Serafim about this, he answered, "Do not be embarrassed by it. The Savior said, 'The poor you will always have with you, but you will not always have Me . . .'"

Toward Easter, Fr. Serafim summoned me. Passion Sunday fell on the first of May. The day that demanded absolute quiet turned out to be on the most bombastic and noisiest day of the year. At this time, participation in the [holiday political] demonstration was obligatory. The night of Passion Saturday I spent in Losinka. Immediately after the end of the liturgy, I had to go to the demonstration and, from there, without going home, to Zagorsk.

Having found myself among my comrades from work, I felt, with special sharpness, the false pretenses of my situation. As it were, I was seemingly with them, but in reality, I lived in another world, which they considered inimical.

It seemed to me that I had to tell them everything or depart from them forever. It was impossible to live any longer such a double life, unworthy of an honest person, I thought. I thought this way, because at that time, the meaning of the following words did not come to me: "For I will not speak of the mystery with Thine enemy . . ." Our faith is a great mystery, and its victory will not be completed in the open world arena. "The Kingdom of God cometh not with observation . . ."

Calmed, before conflicts again took control of my soul, when, having said goodbye to my colleagues on Red Square, I fought through the crowds to the Northern Station.

"How glad I am that you came," Fr. Serafim said when he saw me. "It was very difficult for me," I said. "I felt this," briefly responded Fr. Serafim.

Fr. Serafim did not always give verbal answers and explanations. Often in separate moments, in separate actions, he unexpectedly allowed one to understand what had been unclear until then.

Once, earlier, even before becoming personally acquainted with me, he said to Sister about me: "She is afraid to touch things." This description was extremely truthful. He himself touched things in such a way that revealed their essence. This was a strength and power, which only God's grace gives, that power the Lord bequeaths to his pupils and apostles, having said, "Receive the Holy Spirit."

Each one of his spiritual children many times experienced this in him. The human memory is weak and fickle, but such moments are unforgettable, they remain unshakable, like a crag among the many diverse changes in our spiritual life. Is this not one of the personal proofs, demonstrating the substantiality of the soul?

FIGURE 5. Hieromonk Ieraks (Bocharev), end of the 1920s.

On this particular Paschal night, as in the preceding year, during the religious procession, everyone walked around all the corners of Fr. Serafim's house while singing, "Christ Is Risen." He placed a large cross in my hand, and I had to walk in the front with it. When I took the cross from the hands of Fr. Serafim, it seemed that, in this one moment in time, past and future were united. I did not hold just the cross in my hands; no, I held on to it and all the power that was in it.

Lenochka lived for half a year in Losinka. I often went there after work, and at night left for home. Alik grew. I became more and more connected to him, and this connection gave my heart an inexplicable yearning. Once, I went to Fr. Serafim and told him everything. "Perhaps, it is better that I leave them now?" I asked. "Later I will not have the strength to do this." "It is good that you have brought this up, and you acted correctly," said Fr. Serafim. "Only this is not necessary, entirely unnecessary. Lenochka lived with you for so many years, and what did you do? You looked after her soul. Do you understand me? Live together. We will not, for the time being, talk either about the monastery or about living on one's own."

I did not become accustomed to Fr. Ieraks right away. For a long time, it seemed impossible for me to talk about myself with someone else, except Fr. Serafim. Once, Fr. Ieraks said directly to me, "For what reason do you never drop in to talk with me, since I know everything about you, and I have read all your letters?" I began to call on him, in order to talk about Tonia, who at the time was gravely ill. Once, I talked with him about how people who gathered below said that all believers were enemies of the people and all needed to be executed. "Well, you could say to them: 'Please, execute them,'" Fr. Ieraks responded, smiling.

I knew that Fr. Serafim gave his blessing to Fr. Ieraks to hear confession and even give advice. Nevertheless, in these last instances, Fr. Ieraks usually answered, "Talk with Grandfather (as we called Fr. Serafim), he knows you better," or "he sees farther."

I was very sad that it was impossible to see Fr. Serafim more often, but he reassured me, telling me that even in an earlier time, he traveled to his spiritual father (the Elder Nektarius) in Optina Pustyn' once a year.[40] "We must value that which we have, and the time will come when we have only the Cross and the Gospels."

During the winter, Alik was sick. I looked after him all night, then contracted something myself. When, at last, I could go to Fr. Serafim, he asked me about my spiritual condition during the illness and said, "Sickness is sent to a person so that he will remain alone with God." I acknowledged that

I could not completely find peace during an illness. "What were you afraid of, that you will die?" Fr. Serafim asked. "No," I responded, "I was afraid that, without me, it will be difficult for Lenochka." Fr. Serafim did not respond, but when I was leaving he once more called me and said, "I am glad that you live so harmoniously."

In the winter, it was impossible to travel to Losinka. Lenochka and Tonia often went to the house where Fr. Vladimir served.[41] I did not feel good there myself and almost never went. Once, when I was there, they said to me that Fr. Vladimir was in the other room and wanted to see me. They said I had to go there, even for a short time, to receive Fr. Vladimir's blessing, and then it would be possible to leave. But to me this was such an embarrassment that I could not overcome it, and I left without seeing Fr. Vladimir. After this, pangs of remorse tormented me: how could I offend such a person?

When I talked to Fr. Serafim about this, he reassured me. "These situations happen, when you are not able yet to accommodate something, even when it is very good and entirely legitimate. Fr. Vladimir is a remarkable person, and his role is apostolic," said Fr. Serafim.

I was very surprised, having learned from Tonia that during Lent it was impossible even to attend concerts. I never looked upon music as entertainment, and, to me, it was not understandable why one ought not listen to music while fasting, during a time when we continued to carry out the majority of worldly affairs, which were much more entertaining and distracting than a serious concert. I appealed to Fr. Serafim for an explanation. "I myself love music," he said, "and always attended the theater and concerts, while I was a secular person. Lent requires a special kind of concentration. If worldly matters and concerns distract us, then this causes us suffering, and a concert provides comfort and takes us away from what, during this time, must solely occupy our heart. The problem is not the content of the music. Even if you wished to listen to 'Requiem' during Lent, I could not give you my blessing for this."

In Passion Week, I fell ill. Long ago, they had proposed that I should have an operation, but the matter had been set aside. This time the doctors said that to put off surgery any longer was impossible, and they insisted that I must have the operation in the next few days. On Passion Sunday, I had a high temperature and did not get out of bed. Lenochka and I were invited to the Easter service in Zagorsk. The weather was damp, and toward evening a strong wind and rain began. Naturally, the household considered a trip in such weather, with a high temperature, to be senseless. All the same, we decided that it was necessary to go, but I promised Papa that tomorrow from the station I would go to the doctor, although I did not very much wish to spoil the holiday for myself by being in the polyclinic. When we arrived in Zagorsk, it was already dark, and rain poured down.

My head was spinning, and I did not remember how we got to the place. Before the beginning of the service, Fr. Serafim heard confession from everyone. He expressed his satisfaction that all of us had come and referred to the great power in the Easter service.

Toward morning, I felt better and, from the station, as I had promised Papa, I went to the polyclinic. I told the doctor that all week I had lain in bed with a high temperature and that, to me, meant an operation. How surprising and bewildering it was, when the doctor almost became angry with me. "What kind of operation are you talking about, lady?" he said. "You don't need any kind of medical treatment." On the next day, I went to work, and the illness had completely passed. Since that time, more than thirty years have gone by, and not once has the illness returned.

Holding on to Christ's Garments

Once, an acquaintance, for some unknown motive but most likely out of inexperience, gave me Nilus's book "Elders of Zion."[42] This book so severely affected me that I barely avoided falling into spiritual confusion. I expected very terrible things could come from this. I did not sleep at night, and I had a feeling that I would be asked for a response, which I was not in a position to give. I could not conceive of anything more repulsive than this book. Under the cover of Christian ideology, the most hateful thoughts about humanity were represented in it, the most horrible slander was disseminated. The only solution was to talk openly with Fr. Serafim about everything. At that moment, one could not easily visit him. In the circumstances of those times, Fr. Serafim had to leave his own house and stay in a place where he could receive almost no one. All the same, I tried to arrange a meeting, and Fr. Serafim agreed, despite the fact that everyone around him warned against it, considering the danger of that moment. When I came to Fr. Serafim and told him everything, he anxiously said, "They do not understand! Well, how could I not have received you?!" He was very dissatisfied that they gave me this book without his blessing. Fr. Serafim talked with me for a long time and, at the end, said, "Everything that I could, I explained to you, and now . . . forget about this, forget it entirely."

The physiological memory of a person is weak, but his soul does not forget anything. But how great is the power of a spiritual father over the soul, if he can make one forget. He said, "Forget," and I forgot. With his powerful word, he removed the oppressive nightmare from my soul. Such is the mystery of obedience.

In the summer, Sister was diagnosed with tuberculosis, and since she was pregnant at the time, the doctors insisted on terminating her pregnancy. Fr. Serafim said that there could be no conversation about terminating the pregnancy. The word of Fr. Serafim was indisputable, and Lenochka courageously stood up to her doctors and relatives. Thus, even before Lenochka's illness, I told Fr. Serafim that one of our relatives advised her to have an abortion. "Never pay attention to such advice," Fr. Serafim said. "The advice to sin is a terrible thing."

I trusted Fr. Serafim unconditionally, but apart from my will, the danger for Lenochka's health remained all the same. When the team of doctors, who were in agreement with a professor's explanations, allowed her to preserve the pregnancy, I felt great relief.

When I told Fr. Serafim about the extreme worry for Lenochka, he said to me, "You love Lenochka very much, but you must remember that the Mother of God loves her more than you do."

For me, the prospect arose of taking care of Lenochka for two months far from Moscow and of creating the proper conditions for her. When actively and persistently one cares for a sick person, one's soul feels lighter.

Fr. Serafim pointed to Maloiaroslavets.[43] The thought then came to him that Fr. Ieraks, too, might go there in order to have a small respite from his stressful life and feel himself in freedom. We took a room in Maloiaroslavets, and, after some time passed, Fr. Ieraks came there.

I had to meet him at the station. The old conflicts revived in all their earlier power, when I understood what kind of role I now had to play. Conflicting feelings struggled in me: on one hand was the wish to fulfill the will of Fr. Serafim and love, respect and sympathy toward Fr. Ieraks himself; on the other hand, arose the same inner protest against the necessity to conceal and deceive, which I still could not overcome.

Having seen me at the station and giving me only a cursory greeting, Fr. Ieraks silently followed me, as only a person could do who, over a long course of time, had been accustomed to hide; this was very difficult for me.

Living in Maloiaroslavets, Fr. Ieraks immediately felt well, went on long walks around the surrounding areas, and rejoiced in nature and the opportunity to move about freely and mingle with people.

He somehow became younger, and his natural vitality returned.

I calmed myself down completely, and I wished to look after him, to do something nice, as if he were my papa. But with it came a new source of conflict. Papa was alone in Moscow, in the power of strange, alien people (as I began to suspect), and the reason for my conflicting feelings could have been my estrangement and how I had deprived Papa and given over his care to others. On Lenochka's and my birthday (which was almost the same day), Papa sent us a strange letter, which did not contain the usual affectionate words and good wishes. Papa wrote that what he had attributed only to the enthusiasm of youth (the aspiration to Christianity) had turned out somehow to be much more serious than that, and this created a barrier between us and people close to us. At no time, either earlier or later, had Papa expressed anything similar. In response to this letter, we requested that Papa come to Maloiaroslavets, arranging it so that his visit would take place after the departure of Fr. Ieraks.

The Dormition Fast began.[44] We found a secluded clearing in the forest. Fr. Ieraks took along a book of the church service and conducted the service in the forest. The forest turned into a church. It seemed that all inhabitants of the forest sang praises to Mary, Mother of God. One time a squirrel descended from a tree and, not moving, stood right beside us.

When my papa came, Alik (he was three-and-a-half years old) led him to this glade and said, "It is a pity, Uncle Iasha, that you could not have been with us. Here it was so beautiful!" Better than I, he understood the meaning of "conspiracy" and, like a child, did not fear it.

The day of Fr. Ieraks's departure approached. To go or, more truthfully, to leave with his escort N., he had to depart in the middle of the night, not long before sunrise. For some reason, I suddenly became anxious that Fr. Ieraks would forget to give us his blessing before his departure. This moment acquired some kind of special, vitally important significance . . .

When I went to Fr. Serafim after Maloiaroslavets, the first thing he said to me was "Thank you for Fr. Serafim." By this, he made me understand that everything related to Fr. Ieraks he received as if it was in relation to him, and that, as always, he knew everything that I went through. Similarly, if any one of us happened to leave late in the evening, and he wanted someone to go with us, he sent a request to one of his spiritual children: "Come, accompany me."

My papa, who all his life served as an example of a clean and stern life to the people around him, in his declining years became attracted to a woman, who wanted to marry for the third time, and to this cause lay my "estrangement" in everything.

"You must not grieve about this," said Fr. Serafim. "Now I am your father." He then explained that, for the benefit of Papa's soul, I must not recognize this marriage and should not have any kind of family relationship with

F. A. The fulfillment of these directions caused not a few difficult moments between Papa and me, but in giving these directions, the future showed how wisely Fr. Serafim had acted. One time F. A. arrived especially in order to talk with me. It was very difficult for me, but I thought only about carrying out the obedience. During this time, a friend came to visit me. I was glad for her presence and asked her to help me—that is, to go into the other room and pray the whole time, while I talked with F. A. F. A. wanted to take me in her arms and kiss me, saying that she hoped that I would take the place of a daughter for her. I politely stopped her, formally greeted her, and in the entire ensuing conversation assumed very cold tones. "You wanted to say that you are against me, not as a subject but as an object?" she finally asked. "You understood me entirely correctly," I said. "Then I wish to ask you only one thing," she said, "that your relationship to your papa will not deteriorate." "Don't worry," I answered. "It can only be better." "How can this be?" F. A. was interested. "Because," I said, "great unhappiness has happened to him." After this, we parted.

Soon afterward, another unhappiness lay in store for me. My brother, despairing from the action of Papa, decided to unite his life with a woman who caused unending difficulty for him, especially because she impeded him from meeting with me.

After nearly twenty years following the death of Mama, our family came apart. They gave me a lock and key to a separate door, and Brother had to live for now (after the rearrangement of the apartment) in a dark room, which he called "my coffin." This was an unusually difficult period of life. Between Papa and Brother (who until now had tenderly loved each other) emerged some kind of enmity and misunderstanding because of the living arrangements. It is true that my room, where I had lived with Mama since my childhood, remained the same; as before, the windows looked out to the east, toward the sun, but not everything was the same. I wished to give my room to my brother, but Fr. Serafim did not give his blessing, having said that this will not help him. One time, during the holiday of Mary, Mother of God, Joy of All Who Sorrow, I went to Bolshevo, where Fr. Ieraks then lived.[45] "Here all who sorrow are gathered," he said, and asked me to come more often, since the service took place every day, and one always could find comfort.

Fr. Serafim, on the contrary, cheered me up, saying, "Your situation will get better, and you do not have now the indispensable responsibility to worry about yourself alone. Leaving, you will lock your room, You will fly in and out like a bird, and to the east, sing glory to God."

Alik grew up a bright child, and forgetting about his age, Lenochka and I often shared our worries with him. Thus, while still living in Maloiaroslavets, Lenochka talked with him about her pregnancy. He took this news in his own way and lived in a state of intense waiting. The child, still unborn, represented to him some kind of mysterious stranger, the reminder of which instilled fear in him. When they bought a blanket and other items for the future child, Alik was afraid to go into the room, or he kept a great distance from these things. When I told Fr. Serafim about all of this, he was very dissatisfied: "You should not have talked to him beforehand about these matters. The waiting for over a half-year is not only difficult for such a young child, but also for grownups. Was it necessary to keep him in such tension? Only after the child was born, should you have said to Alik, 'God has sent you a brother,' and he would have had peace in his soul."

Fr. Serafim devoted a lot of attention to questions about education and often gave me various pieces of advice. I always strolled with Alik, devoting to him almost all my free time. Fr. Serafim attributed great significance to these walks. "It is not necessary to talk much with him. If he raises questions, you should answer, but if he quietly plays, read to him the Jesus prayer, and if this is difficult, then recite, 'Lord, have mercy.' Then his soul will be strengthened." In the capacity of a model teacher, Fr. Serafim cited Pushkin's nanny. While occupied with her knitting, she did not abandon the prayers, and he felt that presence, even when he had already grown up and lived apart from her, which was reflected in his poem "To Nanny" (K niane).

When Lenochka built the dacha, Fr. Serafim was very interested in it. "I was not there," he said to me, "but mentally I walked around the entire dacha." He wished that a tall fence stood around the dacha, so that Alik could then freely walk alone around the garden.

One time Lenochka asked Fr. Serafim to permit her to take her son to church, in order to show him the grandeur of the church. Fr. Serafim gave his blessing, but Alik did not feel good there. "It's better to go to Grandfather's or to Losinka," he suggested. When we talked about this, Fr. Serafim said, "If he feels and understands this, then, at the present time, it is not necessary to take him to church."

Until he was five years of age, Alik received Communion calmly, but at this age, for some reason, he began to be very anxious before taking Communion.

Then Fr. Serafim decided that the time had come to acquaint him systematically with the content of the Holy Scriptures, since he already perceptively related to everything. Since neither Lenochka nor I had decided to take this responsibility on ourselves, Fr. Serafim assigned the matter to Marusa[46]—one of the very closest people to us, who beautifully managed this task.

Fr. Serafim did not allow us to take Alik to the theater or to the movies until the tenth year of his life. "If you want to furnish him with satisfactory experiences, it is better to buy him playthings," he said.

Lenochka's second son—Pavlik—was born in December 1938, but they succeeded in baptizing him only in April. We very much wished for Fr. Serafim to baptize him, as he had all three of us. But it turned out otherwise. I do not remember exactly how this happened: someone came to tell us that it was impossible to go to Fr. Serafim on this day (as it turned out, this was a mistake). Deciding not to postpone the baptism, we went to Bolshevo, and Fr. Ieraks baptized Pavlik. Fr. Serafim was the godfather (in his absence), and I was his godmother. After the baptism, one of our acquaintances congratulated me and said, "You have a godson; do you love him?" I was perplexed by this unexpected question and answered, "I do not know."

Afterward, this answer so tormented me that I talked with Fr. Serafim about it during my next confession. "You answered entirely correctly," he said. "You really do not know yet what a godchild he is and how you feel about it." Then he began to talk with me about the children, Alik and Pavlik, and about my relationship with them. In speaking to me, he was looking to the future. "They will more and more exist in your soul," he said. "And in their soul will remain your inward appearance"—I understood that he spoke about what will remain alive after my death—"like a picture that we saw once in an art gallery."

I once brought Fr. Serafim verses in prose that I wrote under the title "Ten Songs about a Little Boy."

Returning them to me after some time had passed, Fr. Serafim said, "I so liked the ten songs of yours that I wrote an eleventh one." I very much wanted to know what song Fr. Serafim had written, but I could not bring myself to ask him about it, and it remained unknown to me.

Once, I told Fr. Serafim that I could not stand by patiently, when people incorrectly approached a child, so that even when a person dropped in at an inappropriate time and prevented children from lying down to sleep, in me arose the feeling as though he or she were a personal enemy. Fr. Serafim said, "Your relationship to children is a gift of God, and it is impossible to expect the same thing from others."

The question of why I had not married disturbed several of our relatives. My aunt, Lenochka's mother, was especially disconcerted about this. For a long time, she had dreamed about giving me to one of her acquaintances. In her words, he was a humble person, educated, knew many languages, and had many other virtues. The whole time, under various pretexts, I avoided meeting this person. Aunt then decided to catch me unawares. During some kind of family celebration at Lenochka's dacha, when all the relatives had gathered, she also invited her acquaintance. The guests were on the terrace, and, as always, I remained with the children in one of the rooms. Aunt insistently asked me to go into the room with the guests, if only to converse a little with her acquaintance. "After all, you have absolutely nothing to lose, and perhaps you will like him." She so affectionately begged me that to refuse her would significantly offend her and all the others. I said that I would immediately go out. No sooner had she left the room, instantly, not knowing why, I went out through the back, and, without excusing myself to anyone, went to Zagorsk. When I was on the train, I could not regain my calm: why had I offended all of them over this, why could I not give in, since no one could compel me to marry, and all of this did not matter! What right did I have to go to Fr. Serafim so inopportunely, unexpectedly, without any serious reason!

After hearing me, Fr. Serafim treated this matter not entirely as I had thought. "You acted completely correctly," he said. "Since it is not necessary to marry, then to become acquainted is not necessary. And all of a sudden to like him?"

Fr. Serafim was very interested in my work and often questioned me about it. "And with what would you be occupied, if the Bolsheviks had not taken over?" Fr. Serafim asked me. "Probably, with much the same thing as I am doing now," I responded. "I always only wanted to engage myself in literary work."

Fr. Serafim related to me something from his own life. His father was a stern man, who was not close to his children. His mother, on the contrary, was a kindhearted and sympathetic woman. Understanding the inclinations of her son, when he was still a child, she would say to her daughters (his sisters), "Sergii will leave us and become a monk!"

In his youth, Fr. Serafim worked in the library of the Rumiantsev Museum and contributed to journals. Apparently, in later years, Fr. Serafim also did not abandon his literary work. One time, he told me, he wrote on the topic of marriage. Another time, he asked me to research various understandings of "science." I brought him many notes that I made from the *Encyclopedia of Brokgauz and Efron* and the *Great Soviet Encyclopedia*, for which he was very grateful. Apparently, he needed this for some kind of work. Unfortunately, I did not manage to become acquainted with even one of his literary works.

Once, I told Fr. Serafim that the people at my institute proposed that I write a dissertation. Fr. Serafim became thoughtful. "You will write the dissertation," he slowly said, "and your soul will suffer, and I will cry about it . . ." I asked whether it would always be harmful to me to write a dissertation or just at this time. The question was clearly ridiculous, but I wanted a precise answer. Fr. Serafim explained to me that the benefit or the harm in each matter depends on the condition of the person's soul.

Another time, Fr. Serafim said to me, "To you, at the present time, it would be harmful to work for much money, and even if you gave the money to me, to your papa, or someone else, it doesn't matter. For you right now, it is not useful."

Fr. Serafim told me that each person has his own pathway that corresponds to his spiritual disposition. Thus, also in the monastery, different people received diverse works of penance. For example, some people were sent specifically to search for those who were in need of help and to do various good deeds. "You are not related to such people," he said. "You must not search for good deeds. You must fulfill only that which you are given right now and which has come into your life. In the future, you will have to dry your tears. Do you understand me—tears?" he repeated, placing emphasis on the last word. I understood nothing. "And it is not necessary to search for suffering," continued Fr. Serafim, "for you what you are already bearing and what is all around you are sufficient." I confessed to Fr. Serafim that formerly I was prepared to repeat after Alyosha Karamazov, "I also want to suffer," and now I do not have such a desire and even the opposite, a fear before impending trials.

"In Alyosha's case, this was on account of his youth," observed Fr. Serafim, "and in your case . . . from pride."

I wanted to know whether in these instances, when you did not manage to recite all the morning prayers to their completion, it was possible to finish them while busy with other things. Fr. Serafim said that only in extreme cases was it permissible. While engaged in other work, it was better to recite short prayers. "These prayers you can recite always and everywhere," Fr. Serafim said, "You hold the garments of Christ . . ."

Go to Sarov

Before my baptism, I knew almost nothing about Russian saints. Only twice had I come across the name of Serafim of Sarov.[47] The first time was when my uncle talked to me—he was a writer, a doctor, and "less than five minutes a communist," as he said about himself. He was sent, together with other representatives of the press and medical staff, to exhume the remains of saints, for "denouncing," etc.[48] He had to go to a series of sacred places, including Sarov. What he related about these trips, I do not remember now and at that time did not have much of a desire to listen to him.

The other time I encountered the name of Serafim of Sarov came several years later, while working in the travel center of the Library of Politprosvet [Political Education].

At that time, much antireligious literature was published, which had before it the task, in Krupskaia's words, "to profane sacred icons."[49]

When they sent me certain books at the center, I usually put them far away in a cabinet, and then, when no one was looking, put them back in the collection. Among these books, my eyes fell upon a small volume, under the title *Serafim Sarovskii*. It told the story that the tsarist government, wishing to divert the popular masses from revolution, invented a new saint. I knew nothing then about the venerable Serafim and could not contradict this lie with anything. In addition, from this book, as from everything similar to it, an oppressive feeling of repugnance and perplexity remained with me.

In the first years after my baptism, I intended to spend my summer holiday in the forest.

Having blessed me before my departure, Fr. Serafim said, "Rest in the bosom of Mary, Mother of God." He gave me the *Diveevo Chronicle* (Diveevskaia letopis') to read and advised me not to take with me any kind of secular literature, even poetry, without which, as it seemed since my childhood, I could not live and apprehend nature.[50] "Wander around the forest," Fr. Serafim said. "Instead of poems, recite 'Lord, have mercy.'" At first, this seemed difficult, but soon I felt that the world began to open itself anew before me. However, only a trip to Sarov clearly showed me how prayers opened up the beauty of nature before a person more deeply and more fully than all the charms of secular art.

I settled into an old, ramshackle hut in a village unknown to me on the edge of a large forest.

Over the course of two weeks, I did not bother myself either with any responsibility or with any company except the *Diveevo Chronicle*, which I wasn't even reading (can one really call it reading?) but was gradually absorbing, together with the quiet, rustles, and aromas of the forest all around me.

Not everything in this book was equally comprehensible and assimilated by me. But what had been foreign and little understood receded into the background, and, an indelible image was left in my soul, close to my heart, of the sacred Serafim and the Diveevo and Sarov inhabitants.

Did I at that time have a thought or desire someday to pay a visit to these places? No, in similar instances, thought follows feeling, and desires remain silent.

If one wishes something from the self or for oneself, the Lord wishes something else for us and guides our life along a path known to Him alone.

Two years passed. The opportunity came for me to take a holiday in the Crimea on the shores of the Black Sea. A room for me had already been reserved, and I dreamed about the prospects of a sky-blue sea, the aroma of roses, and the starry southern nights. There remained only to go to Fr. Serafim for his blessing. But Fr. Serafim, after listening to my story about the proposed trip, said, "No, this is not what you need. For you, the Crimea will scatter your thoughts, and it is necessary for you to gather them. It is better to go to Sarov!"

It is difficult to convey the impression that these words produced in me! How pale and dull my dreams about the Crimea seemed to me.

It is possible to have a desire to go to the Crimea and to ask a blessing for the trip, but without the blessing, it is impossible even to want to go to the Crimea. Only upon receiving the blessing does consciousness of one's unworthiness give way to the sense of peaceful confidence, which covers up the personal "I."

The words "Go to Sarov" produced a strong impression on everyone who came to Fr. Serafim at that time, but they responded to these words in diverse ways. Several were bewildered: "Why go to Sarov now, when everything there has been destroyed and nothing remains?" "Formerly, you might have had a look, but now what . . . ," they said, sighing. They expressed even the thought that, under present circumstances, a trip to Sarov was both inexpedient and unsafe. Only K. I.[51] quietly and simply, as always, asked me to bring her water from the Sarov springs. "If you are honored to be at the Saint's," she said to me. These last words deeply imprinted themselves on my heart and helped me more properly get ready for the forthcoming trip.

At home, I informed them that I had changed my plans, and I was going to Sarovskaia Pustyn'. Papa was not surprised, knowing my love for the forest and solitude, and said, "Do what is most enjoyable to you." Brother, with his own peculiar sensitivity, more deeply understood the goal of my trip, attempting to explain it to himself as analogous to the feeling he experienced, during his ascent to the peaks of the Caucasus Mountains, on the line of the eternal snows, when he left the whole earth far behind.

"Well, what is this, you are setting out to your own Elbrus," he said to me. I was very glad of his sympathy.

I was supposed to go see a woman by the name of Polia. She was to give me a letter to her friend in Diveevo, where I had to stop. Polia worked in one of the large, newly constructed Moscow factories and lived in the dormitory. I went to search for her. For three days, I futilely wandered around the gigantic factory. Polia was nowhere to be found.

Surprisingly, however, these failures did not produce in me anxiety and disappointment, as usually occurred in similar instances, but, on the contrary, increased my conviction that everything would be as needed and Polia found, if not by my own efforts, then by a miracle. In reality, on the third day, after returning from a fruitless search for Polia, I met between long rows of brickwork two women from another factory. After talking with them on the road to the tram and telling them about my lack of success, unexpectedly, I discovered that they knew Polia and even lived with her in one dormitory. It seemed that they had directed me to the wrong factory.

When I returned home, they told me that, in my absence, they had sent me a message about the earlier mistake. Now I had entirely no reason to complain about the loss of three days and could only thank God for what had taken place.

On that evening, it was already too late to go to Polia, and on the following day, I set out to see her. In the dormitory, everyone knew "Aunt Polia" and loved her. A young woman, strong, energetic, and obviously cheerful and sociable came out to meet me.

She led me to her room. I passed her the note, which they had given to me at Fr. Serafim's. Asking nothing, she then wrote a short letter to Nastia and gave it to me. She asked me to convey greetings to Nastia, and she said that yesterday I would not have found her at home, since she had gone to see her Mother Superior. The talk about Mother Superior Mariia thus did not correspond at all to the surrounding environment, and Polia herself did not resemble a nun in any way. In her behavior, however, was such sincerity and simplicity that every thought about conflict or masquerade immediately disappeared. We parted as though we had known each other for a long time, and when I returned, the very factory, with its shops and dormitory, seemed less foreign to me.

Everything that related to my trip to Sarov, each detail, each small event, as I remembered them then and even now, seemed the fulfillment of a special, deep thought, which is always present, but which we, submerged in vanity, are rarely conscious of in the seemingly insignificant events of our fleeting life.

Boarding the Arzamas train was difficult. Brother, who promised to accompany me to the station, did not manage to arrive in time. Almost at the moment the train left, I saw Papa through the train's window.

It was the second time in my whole life that Papa and I encountered each other spiritually. The first time was in the small monastery of Optina Pustyn′ (it was then already a resort) on a quiet summer evening, full of the aroma of flowers, when an elderly gatekeeper, in a quiet voice, said something about the Second Coming. The third time took place two months before Papa's death, on St. Nicholas's Day, when Papa lay unconscious, in a strange room, and, alongside him, I recited the *akathist* to St. Nicholas.[52] When I finished reading, he regained consciousness and in response to my words, said, "St. Nicholas made a present of you to me," he responded with such a bright smile that I understood; the words of Fr. Serafim, "Before death to him everything will be revealed in the light," was fulfilled.

Marusia bid farewell with me through the window, and I felt that with all her soul she wished to go to Sarov with me.

The train departed. I traveled alone to a place unknown to me, which earlier had so many visitors but now was almost a deserted region, and I was going to St. Serafim for the living water for everyone whom I love . . .

In Ravaged Sarov

At dawn, I arrived in Arzamas and went to find the means to cross into Diveevo.[53] I had been instructed not to ask those around me about Diveevo (in order not to awaken any kind of questions and suspicions) but to name another, nearby village (I do not now remember its name).[54]

It seemed that the autobus, which they told me to take, did not go every day, and no one could explain to me how to reach the goal of my trip. Thus I spent several hours in Arzamas, in painstaking search for transportation, unsure this time that everything would work out by itself.

It was already late when I saw a cargo truck on which they had loaded gas. From their talk, I understood that they were transporting the gas to a machine-tractor station, located in Diveevo. I asked the workers to take me with them.

The day was scorching hot. The truck quickly proceeded through clouds of dust. There was neither a small tree nor a slight breeze . . . The barrels moved about and smelled of gas.

Along the way, the truck picked up two or three women. They talked about the weather and the harvest. Toward evening, we drove up to Diveevo. I expected to see the forest, but here, and along the road, the forest was nowhere to be seen.

The truck stopped. Everyone around went about their business, paying no attention to me. I found myself in the middle of a small stone square but in a lively settlement. The windows of homes were open. These were monastic constructions, which now housed the office and administration of the sovkhoz.[55] Many people, apparently coming to work from various places, bustled around.

In the light of the fading summer day, silhouettes of the locked shutters of the church and the chapel sharply stood out. I approached one woman and asked her to show me where Nastia lived. It turned out that I had only to cross the square. Not without anxiety, I went up to the house, and after leaving my things by the gate, I went to meet Nastia and gave her the letter from Polia. After reading the letter, Nastia gave me a choice: to stay alone in the shed or stay in the hut with her and her children. I preferred to stay in the hut.

From the age of three, Nastia had been educated in the orphanage of the Diveevo Monastery, and then had married. Her husband worked in Gor'kii, but she lived here with their two small daughters and two white goats.

The oldest daughter, Mania, ran around the fields the whole day, and little Tonia quickly crawled on all fours around the entire house and at night slept in a cradle, suspended under the ceiling. I lay down on the floor, and I was ashamed for them to spread out clean sheets and pillowcases for me over the sheepskins. In Nastia's home, there were no linens. She slept with Mania always on the floor, on an uncovered mattress, which by day they carried into the garden and, at night, spread out in the hut.

Little Tonia had no clothes, if one did not count the single swaddling cloth for all occasions of life.

The children quickly became used to me. I was the dry nurse to Tonia in the evenings, when her mother tended to the goats, and Mania went with me to the bazaar.

During this year, getting food was difficult, and even bread could not always be obtained. Nastia and I ate together and divided among ourselves everything that we had.

I liked Nastia immediately. She was restrained and taciturn, but her silence was not burdensome. She did not complain, but she had a critical relationship to both the past and the present, and, concerning spiritual subjects, she manifested great care and sensitivity.

Only before my own departure did I begin to feel how dear the monastery in which she grew up was to this simple woman.

Nastia told me, as she much as she could, about the churches, the chapels, and the graves, about the *kanavka* of St. Serafim, and about the brooks and waters.[56] I began to wonder around Diveevo and soon saw that it lived a double life. On the surface was the anthill, the newly arrived people with their anxieties and labors, and in the depths the life of the monastery glimmered, and it kept alive the venerable memory of the saint.

In the chapels, inextinguishable lamps burned; on the graves, a solicitous hand was discerned, and often passersby, especially peasants from distant villages, made the sign of the cross to the images, which had been left on the pediments of the locked churches.

I never saw such signs of the cross as in Diveevo and Sarov. It was as if each person, who came in faith to these places, felt that here he did not pray the prayers only by himself, but the prayers of St. Serafim inspired his prayers.

Undoubtedly, the most miraculous things in Diveevo were the underground springs. After the closure of the monastery, they thoroughly covered them, in order to blot out in the people the memory of their divine power. This, however, did not help: both there and here, the spring water broke anew through the surface of the land. In the beginning, I was surprised, when I saw how someone from among the passersby bent down to the ground and attentively looked and listened to something. Coming closer, I heard an enthusiastic whisper: "the spring has opened up!" They covered the spring again, and it again opened up—a living symbol of God's inexhaustible mercy for the human thirst for faith.

People had accorded several springs a special love and given them the names of people who opened or protected them.

Ten days passed, and all the time I had still not succeeded in going to Sarov. Nastia was very distressed for me and went to all kinds of trouble to find someone to accompany me. To go without accompaniment was impossible, since, not knowing the road, it would have been easy to get lost in the forest, and it was now difficult to find things in Sarov for someone who had not been there earlier.

The local inhabitants already looked askance at me, since they did not understand who I was and what I was doing here. Representatives of both groups of the Diveevo population began to regard me suspiciously.

One time in the evening, I sat on a hill and made notes from the book of Simeon the New Theologian.[57] Several workers from the sovkhoz came up to me and in a reproachful tone asked: "Are you deducting the expenses for the flour?"[58] Then they softened up, sat down next to me, and one of them asked me to take dictation for a letter to her fiancé, who had left her.

Another time, at noon, I sat down to rest by the river. An unusually dressed young woman with a thin and beautiful face came up to me. This was one of those nuns, who, after the closure of the monastery, did not go "into the world," but remained in seclusion to live in the suburbs in a state of impoverishment.

"What are you doing here, servant of God?" she sternly asked me. "I am resting," I answered. Glancing at me, she calmly said, "Rest with God," and left.

Several long days passed. Nastia found someone to guide me. This was an old nun, who had lived in the monastery for more than fifty years. They called her Matrona Fedorovna. She was tall, a little bent over from old age, and her head lightly shook. She wore a black headscarf and, in her hands, she carried a large cane.

We agreed that she would come to us on the following morning, at dawn, and we would set off for Sarov.

When daybreak had only brightened the sky, Matrena Fedorovna rapped on the window. No one said a word. Everyone crossed himself or herself, and we set out upon the path.

All around us stretched spacious fields. We were alone. The road, twisting around, pulled us along with it into the distance. In the soul, as an echo from afar, leaving the world behind, the words of the poet resounded: "Alongside the blind old man to go there, / where no one is going" (R. M. Rilke).

When we arrived at a nearby village, we added still another traveling companion. This was a local peasant woman, whose daughter worked in a factory in Sarov. She was going to see her daughter, and Matrena Fedorovna made an agreement with her about lodging for the night.

The new traveling companion seemed talkative. She and Matrena Fedorovna engaged in a lively conversation. I walked behind and listened to their tales. I heard just about everything: the destruction of the monasteries, the suffering for faith in our time, the countless cases of miraculous deliveries and healings, the terrible punishments of those who defiled the sacred, and all sorts of dreams, visions, and prophesies. To such an inexperienced person as I, it was impossible to discern where the boundary of truth ended and fantasy and folklore began.

Folklore does not always distinguish between the two. These tales of provincial people only approximated the lives of saints, and they often resembled fairy tales or the metamorphoses of Ovid.

The closer we approached Sarov, my traveling companions became more silent. From out of the forest, cupolas appeared, and soon the entire Sarov Monastery arose before us in the form that we had seen more than once in pictures.

The day moved toward evening, and we wanted soon to find a place to spend the night. The huge churches were empty, but all the inhabitants' homes were tightly packed. The inscriptions [signs] said that we were within the boundaries of the Mordovian Autonomous Republic.

On the street, we encountered beautiful Mordovian women in national costumes, but the majority of the population consisted of young teenagers, mobilized from various places at work and in FZU schools.[59] They lived in dormitories. There it was warm, dirty, and noisy.

The daughter of our fellow traveler lived in one of the small rooms of the dormitory. She was still a very young woman. She had a three-year old daughter, the father of whom had disappeared into the unknown. The child agitated and oppressed Mother Mariia and the grandmother, who did not conceal their feelings and wished for her death.

All of us lay down on the floor of the small room; exhausted by our walk, we soon fell asleep. Through the window came shouts and laughter, which did not quiet down for a long time. When I awakened, it was already light. Matrena Fedorovna stood in prayer.

We could go to the waters only at ten o'clock, and therefore I still had plenty of time to look around the environs.

When I went out onto the street, the settlement still slept. The Sarovka River peacefully reflected the bushes on the riverside. Quietly and majestically, the monastery towered above. One felt that, although here existed neither the former splendor and magnificence nor the monks, nor the sacred icons, the grace of God had not left these walls, and St. Serafim continued to carry out divine service in heaven.

I had experienced something similar before, even before my baptism, in Optina, although at that time, I could not have given myself an account of it. Traces of prayers and spiritual feats were imprinted in me, and they remained in the surrounding nature so clearly that they seemed almost accessible to one's external consciousness.

For the most part, the churches were locked, but in one large church, the door remained half-open. I very much wanted to go inside and find out whether paintings or writings on the walls remained. The heavy door gave way with difficulty. I peered inside. Inside, the church was empty, the art was painted over, and grass had overgrown part of the premises. Soon I became convinced that I was not alone. Before me, a cow stood, and she looked at me with her large round eyes. Whether she had separated from the herd and accidentally found her way there, or for some special reason, someone had left her here for the night, she obviously did not like it and mournfully bellowed. I decided not to open the door wider, fearing to release the cow and with that to cause loss to her owner and bring unpleasantness on myself, and I hurried to leave.

Taking with us a dish to obtain water from the Sarov waters, we were led along a further path. Matrena Fedorovna brought with her the *akathist* to St. Serafim.

Despite the fact that our talkative fellow traveler was with us, we walked in silence. Everyone felt that in this forest one must not talk and should only pray.

Here was not that double life that we observed in the settlements of Diveevo and Sarov. Here the power of St. Serafim fully prevailed. Each person who entered this forest came to the saint. People also talked, acted, and moved here somehow differently than in other places, as though they were afraid somehow to violate or interfere in something.

I knew then that to the present day hunters did not kill bears in these woods, in memory of the bear that St. Serafim fed from his hands.

On the crossroads, by the road to the waters, stood a cross. Earlier on, it had been the Crucifixion. Now, it had been taken down and damaged, and the wooden cross was broken in many places.

People who were here earlier remember the monastery in its former flourishing state, think that now in Sarov nothing is left, and perhaps experience only sorrow or indignation at the sight of the broken cross. They do not share my feelings!

The neglected and broken cross in this blessed forest, it seemed to me, made a closer and more tangible symbol of the Savior's suffering than the artistically represented and protected Crucifixions in wealthy and resplendent churches. In the wooden debris, one felt "the blessed tree, on which Christ, the Lord and Savior, was crucified." Crucified and Stained with Blood, He saved the world!

This tree expressed the love of God to the world and humanity. Do not holy places, desecrated and ravaged, really become for us still more sacred and dearer remembrances of the sufferings of the Savior, the Lord Jesus Christ? From here, from the Cross, is granted love, which forgives and blesses everyone!

I picked up pieces of wood, broken off from the cross, and took them with me.

The closer we approached the main springs, the more often we encountered people on pilgrimages. Many of them had walked tens of versts on foot; several carried children with them. They walked in concentration, timidly, trying to be unnoticed, in solitude. In each heart was kindled the all-unifying light of faith in the gift of healing, with which God blessed the saint.

Each of those who came stopped at the place where the rock was located, on which St. Serafim had prayed for many days and nights.

The rock they [the authorities] attempted to destroy: they blew it up; they smashed it into small pieces, but, all the same, fragments could be found at a distance all around. I saw children and grownups carefully collecting the smallest pieces of rock in the grass. The wells were broken, but the spring of clean water gushed from under the earth.

Matrena Fedorovna, with a prayer, sprinkled herself and me with the miraculous fresh water, and she proposed I read aloud devotional prayers to St. Serafim. In another setting, I would have been embarrassed. Here, everything subjective disappeared and lost its independent significance. Sarovskaia Pustyn' propagated the works and achievements of St. Serafim; he ennobled her thickets and forests with his prayer. In this objectivity of the spiritual world, all questions about the theory of knowledge dissipated. God Himself, this world's creator, is the criterion of truth. He Himself is the Path, the Truth, and the Life. The boundary between the material and the spiritual faded out there, where the grace of the Holy Spirit filled the stones and the springs . . .

At the spring, we bade farewell to our fellow traveler. She left for home, and Matrena Fedorovna and I moved further on. The forest became thicker, and fellow travelers appeared no more. If it were not for Matrena Fedorovna, I would not have known where to go. But she knew all corners of the Sarov forest. What a wondrous feeling you experience in this forest, when it envelopes you tighter and tighter on all sides. One can almost not believe that this is still our land that flows into the sky and dissolves in it. Here is the glade in which the saint fed the bear, and here is the cave, in which he also concealed himself during his ascetic life.

Matrena Fedorovna proposed to take in remembrance a handful of earth from the cave. We came to its exit and, unexpectedly, we heard a human voice. From the cave a youth, almost a child, sixteen to seventeen years of age, came out, and, taking me in at a glance, asked, "Looks like you are from Moscow?" "From Moscow," I answered, and he half asked, half assuredly added, "Does Moscow not forget St. Serafim?!"

Then he began to speak about the vanity and futility of all that is earthly. "Take the tsars," he said. "They were proud, supreme, and what of them remains?" The youth proposed that we walk with him. Not a great distance away, in the very thicket of the forest, we saw a birch tree. On the birch tree was a cross, and under the cross, an image of St. Serafim. Below, in the bushes, some kind of human form moved. It was impossible immediately to make out who this was. Only by looking closely, we saw that it was a monk, dressed totally in black, blind or half blind, and his hair overgrown to such a degree that his face was almost invisible. The monk and the youth asked us to sit down, and the hosts engaged us in conversation. It turned out that in both summer and winter, they lived in the forest. About their whereabouts, very few knew. The parents of the youth lived in one of the nearby villages, and worked in a kolkhoz. He had studied in school but, wishing to depart the world, went into hiding from his parents' home and settled in the forest with the blind monk. From time to time, he returned "to the world" to acquire the things necessary for life, and again went away into the forest.

With interest, the blind monk began to ask about Moscow and Moscow life, as though about something far away and a little frightful. The discussion with the blind monk, his dark and almost hostile attitude toward modernity, troubled me. Only by venerating the cross and the image of St. Serafim on the birch tree, with renewed strength, did I feel the proximity of St. Serafim. From his youth, he loved Christ, and he met a robber with the words "my joy," which, through his burning love, covered up and reduced to ashes every human hostility and evil—and my heart again became light and calm . . .

The youth cordially accompanied us and, attentively having looked at me, said, "Look at life, but more simply, and live in simplicity." When I departed, he cried out to me the following: "And do not forget St. Serafim! . . ."

We spent one more night in Sarov and started on our way back. This time we walked not directly but stopped in every village. Matrena Fedorovna walked up to homes well known to her. Never before had I observed anything like it. It was difficult to say what she was doing: whether she was a pauper begging for handouts or a master collecting tribute from his subjects. They gave to her not out of compassion but out of duty, not for her but for God, and consequently, also for themselves, for saving their souls and the well-being of their homes.

She collected with the knowledge of her right to a share of their labor. After all, she prayed for them!

Toward evening, we came out into a field. The harvesting of wheat was taking place. Seeing that we were coming from Sarov, several workers questioned us about the condition of the springs; others shared their own memories. One woman stopped for a minute with sickle in hand and pensively said, "Grace is everywhere, if only there is faith!"

When we arrived in Diveevo, it was already late. Nastia had waited for us. Her mood was animated. Somewhat embarrassed, she took from a trunk an icon of the Holy Martyr Faith and gave it to me.[60] "When they were closing the monastery, I took it from there and put it away, and now you take it in remembrance. This is your saint; place it somewhere in the icon corner."

Then she searched still more for pictures with a representation of the icon of St. Serafim of Sarov and separate moments from the life of St. Serafim, and she gave them to me.

Matrena Fedorovna spent the night with us, and in the morning she left, having promised to give me a piece of the rock on which St. Serafim prayed, if I would come see her in Slobodka.

Two days later, I set out for Matrena Fedorovna's. A hot midday set in, and the sky was cloudless. I needed only to cross a small meadow and ravine.

The hut in which Matrena Fedorovna lived seemed unfit for habitation. The local kolkhozniks had returned it for the use of Matrena Fedorovna and another elderly nun, who lived with her.[61] Someone had given them a goat and a pair of chickens, so they also lived there. The second nun was completely feeble and barely moved. In the home, everything was dilapidated, and there were almost no furnishings. Matrena Fedorovna allowed me to look at the monastery books she had preserved and in parting gave me the promised piece of rock.

When I went out into the street, the wind came up. I thought a storm was approaching, and I needed quickly to make a run for home. No sooner did I run across the road than an unknown woman cried out to me, "Run quickly to the house." I did not understand what the matter was but decided to do as she said.

I had barely managed to reach the home of Matrena Fedorovna, when everything around darkened, making it impossible to discern surrounding objects. The sky became dark yellow, and it was difficult to breathe. I cannot say whether this lasted for a long time, but for an instant it seemed that the light grew dim. "How serene and calm everything around was only several minutes ago," I thought. "This is the way the day of the Final Judgment will come," said Matrena Fedorovna, as if responding to my thoughts.

A strong gust of wind struck, which nearly blew down the tumbledown hut, and a large hailstorm began. Both nuns whispered prayers and, with shaking hands, placed cups with the sacred water between the windows. When it became light, all the windows in the hut seemed to have broken into pieces . . .

In the settlement, people picked up the broken glass and, shaking their head, said, "It is like it is after a bombardment!"

I very much wanted to stay in Diveevo until August 1 (the day in memory of St. Serafim, according to the New Style calendar). But the representatives of local authority began to be interested in why and for what I had come, where I worked, and so forth. I was afraid to create some kind of complications for Nastia and hurried to leave. Before my departure, I wished still to see the icon of the Kazan′ Mother of God, revered by the local population, and located nearly a kilometer from Diveevo.[62]

In the evening, on the eve of my departure, I went alone in the designated direction. The sun was setting. On the road, it was quiet, without any people. In the field, at a distance from any dwellings, stood a stout wooden house. It was locked, but through the window, one could see what was inside. Inside the house, it was marvelously clean and silent. There was nothing there, except the large miracle-working icon of the Kazan′ Mother of God. Wild flowers surrounded it. Lamps burned. Through all the turmoil that had taken place in the monastery, this icon remained inviolable.

They closed the churches, they silenced the bells . . . but the Zealous Defender devotedly poured out love and bestowed grace on the entire suffering world . . . Sunset colored the sky. It grew dark. The brook murmured quietly.

I returned to Moscow with a joyous feeling. In ravaged and desolate sacred places, I found the sacred not destroyed, but all-embracing, radiant with heavenly purity, and triumphant!

The day I came from Sarov to see Fr. Serafim was, for him, some kind of holiday. I had never seen him in such a joyful state of mind. "Tonechka, come look, your daughter has come, a real Sarov person," he called out to Tonia and, then still turning toward Tonia, Fr. Serafim said, "Tonechka, just think, only just think . . . Verochka—was in Sarov!"

Fr. Serafim was overjoyed because, finally, after so many years, at last, he had a living greeting from those sacred places dear to his heart. He might now learn what remained there and in what condition was everything he held dear and knew so well, and because, finally, after so many years, he had managed to send one of his spiritual children there, and because this, in fact, was me.

Fr. Serafim inquired about everything. He knew every small corner there, knew many people personally, and at one time had heard their confessions. In my confession, Fr. Serafim requested that I tell him only about the spiritual side, and everything concerning the external facts to relate later in front of the others. When I told Fr. Serafim about the feeling that remained at the end of my trip, that I had not only visited Sarovskaia Pustyn′, but had been at St. Serafim's place, he responded, "In essence, they are one and the same thing."

When we went out into the general room, I showed the presents that they gave me in Diveevo: the icon of the Martyr Faith from the Diveevo Monastery, the large picture with portrayals of the Sarov cloister, the appearance of Mary, Mother of God, to St. Serafim, and others.

"Your trip was not easy," Fr. Serafim repeated several times.

"Father, Verochka showed these pictures to her brother," Tonia said.

"As it is," Fr. Serafim said, "that is also necessary; it is very good that she showed them."

It Will Be More Difficult

The attempt to portray in words the internal character of Fr. Serafim presents such great impertinence, does it not, since I, as one can understand, am not in a position either to relate or to comprehend, even to an insignificant degree, all the multifaceted elements of his soul, all the diversity of his activity, and still more to depict the blessed atmosphere, which was created around him and emanated from the depths of his heart and dedicated to the Lord and Mary, Mother of God, to describe the depth of his understanding of the human soul and those pathways and predestinations, which the Lord opens only to his selected ones, and finally, to portray his great love for his homeland and for the Church, for which he suffered hourly. It is impossible to forget those moments of the liturgy when Fr. Serafim prayed about the "suffering Russian power" . . . One has to marvel at the breadth of his heart. It seemed he was prepared to receive everyone. The relationship of Fr. Serafim to each human soul may be defined by one word—"solicitude." When a person came to Fr. Serafim with unresolved questions or with great anxiety in the heart, as it happened, when he first made the sign of the cross over this very troubled heart, the anxiety disappeared, and then he began to explain, in an affectionate manner, what was not understood: "My beloved child!" And from these words, so strong did the soul become that it seemed prepared to meet all trials.

In concert with this, Fr. Serafim never tried to mollify external and internal difficulties.

"When Alik was small, we fed him porridge, and when he was older, we began to give him solid food," Fr. Serafim said to me. "The same thing with you. At the present, much is difficult for you, and it will be still more difficult in the future." This was clear and understandable.

He talked about the path of the Christian life. You see, the Lord himself said, "Whoever does not take up the cross and does not follow me cannot be my follower."

When bidding farewell, Fr. Serafim always followed the departed with a long attentive look. It was good to feel this gaze on oneself, which, it seemed, would accompany you everywhere until the end of one's days. How often does a person wish now, if only on the other side of life, to see again that same attentive look and to hear his voice, conveying the tender words, "My beloved child."

Fr. Serafim himself was often surprised that our peculiar form of life, in such a complex situation, went on without serious external complications. "It is surprising how the Lord takes care of you!" he said.

Besides his spiritual occupations—the elder's leadership and his pastoral and theological literary works—Fr. Serafim, in his seclusion, played an active part in the life of the Church, met with many of his like-minded church activists, and carried on a continual correspondence with them. In addition, there was not one question in which he was uninterested. He followed current events and worried about them with everyone.

The beneficial strength of his blessing was so great that it conquered the soul of each person with whom he came into contact. One time, he related to me the following example from his life. This was during that period when people were trained to relate to spiritual people without any respect and even to make fun of them. Fr. Serafim said that, for some reason, he had to go through the forest on a holiday. He encountered two young workers, who had had a drop too much. Coming alongside Fr. Serafim and laughing, they addressed him with the following: "Father, bless us to drink!" Fr. Serafim did not answer. They, however, did not leave him in peace and continued to walk beside him, persistently repeating these same words. Then he stopped, turned to face them and, crossing them, said, "I bless you . . . not to drink." This had such an effect on the young people that they asked his forgiveness, told him about their lives, and then came to him more than once for advice and blessing.

Fr. Serafim spent free time in his small garden, enclosed by a tall fence, behind the house. He loved to transplant young saplings and tend the flowers.

When Fr. Serafim went out into the garden, many white chicks surrounded him, walked behind him, and sat on his shoulder.

On holidays, when many guests were at Fr. Serafim's table, he was in such a joyous and affable spirit, and he joked and rejoiced in the little joys of his spiritual children, so that everyone felt entirely free and unconstrained. It seemed almost immaterial that each unfamiliar knock on the door, each accidental passing person, whether it was the postal worker or someone else, could disturb the peace of the small house, and its owner would have to hide. Such incidents often took place. Everyone knew and felt this, but there was no fear. Being near Fr. Serafim, each person felt under the Protection of Mary, Mother of God, and feared nothing.

They sought advice from Fr. Serafim about everything, even about any kind of purchase or about a style of dress, about a repair or the building of a house. He had a very good practical orientation and not only gave advice about many questions of household management and construction, but he also could perform many tasks and loved it when it seemed that everything was executed well and in good order. He found time to help the children of relatives in school assignments (those whose house he lived in), who found it difficult to learn. Fr. Serafim loved to draw, to design various constructions and crafts. One time, he gave Lenochka the blueprint of a sofa that one might convert into a sofa bed, and vice versa. Someone often spent the night at Fr. Serafim's, and such things were very necessary. He asked Lenochka to show [the blueprint to] the joiners who worked on her dacha, and to ask them whether they thought such a piece could be built. One of the carpenters said that, although he himself could not do this, he had seen such a piece of furniture when he lived in Finland. Fr. Serafim was very satisfied that his project turned out to be correct.

Loving life in all its manifestations and intellectual and physical work, Fr. Serafim also never abandoned the "consciousness of death." One time, at his request, Lenochka brought him nails for some kind of construction work. After examining the nails, Fr. Serafim put aside the very best and gave them to K. I. so that she might hide them. "These nails are valuable," said K. I. to Lenochka significantly, but Lenochka did not understand to what this referred. When Lenochka arrived on the day of Fr. Serafim's death, she saw these nails. They were to serve for constructing the coffin. For several years before this, Fr. Serafim saved them for the day of his burial.

Fr. Serafim attributed great significance to a reverent relationship to death. He very much grieved, when during the war, people tossed around the slogan "contempt for death." "Where will this lead next?" he said.

Nothing seemed to Fr. Serafim to be too small or unimportant. He took an interest in everything, knowing that behind each thing that belongs to a human being was concealed some kind of movement of his or her soul. Sometimes, a person brought something to him, for example, an apple or an orange. With gratitude, he accepted everything, and then often returned his gratitude to the carrier, and this action conveyed to the recipient a special joy and comfort. You see, in our everyday life we were almost constantly losing the feeling that everything we have, each piece of bread, was God's gift. Without God's blessing, things become agonizingly dead, they cease to give joy, become either of no consequence or inimical. Fr. Serafim, with one word, one touch, or by his presence, restored the correct relationship to things. Summoning God's blessing, he restored life to things, and the joy of life to people.

Once, when I was sick, Fr. Serafim sent me, glued on cardboard, a dried flower pressed under glass. Sending it to me, he said, "With great love, a servant of God gave me this item." I did not know who this "servant of God" was. But it was somehow of great value in that Fr. Serafim wanted to give to me, through this flower, the love of an unknown soul.

At table, Fr. Serafim himself divided and served the food, telling stories about everything, sometimes narrating something or reading aloud.

When someone recounted something about early gifts or especially interesting manifestations in children, Fr. Serafim always said, "Take care; it is necessary to take care!" Talking about a child, he spoke as though he had in mind not only a given period of his development, but also his life as a whole.

Once, Fr. Serafim said to me, "It is good that you are so attentive to Alik, but, having become accustomed to this, he will demand the same kind of attention from his wife." It seemed to me that Fr. Serafim was joking (Alik was only five years old), but he spoke seriously.

During this period, I often found it difficult to give myself an account of my real relationship to a whole series of things and what had already taken place in the past, and this complicated my relationships with former acquaintances. I wanted to ask Fr. Serafim to help me gain an understanding of this issue.

I asked this question, using a concrete example. "Father," I said, "when, for example, I went to the Library for Foreign Literature, I felt that I did not know, as before, whether I was interested in the fact that a new writer had appeared in America, or whether this does not much concern me?" "It does not concern you," Fr. Serafim firmly answered.

From childhood, I loved poets; poetry was the life of my soul. Fr. Serafim deeply understood and loved poetry, but, as far as I could tell, he understood poetry as some kind of preparatory stage in the development of the soul. I say "educated" because Fr. Serafim was an educator in the very highest sense of this word—in the art of the making of the soul, of that art, the material of which is neither the marble nor the paint, but the finest movement of the soul, that striving toward the divine, which the Lord invested in His intelligent creation.

In my communications with Fr. Serafim before my baptism, I often used the thoughts and words of poets. He always passionately responded, allowing me to understand that in them are only allusions, and these allusions are revealed in full in the world of the spiritual life; in the world of religion is where these allusions are fulfilled and become reality.

When I sent a quatrain by Tiuchev in one of my letters,[63] "To us, it is not given to guess/How our word will be—/But to us, sympathy is given,/As to us is given grace," Fr. Serafim warned me that I did not yet understand the full meaning of these words, and he reminded me of the words of this same poet: "Under the burden of the cross,/All of you, dear land/In the guise of a servant the Heavenly Father/Walked, blessing."

At another time, I used Blok's verses from the drama "The Rose and the Cross" to express the thought that occupied me, "joy—suffering—are one."[64] In response, Fr. Serafim wrote me that this thought is deeply Christian, and the road to its true understanding is only in the spiritual life.

By the way, Fr. Serafim greatly valued Gogol and, recalling his article "Meditations on the Divine Liturgy," said, "I cannot believe that a secular author wrote this."[65]

After my baptism, Fr. Serafim began to lead me to another understanding of the relationship between poetry and religion. I understood them one-sidedly, only their proximity, according to the thoughts of Zhukovskii: "Poetry is the earth's sister of heavenly religion."[66] The opposition between poetry as the art of fallen man and religion as the means of salvation I understood later, and only thanks to Fr. Serafim.

Fr. Serafim did not advise reading poets during a secluded stay in nature. Having returned home after the trip to Sarov, where verses were then entirely inappropriate, according to habit, I opened Blok and read a poem well known to me, "To the Muse," but the lines opened up to me, and I now read them in a different way. Addressing the muse, the poet says: "There is in your concealed melodies/Fatal news about death."

"Yes," I thought, "there is the news about death, but here is the news about salvation . . ."

At the same time, when there was talk about my brother and how to bring him closer to a spiritual life, Fr. Serafim said, "Read poetry to him."

Such is the "dialectic" of the life of the soul.

I told Fr. Serafim that one of my acquaintances often accused me of insincerity and even of pharisaism. "Don't try to vindicate yourself," Fr. Serafim said, "and you will be at peace."

Fr. Serafim never refused to help, even if they were people whom he did not know personally. When Natasha,[67] who lived in Leningrad, sent her friend a letter, in which she revealed her extremely difficult spiritual situation—how she, in the place of genuinely spiritual values, had begun to chase after "green emeralds," those things of dubious value (in essence, demonic idols), which European art of the nineteenth and twentieth centuries often attempted to present as attractive in appearance—Fr. Serafim himself decided to write her a letter for someone to rewrite and send on his or her behalf.

Fr. Serafim strictly related to each state of exaltation, which he looked upon as an infringement on the structure of the soul, on spiritual integrity, and as a "fascination," extremely dangerous for the spiritual life. When A. came, she demanded that Lenochka go with her to look at this "miracle," which, in her words, had happened to her. She had found an icon of the Savior standing in a church, felt that it was destined specifically for her, and had taken it herself and temporarily placed it in my room. When they told Fr. Serafim about all of this, he became agitated with A.'s deed and said, "This is not a miracle, but robbery."

Once Fr. Serafim conducted a long conversation with someone, and I sat alone in another room. Going out for a minute for something in this room, Fr. Serafim stopped and, unexpectedly, asked me, "Have you ever been attracted to theosophy?" (Apparently, the conversation in that room was precisely about this subject.) "No," I responded, "I have met people who were interested in these questions, but for me these things are repulsive." "Thank God," said Fr. Serafim, and he went out to continue the discussion without interruption.

Fr. Serafim highly valued work and considered libelous to Christianity talks about work being a curse for a human being. Work, like science—in his words—had its beginning even before the fall of man, when God gave man Eden, which he was to "preserve and cultivate."

He considered it very natural to have a lively interest in and even a passion for work. I remember once, in confession, I told him how, having gone to work on a Christmas holiday after an early Christmas service, I completely forgot that it was Christmas, and I remembered this only after finishing work, when I came out on the street. Fr. Serafim said that, if it were possible not to work on this day, it would be very good, but if it were necessary to work, then it would be completely natural.

He related very negatively to those whose unscrupulous relationship to work they attempted to conceal by citing reasons of "principle." Under no circumstances did he allow thoughts about sabotage or deception in fulfilling civic responsibilities. When a spiritual person, however, proudly occupied himself with social activity, Fr. Serafim considered this phenomenon distressing.[68]

"In spite of my deep respect for Fr. Pavel Florenskii," he said, "to me it was distressing, when I once met him on one of Moscow's central streets in a great hurry on matters of GOELRO (state electrification), with a packet of papers in his briefcase."[69]

Fr. Serafim was very inquisitive. Once, I arrived for confession with a heavy feeling. During the holiday, instead of going to the house where they had an all-night service, to which they had urgently called me, I preferred to go to a lecture about teaching the blind and deaf, an issue that was then, for Moscow, a novelty. Fr. Serafim said, "This is very interesting. In spite of my holy orders, I willingly would go to hear such a lecture."

"Do not be troubled by this," he said. "Each bird has its own altitude. The eagle flies under the clouds, and the nightingale sits on the tree branch, and each of them glorifies God. And it is not necessary for the nightingale to be an eagle."

In 1941, Lenochka's husband was arrested, accused of some kind of abuse of power at work. The accusations remained unproven. Fr. Serafim saw the internal meaning of everything that had taken place and responded with great passion. When they told him that there were sixteen files of charges, Fr. Serafim said, "Mary, Mother of God, will take care of everything." A year went by, and that is what happened.

Life on the outside was complicated. I had to take upon myself almost all worry about Lenochka's family. In addition, my worry grew about her personal safety. But my relationship with Fr. Serafim removed the bitterness of all life's ordeals.

On May 1, I had to go to a demonstration. I decided to take Alik with me. On the one hand, I wanted him to get fresh air, and on the other, I wanted to acquaint him with my comrades, so that if I had to enroll him in the kindergarten or sanatorium, he would not be a stranger to all the other children.

The weather was beautiful, and everyone was in a good mood. They asked Alik if he wanted to go to Red Square, to which he answered in the affirmative. In a word, everything was good, but in my soul I was not peaceful. What right had I to take the child to Red Square without having asked for a blessing? When I told Fr. Serafim about what I had done, he was not happy: "Your responsibility was to go to the demonstration, but you should not have taken the child."

"But why?" I asked. "I had such a good feeling. I felt that the people around were my friends, and I wished that everyone felt good."

"But you do not know what others felt," curtly answered Fr. Serafim.

One time Fr. Serafim gave me a candle and said, "When you have anxiety in your soul, light this candle and read the Canon to the Mother of God 'Distressed by Many Temptations.'"[70] After several days, late in the evening, they summoned Papa for questioning (as it appeared then—about a person unknown to him, who by chance dropped in on him at work). I lighted the candle that Fr. Serafim gave me and read the canon unceasingly until four o'clock in the morning. At four o'clock, Papa returned. From this time on, this canon became my constant companion in all the difficult minutes of my life.

Fr. Serafim aspired every hour to turn the hearts and minds of his spiritual children toward Mary, Mother of God. He prayed to Mary, Mother of God, both in greeting and in parting with each person who came to him.

He did not like to force the will to do anything; obedience must be by free will. Those who wished to think differently did not understand the essence of his guidance.

"Through her lack of development she talks like this: 'Fr. Serafim commands, Fr. Serafim does not command,'" he said to one of his spiritual daughters. "Fr. Serafim does not command anything."

Once a young woman, upset that Fr. Serafim did not give her the blessing to go to her fiancé in exile, said, "No longer, Father, will I come to you." "You yourself will not come. Mary, Mother of God, will bring you by force," Fr. Serafim responded.

One time, I asked what the meaning of the words "eternal memory" was, because the memory of a person or even of humanity cannot be eternal.

"Eternal memory is the memory of the Church," Fr. Serafim answered.

Fr. Serafim usually began a sermon with the words, "Well, how are we all doing?" Thus, in this way, it had the character of a discussion of all of life, of all of that which could have entered our consciousness in either a correct or a distorted form. Fr. Serafim saw deeply and knew better than I what had transpired in my soul, and he illuminated for me the dark aspects of my personal actions or worries.

"You see how difficult it is to understand," he said, referring to the danger a life without direction presents for the soul, how easy it is to be enticed by elements of the world or by the temptations of one's own self-deception and self-delusion. Sometimes, if I had not managed to be at Fr. Serafim's for a long time, I put my confession in writing and sent it through close friends. Visiting Fr. Serafim, I would find this letter in his hands, with various places underlined in red pencil. He would become acquainted with it in advance and would note those places to which he considered it essential to draw my attention.

One time, when I came to Fr. Serafim, a man unknown to me was sitting with him and writing something. This was Fr. Pyotr. "Take the blessing," Fr. Serafim said. I went up to Fr. Pyotr. He rose and blessed me. Afterward, Fr. Serafim said to me, "You will not remain alone: if I cease to be, Fr. Ieraks will be here; if not Fr. Ieraks, it will be Fr. Pyotr."

Fr. Serafim expressed the wish to walk with me to one of suburbs of Zagorsk, where an especially revered image of Mary, Mother of God, was located. I was extremely surprised, since Fr. Serafim seldom left the house, and moreover, for such a distance I did not understand why he wished to go with me. Undoubtedly, this must have had some kind of special significance for me. On that day, I had to hurry to go back to Moscow and asked to postpone the walk until my next visit. Until now, I cannot forgive myself that I neglected Fr. Serafim's proposal for the sake of some kind of household matter. I should have dropped everything.

On my following visit, our walk could not have taken place, since it corresponded with the memorable day of June 22, 1941, and Fr. Serafim could not leave.

The War

June 22, 1941, was Sunday and the holiday of All-Russian Saints. The weather was beautiful, and I, in very good spirits, was getting ready to go to Zagorsk. Right before my departure, Alik asked me, "Find out, please, from Grandfather, will there be war when I grow up?"

At Fr. Serafim's also, everything was calm. When I arrived in Zagorsk, it had begun to rain. "The rain will pass, and Father and I will go where he planned," I thought. At twelve o'clock, people began to arrive at Fr. Serafim's house. Some said the word "war." It seemed strange, lacking sense, but each of the arrivals, and there were more of them, brought the same news, behind which grew the unbelievable monstrous reality of an enemy's sudden invasion into the depths of the country.

I wanted to confirm [this news] again and still again. Molotov spoke on the radio; he named the cities occupied by the enemy, the cities that enemy aviation had already hit. War! Moscow in wartime conditions! Moscow suddenly seemed far away from Zagorsk. What mercy of God that I found myself on this day at Fr. Serafim's! The spiritual children of Fr. Serafim's arrived from Moscow, from nearby places, to receive directions, how to be, what to prepare, where to put their family, children, and possessions, whether they should remain in place or leave in the evacuation, and so forth. Fr. Serafim had to take upon himself all the burden of their decisions; he had to consider and define the place and fate of each person, to calm everyone, to inspire faith and confidence and the right relationship to the coming ordeal, according to the strength of each person. Finally, my turn in line came. When I approached, Fr. Serafim said, "Well, here, the shower has passed, but You and I will not go on our walk anymore." I was very agitated and said that

I would willingly cast everything aside and go to the front as a sister of mercy. Fr. Serafim stopped me. "Passion speaks in you," he said. "Your place is not there. You must protect the children. Tomorrow, transfer Lenochka with her children to Zagorsk; find a room somewhere nearby. In Moscow, children can perish, but here St. Sergii will protect them."

Taking his leave, Fr. Serafim blessed each of his spiritual children with special warmth. He knew that heavy trials awaited each one of them: for some—death, for others—the loss of loved ones, for a third group—sickness and isolation, for many—prison, and for everyone—deprivation, hunger, and danger.

"The martyrdom of Russia is beginning," said Fr. Serafim.

And on this terrible day, with special irresistible strength his words rang out: "With your grace, defend, save, forgive, and protect."

When I returned to Moscow in the evening, the city had become unrecognizable. The gay and welcoming lights shone nowhere; darkness enveloped everything. They say that Patriarch Tikhon, approaching the last days of his life, said, "The night will be dark and long." Precisely this way, it seemed, were these long wartime nights without lights.

Lenochka was alone with the children. They impatiently awaited my return. All of life had changed from morning to evening on this endlessly long day. Both Lenochka and Alik were very glad that Fr. Serafim had given [them] the blessing to go to Zagorsk.

At night, people went with their children to an air-raid shelter, since in the evening an air-raid alarm sounded, for what reason we did not know, whether this first "alarm" was real or educational. In the morning, we began to gather our things. It was already night when we reached the village of Glinkovo, three versts from Zagorsk. We were probably among the first "resettlers" from Moscow, and our cortege presented a strange impression. All our things we literally carried ourselves. Alik shuffled tiredly behind us, and Pavlik at times had to be carried. Somewhere, we arranged to spend the night in the very first hut we came upon, since it was already late, and, on the following day, we settled down into a more stable situation.

Established in Glinkovo, the four of us set out to go to Fr. Serafim. Walking three kilometers with small children on a hot day was not easy. When we reached Zagorsk, Fr. Serafim said, "The pilgrimage to St. Sergii begins."

"You will live here, as youth living in the fiery furnace," said Fr. Serafim. In reality, by the side of Fr. Serafim, it was impossible to feel otherwise. Panic could be seen everywhere; people rushed about; they evacuated children, drove the cattle away, and carried off machinery. Enemy airplanes sometimes came so close that it was possible to distinguish the imprinted swastikas on them; at nights, over Moscow, glowed the fire from the enemy's incendiary bombs. But Lenochka and the children felt themselves secure. When I was in Moscow, and Lenochka left to stand in the endless lines for bread, the children remained alone. Simple-minded neighbors said to the children, "They will kill your mama and aunt, and you will be sent to a children's home." "We won't go to a children's home," Alik whispered to Pavlik, "we will go to Grandfather's."

Relatives, acquaintances, and colleagues did not understand our "lighthearted thinking," and it deeply disturbed them. "Why did you not take the children into the deep interior? What right do you have to risk the life of children?" they said. But we knew: St. Sergii would protect them. "Here the enemy will not be, even if he comes very close, and even if he succeeds in taking Moscow," said Fr. Serafim.[71]

"In the day of national calamity, Sergii will rise up," said the historian Kliuchevskii. After a whole series of centuries, he again stood ready to guard the fatherland. The enemy occupied all cities near Moscow, except for Sergiev Posad—Zagorsk.

Fr. Serafim said that this war did not accidentally begin on All-Russian Saints Day, and its significance in the history of Russia would be very great. To the question "Who will win?" which they asked him, he answered, "Mary, Mother of God, will win." Many asked how to pray about the outcome of the war. Fr. Serafim answered, "Pray: 'Your will be done.'"

The fascists seemed to me the carriers of a dark power. One time I said to Fr. Serafim, "It seems to me that no Christian can be a fascist." "Not any Christian can accept such a cross," said Fr. Serafim, and made in the air the sign of a swastika.

Our institute quickly evacuated. The panicked flight of people produced an oppressive impression on those who, still not having experienced anything, were actually "perishing from fear of the coming disaster," suddenly overestimating everything, destroying material and cultural valuables, which they had created by their own labor—having forgotten, it seemed, in that moment even about their homeland and its future. No one understood why I was not leaving.

Several days after the evacuation of the institute, I went to work in the library of the Red Bogatyr' factory. Once a week I had to be on duty at night, and after the night duty, I left for two days in Zagorsk.

F. A. left for Sverdlovsk, and Papa remained with me. The lack of food products became more noticeable. Once a week, Papa and I collected everything that we could get, and I took them to Zagorsk. "I do not need anything;

take it to the children," Papa invariably said, on the sly, handing over everything to me that they brought for his personal use.

On almost every trip, I tried to visit Fr. Serafim. One time, when we were conversing, an air raid began. Fr. Serafim interrupted the conversation and began to pray. "And in times of an attack, you should always read the prayer "Victorious Leader" (*Vzbrannaia Voevoda*) in the factory during your night duty, and then they will not bomb the factory," he said.[72]

Night duty turned into hours of surprising experiences. I was alone on the upper floor in a huge four-story empty building. Below were only an old security guard and a chained watchdog. All around, it was full of emptiness, a city engulfed in darkness, pierced by the wail of sirens and the whistle of fragments of projectiles. I did not know whether they had hit our home and whether I would still see those close to me. But I was not fearful. I slept a completely peaceful sleep, and when the alarm began, I got up and prayed to Mary, Mother of God, as Fr. Serafim had instructed me, and then I fell asleep again until the next alarm. In the morning, I found out that an incendiary bomb had fallen nearby and burned the market. I remembered the words of Fr. Serafim: "They will not destroy the factory by bombing."

In those days, when I could spend the night at home, my brother and I did watch in the loft, where we could observe the air battles in all their horror, together with their fascinating grandeur. The war slightly opened the curtain of the other world. The war was not only between armies, between peoples; the war went somewhere deeper, into the heart of man, into the heart of the world. It seemed that all the powers of light and darkness came out to battle . . .

"Mary, Mother of God, will win!" . . .

"All of us must die, but only you and I will not die a violent death," said Fr. Serafim during one of my visits. "And from hunger you and I will not die, although we have little bread now, and there will be still less."

I told Fr. Serafim that I had brought the children several loaves of bread, which, with great difficulty, I had managed to obtain, and when I met a familiar elderly nun, I very much wanted to give her a loaf, but I did not know whether I had acted rightly and had the right to do this . . . Fr. Serafim said, "If you were bringing the loaves for the children, then to give them to someone else is not your responsibility, but if you are disposed by the heart to give one of them, the Lord will return five." Thus it was and would always be, as Fr. Serafim said.

In this difficult time, through very miraculous means, the Lord fed us. Everything essential appeared completely unexpectedly and at a time when, it seemed, help would come from nowhere. The evangelical miracle with the multiplication of bread, it seemed, was repeated hourly. One time, an entirely strange woman gave me ten eggs at such a moment, when I could not obtain anything for the children. She had brought the eggs for her relatives. It turned out that they were not in Moscow, and to carry eggs to the village was inconvenient, and she gave them to me, because, at that moment, I came upon her on the road.

On Christmas Eve, I was getting ready to go to Zagorsk with empty hands. I, however, did not abandon the conviction that the Lord would provide something for the children. On my way to the railroad station, I unexpectedly met a young woman, who before the war had been Pavlik's nurse. With joy, she gave me products she had only just received from the factory, which would enable us not only to feed our children but also to put up a Christmas tree and invite the village children. I will never forget this first wartime Christmas tree.

In this, as it were, very mundane sphere of life, some of the coverings blew off, and the depths of things were laid bare, through which the mysterious connection between people became more visible. Once, someone at work gave me one piece of candy. I decided not to eat it, since I felt it was intended for someone else, but I did not know for whom. That same evening, I stood in line at a store. The store was full of people. Suddenly, from the crowd, a woman emerged, and asked if anyone had a piece of candy. She was going to the hospital to visit a sick person, and she very much wanted to bring him a candy. It goes without saying that I gave the unfamiliar woman the candy, which was clearly destined for her.

Once, in the morning, Papa, who had the beginning of severe malnutrition, said, "I am dying without sweets." The further development of the sickness and its tragic end showed that this was not an exaggeration. I had nothing to give him. With a grave feeling, I went to work. There I was alone in the room. I asked Mary, Mother of God, to show me the way, how I could get today what Papa needed. From weakness, I began to doze off. A knock on the door awakened me. A familiar teacher entered and brought a little sugar, which she had received for her students, who, for some reason had not appeared for their lessons.

After this event, Fr. Serafim instructed me to divide the butter and sugar in equal portions between Papa and the children. "Now he is weak as a child," Fr. Serafim said, putting me on notice that Papa would not live much longer.

When I told him about my brother, about his tragically complex personal life, Fr. Serafim with particular apprehension said, "I do not know how the Lord will lead him out of this!"

Fr. Serafim said that he always prayed for my relatives, and only during the liturgy was it not permissible for him to pray for them. He said that it would be easy to convert my brother if a personal meeting were possible. But during these circumstances, it was out of the question.

The war strained all feelings to unprecedented limits. When the enemy occupied towns, it seemed that people close by were dying, and when an air attack destroyed houses in Moscow, it seemed like parts of your own body were destroyed.

One time, when I went to Fr. Serafim, he was very busy and proposed that I walk around the city, and, at the same time, find out whether they had brought in kerosene, which was already difficult to obtain.

At the outset, it was pleasant to me to stroll around the open space, and I even collected a bouquet of cornflowers. Having reached the central square of the city, I read an announcement that enemy troops occupied Smolensk. It seemed to me that the day darkened and the flowers lost their charm.

I hurried to return to Fr. Serafim and told him about my experiences. "Well, you see," he said, as if wishing to bring to my consciousness the meaning of these unclear feelings taking possession of me. Suddenly, Fr. Serafim asked me, "And what will you say when they ask you why you did not evacuate with everyone else?" "I will answer that in Moscow I was born, and in Moscow I will also die," I said. "You answer correctly," noted Fr. Serafim. Then he added, "And when in Moscow the turmoil begins, cast aside everything and come here." "But what about Papa and Brother," I asked? "You propose that they go with you, but, if they refuse, you cannot do anything more."

The turmoil began on the night of October 16. I was on duty alone in the building that housed the factory library. Having checked on the darkening and the boarding up of all the doors and windows, I lay down to sleep on one of the tables, placing books under my head. A rucksack of groceries lay under the table. Suddenly, an unusual noise awakened me. On the second floor, at that time, a trade school and a radio were located there. I sat motionless, listening to the news. One terrible thing followed another. One after another, towns near Moscow surrendered. Finally, in a heart-rending cry of the soul, came the words: "The enemy has broken through the line of our defense; the country and the government are in mortal danger."

The unimaginable began. The trade school with its teachers left on foot for Gor′kii; workers in the factory left for who knows where, traveling with their families to a village, and they seized the state's fiscal property. In their cars, in the night, the authorities secretly "evacuated" into the deep interior.

Moscow abandoned work, people aimlessly "wandered" on the streets. The life of the country suddenly broke down, like clockwork.

At the station, there were no electric trains, and, in the city, there were no cars, and the metro did not work. On the streets, enemy airplanes shamelessly dropped pamphlets in which was printed the following: "Moscow is not the capital. The Urals are not the border," etc.

This was a monstrous moment, which, happily, did not last long.

It took more than twenty-four hours to get to Zagorsk. Direct trains went rarely and came to a standstill during an air raid attack. When I finally reached Zagorsk, I sighed with relief.

I asked Fr. Serafim whether I might remain here and not return to Moscow. "No," Fr. Serafim said, "Rest a little while, and then you need to go and work in Moscow." Such an answer Fr. Serafim gave not only to me, but to many who put the same question to him.

The enemy troops came so close to Moscow, making railway connections difficult, and the passage, even at such a distance as Zagorsk, required special permission. My trips to Zagorsk continued to be regular, but each of them became a miracle—a miracle that St. Sergii accomplished through the prayers of Fr. Serafim.

Severe physical weakness, caused by the onset of malnutrition, increased the effect of the ban on railroad travel for private matters. When they asked me, "Will you be going to Zagorsk tomorrow?" it sounded like mockery. This was entirely impossible.

On the following day the struggle began, which took place not in me but in my consciousness and will, a struggle between the elements of the world raging in Moscow and the beneficial powers coming from Zagorsk. I myself was almost passive, trying only more often to repeat the prayers, recalling the words of Fr. Serafim: "Take hold of the garments of Christ!" In those difficult days, we felt the vitally important meaning of these words with a particular clarity, which was impossible in everyday life. It was as though a thick layer of impassable ice covered the entire world around us, and the single icebreaker was prayer. Without it, it became literally impossible to take one step. This was entirely obvious.

The journey to Zagorsk required many different stages, and until one stage was completed, I did not dare think about the next. [It was extremely challenging] to obtain everything needed for Lenochka and the children, procure the registration forms and certificates, go to the station, pass through the cordon of controls and police in the station and in the train, to go to Zagorsk (many times it was necessary to get off the train, if the registration seemed to the police officer insufficiently convincing, and to go several stops on foot, and then to transfer to another train), and, after getting off the train, reach the place. Each of these steps presented almost insurmountable difficulties; sometimes, complete darkness engulfed us, and neither habitations nor the road were visible, or snow blanketed everything, making it impossible to guess where to go.

But at each stage came unexpected and accidental help, and obstacles were resolved, one after the other. When the road was completely closed, and only the permission of the town commandant allowed passage, I asked Fr. Serafim, "How can I come the next time?" thinking only about the worldly, like the apostle Peter at that moment when the Lord called him "a person of little faith." Fr. Serafim responded, "With God's help!"

The power of Fr. Serafim's words consisted in their complete conformity with life, and in all life a gradual revelation of meaning, which he served as the messenger.

During the war, Fr. Serafim could not consistently remain in one place, since they [the police] often checked the composition and documents of the population; from time to time, he had to leave the house and live in the homes of others of his spiritual children.

The atmosphere in Moscow became so difficult that I dreamed of living, if only for a little while, in Zagorsk. "I know that things are very difficult for you," said Fr. Serafim. From what he knew, the difficulties had acquired another meaning and reduced the burden.

Once, walking in the evening darkness, I stumbled into an antitank barrier, of which there were so many on all the streets, and so powerfully was I hurt that I had to take sick leave. Somehow I managed to reach Zagorsk, where I walked to the polyclinic for bandages. By such means, my wish was fulfilled; I could remain in Zagorsk for almost three weeks.

As Germany's hopes for a quick war did not come to fruition, the policy of fascism in the occupied places became even crueler. The most terrible of all was the total extermination of the Jewish population. All the same, ghosts from the depths of history swam up to the surface, and became an incredible fact of the present.

During that time, we experienced immensely more than commiseration. In those terrible days, everyone feared something or other most: for one person it was chemical warfare, for another—death by hunger, for a third—to fall into the hands of the enemy, etc. In my case, I feared the thought that the Germans might come, and they would find me in some kind of "privileged" situation in comparison with others. This would be moral death. I desperately wanted to die, to prove to myself and to everyone that my attraction to Christianity was not an act of estrangement but an act of love for my own people. "You can pray for others, and for yourself at the same time as for others," said Fr. Serafim. He decisively rejected my words about "privileged." Life and death are in the hands of God, and privileges cannot have the smallest significance.

I discovered a similar lack of understanding another time also, when for some reason (about what topic I cannot remember), I tried to claim that I did not have the right. "About which rights do you speak?" asked Fr. Serafim. "For what do we have the right? Do we have the right to receive the Sacrament? Not according to our sins, of course, but the Lord tolerates us."

On one of the troublesome days, it was necessary to clear up a question that agitated all of us. Lenochka's husband urgently demanded that she move with the children to Sverdlovsk, where, at the time, he worked at a military plant (he considered their future living conditions near Moscow to be extremely dangerous). I set out for Fr. Serafim's with Alik and Pavlik. I had to carry Pavlik a large part of the way in my arms. After seeing us, Fr. Serafim became very joyful. "For all your care Mary, Mother of God, will not forsake you," he said.

When everyone sat down at the table, Fr. Serafim placed Alik and Pavlik next to him. There were fairly many people at the table. "Who are these children?" a woman, unfamiliar to me, surprisingly asked, when she entered the room. "Mine," answered Fr. Serafim.

The Last Days and the End

In those days, Fr. Serafim had already begun to feel ill. For a long time, we did not know what his illness was, thinking that he suffered from malaria. I understand now that he did not want to darken the life of his spiritual children with the expectation of his near end.

During my stay in Zagorsk, one more time I was with the children at Fr. Serafim's. "Your children are surprisingly good. They are, after all, your children," said Fr. Serafim. We sat together in the small garden at Fr. Serafim's. Alik brought some kind of flower and, showing it to Fr. Serafim, said, "You see how good it is." "Yes, yes, darling," answered Fr. Serafim, "it is good, as you are."

Fr. Serafim expressed the wish that he would hear Alik's first confession, although he was not yet seven years old (obviously, he knew that he would not live until the time when Alik would reach seven years old).

After his first confession, Alik conveyed his impressions: "With Grandfather, I felt as though I were in heaven with God, and at the same time he talked with me so simply, the way we talk among ourselves."

One time, Fr. Serafim said to me, "For your sufferings and your serious education, this very Alik will be a great person."

The illness of Fr. Serafim intensified. A large part of the time, he did not get out of bed.

When I came to see him with the request to perform the thanksgiving service on the anniversary of my baptism, he said, "Ask Fr. Pyotr, I do not have the strength." Then, in a more cheerful voice, he added, "You and I will still hold a service of prayers . . ." I did not understand what he meant by this.

When I returned to work, the factory was already being prepared for evacuation to Omsk. I had either to go with the factory or be discharged from work. The latter threatened deprivation of the ration card, which, at the time, I received in the factory for the whole family. Fr. Serafim gave his blessing to take the discharge and not to go anywhere. This I had to obey, but I did not know how to obtain it [the ration card].

In the morning, I went to see the factory administration. To all my arguments, they answered that this was wartime and everyone had to go; they did not allow for any other kind of circumstances.

One thing remained—a prayer-icebreaker, which could pierce the impenetrable wall of ice.

The whole day I went from one authority to another, trying not to weaken my internal focus and almost mechanically answering all the questions presented to me. The hours passed. All kinds of new obstacles emerged, one more unexpected than another. The day seemed exceptionally long and filled with some substance incomprehensible for me—of a peculiar struggle.

What a surprise it was when, at the very end of the workday, they gave me not only the document for my discharge, which I had sought, but also all four ration cards for the following month that completely exceeded my expectations and appeared inexplicable. By such means, I found myself free.

This, on one hand, gave me the possibility, having gone to Zagorsk, to stay there for as much time as I needed, but, on the other hand, it meant the loss of needed earnings. Several times, I turned to Fr. Serafim with the request to permit me to begin work as a nurse or a nurse's assistant in the hospital, or simply do physical labor. Fr. Serafim categorically denied all these proposals, saying that I might do only "suitable" work. Thus, by the blessing of Fr. Serafim, I awaited that moment, when, although in very unusual circumstances, I could resume my former work in the clinic.

"If the Germans enter Moscow, terrible things await," said Fr. Serafim.

The closeness of the enemy was felt in everything; air bombardment became so habitual that we almost paid no attention to it. Papa often rushed about the room with such an anxious appearance that it was painful to look at him. "I cannot [believe] that they are so close," he whispered. At night, the windows were tightly covered, and no one knew what went on out there. Therefore, in the morning after hearing the sounds of our radio, we felt great relief.

During our nighttime duties in the attic of the house, I usually took with me the "Akathist to the Passion of Christ," and Brother often asked me to read to him. I read separate pieces, which made a deep impression on him. One time, he managed to come for three days to Zagorsk. Knowing nothing and not suspecting anything about the existence of Fr. Serafim, he felt immediately the atmosphere in which we lived. "I fell into your orbit," he said. This was the great mercy of God. St. Sergii helped us get him away for these short days from that chaos, external and internal, among which he lived, always estranged and always unhappy. He deeply felt that peace and grace, which flowed into everything here, even into the air, into the bells of the church, into the patchy sunlight on the snow, in the marvelous quietness, in some kind of inexplicable silence, which is not from us, not from the interchangeable circumstances and unequal ways of the fate of a human being in the world. "The goal of our life is peace," Fr. Serafim said to me one time, but I did not understand what these words signified. Peace, about which Fr. Serafim spoke, is the "silence of greatness," which the Gospels proclaim. The entire evening, we talked about Zagorsk and St. Sergii.

On the following day, Brother set out with Lenochka to search for potatoes. On the road, they were caught in an air raid. They managed to hide in one of the buildings of the lavra that remained open, and they stayed there until they heard the all-clear signal.

How he did not wish to return to Moscow! Once he even expressed the thought, "If I live until the end of the war and the fascists are defeated, I also will be baptized." When Lenochka related these words to Fr. Serafim, he said, "With such words, he, perhaps, will be saved."

Once, leaving the city in a critical moment of the war, Marusia said to us, "We will see each other here or not here!" "And what about me?" Brother asked.

This question stands before me even now, but the Lord has created in the heart of a person that hope does not die in him, and His ways are inscrutable . . .

Several days after Brother departed, I decided to make use of the attitude that he displayed during his stay in Zagorsk and write him a letter.

In my letter, I tried to reveal to him that circumstance, in which he had not accidentally fallen into our "orbit," and that, in essence, he had always been located within it, to show, through the example of his own life and the life of all our family, that a yearning for a Christian disposition was inherent in one way or another with many members of our tribe. This feeling was well expressed in the poems of our relative—the poet Vasilevskii.[73] In one of the old Leningrad collections, I found his poem, "Palm Saturday" (*Verbnaia subbota*). Walking past a church on Palm Saturday, at the moment when the people praying came out with burning candles in their hands, the poet felt the significance of what was taking place: "The world, worn out from empty dreams / Rests from evil and melancholy."

Not being in a position to fuse, in action, his soul with the celebration, he concluded his poem with the words: "I carry not supplication but sadness, not to my own, but to a beautiful sacred place." A similar mood we find in the writer Gerzhenzon, the artist Levitan, and many others.[74]

I reminded him that, for some reason not understood, either by him or by those around him, from his eighth year he considered the holiday of the Entrance into the Church of the Most Holy Mother of God [The Entrance of the Theotokos into the Temple] as his holiday.[75] I reminded him how, all his life, he had searched for Christian motives in art and music and had valued these motives most of all. I attempted to prove that only then could he understand the true meaning of his yearning and aspiration, when he fully grasped the meaning of these words at the end, which he so loved during the performance of the requiem of Mozart: "Blessed is he who comes in the name of the Lord."

This letter must not be only my letter. It derived strength only if all the thoughts and feelings expressed in it came with the blessing of Fr. Serafim.

Fr. Serafim did not get up from the bed. He kept my letter for himself, to read it attentively. When he returned it to me, he said that he approved and considered essential everything written in it. The sole thing against which he took exception was the address, in which I used not a personal name, but an affectionate word, which was how we were accustomed to address each other. Fr. Serafim said that a name had great meaning and it was necessary to call each person by his personal name, not something else. "Often in a family, they call a person Musia, Liusia, Asia," said Fr. Serafim. "These are not real names. An affectionate name must be as close as possible to the full name. The use of invented names weakens the soul."

Brother received my letter very well and was very, very grateful for it when we met in person. A short time later, however, he sent me a letter in which he rejected what he had passionately accepted not long ago. He denied nothing but turned it down for himself personally; heavy, hopeless moods gained the upper hand.

Fr. Serafim calmed me. "He took everything well, this will help him, and it is better to burn his letter and not attribute to it any kind of significance."

The Germans continued to advance.

At that time, Lenochka lived in Zagorsk itself. The winter set in. Rumors circulated that the German army had crossed the northern road, and Zagorsk would be cut off from Moscow. In one of those alarming moments when a snowstorm engulfed the courtyard, Lenochka and I, in a hurry, having left the children at home, set out to visit the spiritual daughter of Fr. Serafim, Vera Maksimovna.[76] There we met Fr. Vladimir. When he saw me, Fr. Vladimir said, "See where the Lord has brought us together." The common danger made everyone become closer, and we had a simple and good conversation.

The danger that Zagorsk would be cut off from Moscow became sharper and more real. I had before me an agonizing choice: to remain in Moscow and be isolated from Lenochka and the children, or to remain in Zagorsk and part with Papa and Brother.

I waited for an answer from Fr. Serafim, which would resolve all my hesitation. In this difficult moment, however, a direct answer did not come to me.

"Go to Moscow," said Fr. Serafim. "Read there three *akathist*s: The Savior; Mary, Mother of God; and St. Nicholas, and then do what the Lord lays on your heart! . . . Come on Sunday," he added, after a pause.

I understood one thing: Fr. Serafim was leaving us and wished to teach us to be independent . . .

The devotionals were read, but luckily, I did not have to do anything. Perhaps Fr. Serafim had also foreseen this, because on Sunday the situation changed: our army went on the offensive and threw the Germans back from Moscow.

"Truly, the Moscow prelates prayed for the city," said Fr. Ieraks.

After this, trips to Zagorsk became significantly easier. Fr. Serafim did not get up from his bed. I dropped in on to him as often as possible. Sometimes he asked to dictate a letter (Fr. Serafim had always maintained a large correspondence with other spiritual and secular people).

Sometimes I had to bring medicine and blood test results from Moscow. Having investigated the latter, I understood that the illness of Fr. Serafim (cancer) was incurable and he neared the fatal end.

One time, Fr. Serafim said to me, "You do not know what you are to me (he had in mind Lenochka and me). To you this is not revealed. Only there will you know it. You are closer to me than my sisters."

On the commemorative day for St. Serafim, Fr. Serafim suddenly experienced a surge of strength. He rose and celebrated the liturgy with me. It was his last. He did not get up again.

Fr. Serafim then could eat almost nothing, and despite all the efforts of his spiritual children, it was not always possible to find what he needed.

Kseniia Ivanovna—a Diveevo nun—nursed Fr. Serafim the entire time.

She did this with such exceptional gentleness, patience, attentiveness, and with such special concentrated efficiency, characteristic only of people who have passed through the great school of spiritual life.

Once, on the day of St. Spyridon, Fr. Serafim asked Paraskeva,[77] the sister of Kseniia Ivanovna, to bring him a fresh fish from the market. Paraskeva told Fr. Serafim beforehand that to acquire a fresh fish was almost impossible now, to which he confidently replied, "Don't worry, Mother, St. Spyridon will provide."[78]

When Paraskeva came to the market, she saw a small group of women surrounding an old vendor. The old man had brought a few fresh fish for sale. Having noticed Paraskeva, he gave her his fish and disappeared into the crowd, to the surprise and indignation of the women surrounding him.

After returning home, Paraskeva told Fr. Serafim about the miraculous event that had taken place. Fr. Serafim asked her to describe the appearance of the old man who gave her the fish. When she did this, they were convinced that this was none other than St. Spyridon.

The winter approached its end. The first spring sunsets blazed over the Lavra of St. Sergii (the doors of which were still closed), over the fields and roads, along which he himself had walked, prayed, and blessed people—the humble monk and interlocutor of the angels.

Fr. Serafim rejoiced that we had the opportunity to meet in Zagorsk in the early spring. He said to me that this time of the year was unusually beautiful in these places. A special grace filled the air, reminding one about another, higher world and pacifying all feelings, like the song of the lark in minutes of mental anxiety.

The days of "the spiritual springtime" also grew near—of Lent. The last Sunday evening, before I left for Moscow, I dropped in on Fr. Serafim. A woman who opened the door for me said, "It is impossible to see Fr. Serafim; he is very weak and receives no one." I had to go away.

I made my way to the station, not understanding what was going on with me. The world again was losing its reality, as in those days when Mama was dying. But then the Lord took pity on me, and after eleven days in a coma, Mama had regained consciousness, and I could see and talk with her up to the last minutes of her life. Would I really no longer see Fr. Serafim? Would I not receive his last blessing? How would I live in the future? This could not be! I continued on my way to the station; I could not have done otherwise, but in the depths of my soul, I was absolutely convinced that the Lord would not allow me to leave in such a state.

I arrived at the station, went up to the cashier, and bought a ticket. The train was due now, and I would have to leave. Suddenly, I discovered in my pocket the medicine, which I had brought for Fr. Serafim and which, without fail, I had to deliver to him, since it could relieve his suffering. I had entirely forgotten about it. What was to be done? To return to Fr. Serafim was impossible. I decided to go to Sister Kseniia Ivanovna, to Irina, who lived on the same street, and give her the medicine.

"How good it is that you came!" suddenly exclaimed Irina, when I entered her house. "Go quickly to Fr. Serafim! He knew that they did not allow you to come to him, and he was very distressed. He absolutely wishes to see you."

Then, what took place was more than I could expect. I not only saw Fr. Serafim; he called me to himself.

Kseniia Ivanovna led me up to Fr. Serafim's bed and said, "Say what you need, while it is not too late," and left the room. Many thoughts flashed through my head, but all of them in that moment seemed superfluous. I could not speak. Then Fr. Serafim spoke with a quiet and gentle voice, "Say what you need, while I am not completely weak." "Father," I said, "forgive me for everything, for all the grief and unpleasant minutes that I caused you."

"No, no." Fr. Serafim came to life. "Nothing of the sort ever happened. And forgiveness we must ask of each other . . . And convey this to Lenochka." "Now for me there is nothing, except your blessing," I added. "It's better like this," Fr. Serafim responded. "The Lord goes with you in many ways, only live as you are living. Live life a little at a time." Especially quietly and slowly, visibly weary, Fr. Serafim conveyed these last words.

Everyone in the house entered the room of Fr. Serafim to begin the evening service, the reception of Lent.

With a weak, but clear voice, Fr. Serafim himself began singing the introduction to the Great Canon "Helpmate and Protector, Be My Salvation."[79] In the voice of the dying, these words resonated with an uncommon strength. This signified not only the end of an earthly journey but the same words that the Church sang at the beginning of Lent and opened the door of repentance to the faithful, and in that hour, the gates of eternal life were opening before him.

On the conclusion of the service, Fr. Serafim said that they should let me spend the night, since it was already late.

Early in the morning, Fr. Pyotr arrived. Each day, he came to give communion to the sick and then left for work in the bookkeeping office of the factory.

Entering the room of Fr. Serafim, Fr. Pyotr said cheerfully, almost in a gay voice, "Good morning, Father Archimandrite, may the spirit of Lent be with you."

Whenever Fr. Pyotr was at the home of Fr. Serafim, everyone assembled in the kitchen and grieved about the coming separation from Fr. Serafim. When Fr. Pyotr left, he said to us, "We do not know what awaits us; perhaps the Lord will lead him out like His chosen one." Subsequent events proved that Fr. Pyotr was right.

During this time, Fr. Serafim summoned Kseniia Ivanovna to him. "Mother," he said, "bring Verochka cabbages." He was worried that Kseniia Ivanovna would forget to feed me before my departure.

When I prepared to leave, I went to Fr. Serafim in his room one more time. He lay in a semiconscious state. I decided not to bother him. Kseniia Ivanovna herself went up to him and said, "Bless Verochka, she has to go." I got down on my knees beside his bed. He blessed me, and I left for Moscow.

After three days, when I came home from work, Papa told me that they had telephoned me and left an address, to which I must quickly go. I understood everything. When I arrived, I heard, "Fr. Serafim passed away."

They also told me that it had been decided, over the course of a year, to read the Psalter over Fr. Serafim. Therefore, in order that the entire Psalter was read every day, they had divided it among Fr. Serafim's spiritual children, so that each person would read daily one *kathisma*. The sixth *kathisma* they assigned to me.[80]

"Look," one of the spiritual daughters of Fr. Serafim said to me, when I prepared to leave, "at home show no one that you are grieving. And do not cry, for there is the night."

Before his death, Fr. Serafim had thought about all of his spiritual children; he forgot no one. To each person he gave a blessed icon of Mary, Mother of God. To Lenochka, Alik, and me, he gave "Joy of All Who Sorrow," and to Pavlik "Unexpected Joy." He transferred his spiritual leadership to Fr. Pyotr, Fr. Ieraks, and Fr. Vladimir, dividing his spiritual children among them. He entrusted us to Fr. Pyotr.

When I came to Lenochka several days later, she told me the following.

On Tuesday night, she had a dream in which, in the middle of it, she was at the home of Fr. Serafim, and he asked her to read the Gospels aloud. She opened the book and began to read, but he stopped her, saying, "You need to read Luke in the Gospels."

In the morning, she got ready to go to Fr. Serafim. Alik cried and asked her not to leave. This had never happened before. Coming to the home of Fr. Serafim, Lenochka asked Kseniia Ivanovna, who opened the door, "How is he feeling?" "Now he is completely well," she answered. Lenochka understood that Fr. Serafim had died. Kseniia Ivanovna embraced Lenochka, led her to Fr. Serafim, partly removed the shroud, so that Lenochka could glance at his face and lay her hand on his. Then Kseniia Ivanovna said to Lenochka that she read aloud the Gospels. "You need to read from Luke in the Gospels," Kseniia Ivanovna said.

To the question was it possible to come to the funeral, Kseniia Ivanovna said, "No, I comforted you as I could, but you do not need to come to the funeral."

Lenochka went home and told the children that Grandfather had died.

"I knew it," said Alik. "Only it is not frightening at all, he has gone to the Heavenly Kingdom."

Over the course of several days, Alik refused to engage in any kind of play or entertainment. Afterward, they told me that other children also felt the death of Fr. Serafim.

Fr. Pyotr conducted the Easter matins in Fr. Serafim's house. The matins went on very triumphantly.

At the end of the service, Fr. Pyotr said, "Now let us exchange kisses with Fr. Serafim."

We descended on a ladder under the house, where the grave of Fr. Serafim was located.

They had buried him there in his "catacombs," beneath where the Throne had stood, as the Church practiced during the first centuries.

Part II

Fr. Pyotr Shipkov

> In the light of Your Face we will walk
> and Your Name will radiate through the centuries.
>
> —Communion poetry of the feast day of the Transfiguration of Our Lord

In Zagorsk during the War

After the death of Fr. Serafim on February 19, 1942, Fr. Pyotr became our spiritual father.

At this time, Fr. Pyotr lived in Zagorsk, worked as a bookkeeper in a handicraft factory, and simultaneously continued his activity as a priest in the comparatively narrow circle of his spiritual children.

To visit the small number of open churches during that time was not, for us, a blessing. In these churches, priests mainly served who made a whole series of compromises that violated the Church's regulations and traditions. Those who wished to preserve "the purity of Orthodoxy" served secretly. In Bishop Luke's[1] article, composed on his eightieth birthday, he wrote, "The city in which I lived gleamed with a great number of churches, but all the priests of this city were Renovationists. Therefore, accompanied by priests, I had to celebrate the liturgy in my room. There Orthodox people came, not wishing to pray with their unfaithful priests."

The war continued, although the danger of further invasion of the enemy into the depths of the country had passed. Little by little, Muscovites returned from evacuation. In the spring of 1943, I resumed work at the Institute of Mental and Physical Disabilities.

It was difficult to organize the work of medical-pedagogical consultation. Everything was either destroyed or neglected; several buildings were burned during the air bombings. Only single individuals remained from among my associates of the institute in Moscow. Children in Moscow still numbered very few; schools did not meet; doctors, in particular pediatric neuropsychologists, had not yet returned. The first months I worked almost alone, visiting the homes of those few sick children whose parents brought for consultation. Because of the absence of residents and heating, I often wandered alone along the deserted, frozen corridors of the Old Arbat apartments. In one of them, at the very end of the corridor, I saw an old woman; on the stove beside her, two to three small pieces of firewood smoldered, and near them she warmed herself. Everyone had left in the evacuation, but they did not take her; she would not have survived a journey in wartime conditions. "These logs will burn, and I will die with them," said the old woman. In another home, I found only a sick woman with an epileptic boy of twelve years of age, who had only just returned from the evacuation. She remained at a loss about what to do next, since she had lost all the members of her family. How to live? What to do with the child? Where to take him for treatment?

All Moscow, it seemed, breathed with difficulty, as though gravely ill. But for me, beyond Moscow, was Zagorsk, St. Sergii, the grave of Grandfather [Fr. Serafim], and Fr. Pyotr.

In October 1942, my brother perished on the home front: from hunger and from poisoning with toxic mushrooms, and it was too late for an operation for peritonitis. In his diaries, I found the following note: "'Christ will save you,' a beggar woman said to me. Is this necessary for me? Yes, it is necessary, because my soul is enshrouded in a bad nightmare. To it the Savior is necessary." When I told this to my friend Tania K. [now already deceased],[2] she said, "The life of your family is a page from the history of the Church."

The temperature in the room where I lived with Papa did not exceed 10 degrees C. Papa lay sick the whole winter, in a fur coat and a winter hat. On February 14, Papa collected himself to go to work and, after looking at himself in the mirror, said, "I have the look of death in my eyes." In the evening, he did not return home; they had taken him to the hospital directly from work, and he died in the night, in the arms of a nurse, the daughter of his friend. They buried Papa on the day of the anniversary of the death of Fr. Serafim. When they carried the coffin in a large truck, I was entirely alone; not one person close to my soul, no believing person, was beside me. It seemed that a wilderness surrounded me. At the same time, in the truck they carried still one other casket, and next to the casket they had placed a large image of the Savior, holding out his hand to the drowning apostle Peter. On the anniversary of his death, the deceased Fr. Serafim sent this image to comfort me. At this moment, my grief dissolved into joy and hope. I formed a cross of white chrysanthemums and laid it on Papa's casket. One of the relatives in attendance became indignant and wanted to remove it. "He was a Jew," he said. "Leave it where it is," I responded, "He was my father."

After Papa's burial, I became totally weak, and I spent several days in bed at Sister's home in Zagorsk. Awakening early in the morning, I unexpectedly saw Fr. Pyotr at the door of the house. He did not walk but literally ran to us so early, in order to call on me and yet manage to get to work on time. "They told me that you were feeling very bad," he remarked. "I was afraid that your soul was exhausted." But after speaking for a while with me and sensing my mood, he said, "Glory to God!" Then we agreed on a day, when he would take us to Mother Superior Mariia.³ Fr. Pyotr knew and felt that he, like Fr. Ieraks also, inevitably would be arrested, and he wanted us to become acquainted with Mother Mariia and transferred to her guidance.

Sister and I decided to use this occasion to ask Fr. Pyotr, in their absence, to read the burial rites for our deceased relatives. Fr. Pyotr willingly agreed. The beloved brother of my Papa, his wife Liudmila, and daughter Valentina were baptized before the revolution. Uncle Volodia became a Christian, but not by conviction. He remained confident that a divine origin was a fact that all religions held in common, and everything else that divided them came not from God, but from people. He was the single breadwinner of a large family, which consisted of a widowed mother and seven small children. Working on the railroad from the age of fourteen, he sustained the whole family. But one day the tsarist government issued an order that forbade Jews (not baptized) from work on the railroad.

From his youth, Uncle Volodia nourished some sympathy for Orthodoxy and Russian antiquity. In childhood, I remember going with Mama to buy him a present for his birthday. Mama selected a book on Russian history with a beautiful dustcover, which had illustrations of a church with gold cupolas. "Volodia loves such books," Mama said.

During this time, relatives talked about how, coming home after the sacrament of his baptism, Uncle Volodia bitterly cried, thinking that, by making this sacrifice for the sake of the family, he had betrayed his own people, and this now prohibited his burial in the Jewish cemetery beside his own father.

Sister and I were very grateful to Fr. Pyotr for performing the burial service with great feeling, and Sister expressed the thought that perhaps through this burial service and our faith, their "necessary" baptism would be justified.

Once, while in Moscow, I wrote Fr. Pyotr a long letter. His response I cite in full:

Zagorsk, 1942

The grace of God be with you. "I truly understand that God shows no partiality, but in every nation who fears him and does what is right is acceptable to him" (The Acts of the Apostles, 10:34–35).

"Stand therefore, and fasten the belt of truth around your waist, and put on the breastplate of righteousness. As shoes for your feet put on whatever will make you ready to proclaim the gospel of peace.

With all of these, take the shield of faith, with which you will be able to quench all the flaming arrows of the evil one. Take the helmet of salvation, and the sword of the Spirit, which is the word of God" (Ephesians 6:14–17).

"For our struggle is not against enemies of blood and flesh, but against the rulers, against the authorities, against the cosmic powers of this present darkness" (Ephesians 6:12).

"I in them and you in me" (John 17:23). "May they also may be in us" (John 17:21).

"If you belonged to the world, the world would love you as its own. Because you do not belong to the world, but I have chosen you out of the world—therefore the world hates you" (John 15:19).

"Do not let your hearts be troubled, and do not let them be afraid." (John 14:27). "In the world you face persecution. But take courage; I have conquered the world" (John 16:33).

"For to me, living in Christ and dying is gain" (Philippians 1:21).

"My desire is to depart and be with Christ, for that is far better" (Philippians 1:23).

In the Church, there cannot be loneliness, and if we really were its genuine children, then we would have fathers, mothers, brothers, and sisters in the very best and fullest meaning of this word. All the gravity of our situation consists in that even in the Church (I understand, of course, as a visible society of people and with an exterior side), at present the love and the feeling of brotherhood and unity are scarce and have dried up. But how joyfully it is now to people to come together, with the strength of a clean conscience, to kiss each other and say, "Christ is among us." I am neither an ascetic, nor a mystic, nor a philosopher. I humbly serve the Church of the Lord not by my accomplishment or by merit, but solely by His ineffable kindness, receiving from Him the power to bind and determine human sins in His Holy Name; to nourish people with divine food: with the Body and Blood of Christ; to raise up for them prayers before the Throne of the Lord. In the simplicity of my heart and mind [I] bow before Divine Love, Truth and Beauty, with gratitude, I throw myself into the dust before God's unending compassion for us and call upon others to do this. Help us Lord, to carry our living cross and may Your will be done in everything! Prayers and, most importantly, the Mystery of the Sacred Church, and, above all, the Eucharist of the Sacred Body and Blood of Christ will support us on that road, will give us the possibility to continually struggle with eternal enemies, will fulfill our meekness and humility, and will fortify our Faith. They will fill your heart with the peace and joy of the Holy Spirit. The Lord, summoning you to His Sacred Church, will lead you along familiar roads to salvation. "In my Father's house there are many dwelling places" (John 14: 2).

In this letter, Fr. Pyotr clearly expressed an understanding of his personal pastoral service. In it, that rare wholeness of the soul was reflected, "the simplicity of the heart and mind," which, together with impassioned zeal about God and His glory, defined his essence. He understood the Church in its human (and not mystical) side as a unified family, in which no one remained alone. The ideal of the Church for him was a community of people, united in spirit, who, with a pure soul, could say, "Christ is among us!"

Including in his letter a large number of quotations from the New Testament, he attempted to show the weak and depressed soul how God's compassion was endless, what abundant comfort, hopes, and strength could come from the Sacred Scriptures. Human efforts alone, no matter how strained and agonizing, would not lead a person to salvation. God would do this! And, moreover, by ways known to Him alone.

Once I managed to go to Zagorsk to ask Fr. Pyotr to help me resolve a practical question: whether I might occupy myself now with preparation for the defense of my dissertation. This question was difficult because, before the war, Fr. Serafim had not given his blessing to me in this matter. But several years had gone by, and much had changed. Then Fr. Serafim had spoken about another period of my life. Now might one again raise this question?

Fr. Pyotr did not wish to resolve this question alone. Again, he preferred for us to go together to Mother Mariia, to decide it jointly with her or, perhaps, to let her decide.

Mother Mariia said that for me to work on the dissertation was now not only useful but also essential. Fr. Pyotr accepted her counsel and decision. Thus work on the dissertation became for me not something extraneous or neutral in my internal life but a matter of obedience. This knowledge placed new stimuli in my soul and gave me complete peace in my work. In the course of four years of preparation of the dissertation, Mother Mariia looked after me the whole time. In a difficult moment, when the director [supervising professor] of my dissertation turned it down and I was prepared to give up, Mother Mariia said, "It is essential to take this to the end, and while they may not wish to pass it now, they will do so." Fr. Pyotr deeply respected Mother Mariia. Not long before his arrest, he went to her and, in tears, asked her to receive his spiritual children when he was far away. "You will receive mine," Fr. Pyotr would say. Having learned that Alik (then still a schoolboy) had drawn close to Mother Mariia and had spent the holidays with her, Fr. Pyotr said, "I am very glad that Alik is acquainted with Mother Mariia. Wherever he is, the acquaintance with a person of such high sensibilities will be useful to him his entire life. Such people are becoming fewer and fewer, and perhaps, in the future they will all be gone."

While in exile, the entire time he corresponded with Mother Mariia, asking her to look after herself until his return.

On the End of the War. The Rebirth of the Church

During the war, on October 14, 1943, Fr. Pyotr was arrested.[4] After the arrest of Fr. Pyotr and Fr. Ieraks, we had nowhere to go to make confession and receive communion. My psychological condition during that time was very difficult. I was depressed about my brother: he did not live until the end of the war and died unbaptized. During the last, most difficult years, he spent very much time alone, since I, worrying about Sister and the children, almost abandoned him, and he suffered a great deal from this.

I set forth everything in the form of a letter, hoping that it would be given to someone close to Fr. Serafim and like-minded fathers. The letter never reached them. Soon, however, I had the opportunity to meet with Fr. Dmitrii (Kriuchkov).[5] I saw Fr. Dmitrii only one time; soon he was sent into exile, where he spent the rest of his life. The meeting with him made a deep impression on me. He had a surprisingly sensitive concern for my feelings. He said that much in the field of human relationships that seemed significant to us went beyond the boundaries of this life, lost its sharpness and significance, and did not transfer into eternity, and that the friendship between the living and the dead really existed, etc.

The war ended. The long-anticipated word "victory" spread all over the country and far beyond its borders. In the Church, a major event also took place. Patriarch Aleksii was elected.[6] With great interest, both believers and nonbelievers read about his appeal in the newspaper. In the beginning, we did not entirely realize what had taken place, and did not know whether to believe what was written in the newspaper. We soon learned from the newspaper one other bit of joyous piece of news: the patriarch traveled to Jerusalem to give thanks at the grave of the Lord. But for us, nothing changed. As before, we did not visit the church. The spiritual solitude continued.

It was 1945.

Once, returning home from work, I found Alik very anxious. "Nadezhda Nikolaevna came," he said. "She said that a letter came from Siberia, signed by Bishop Afanasii,[7] Fr. Pyotr, and Fr. Ieraks.[8] We may now go to the church and receive communion. She asked that you come to her at work, and she will tell you everything herself."

After the discussion with N. N., we decided to go to church. In order not to call attention to ourselves, Sister went to one church with Alik as the older son, and I to another with his younger brother.[9] Alik was startled, having seen a church full of people and having heard the general singing of the Symbol of Faith [the Creed]. He had not seen or heard anything similar before. Pavlik also was thrilled with what took place around him.

We had still not decided to receive communion again in open churches; rumors circulated that signatures in the letter could be forged. To remain for a long time in such a bewildering situation was impossible, and I decided to go to Mother Mariia, whom Fr. Pyotr so valued and respected. Let her have the last word. Mother Mariia met me with these words: "You went to what kind of church?" Instead of answering, I burst into tears. Mother Mariia calmed me and said that there was no reason to doubt the authenticity of the letter. And Fr. Pyotr, through someone, communicated a message: "One may take confession in the churches, but one must delay friendship with their clergy."

In the Moscow churches a revival began: good preachers appeared in several churches, and entire cycles of conversations on defined themes took place. In one church, these preachers even held special conversations with children. They conducted conversations with slides, illustrating the texts of the Old and New Testaments.

Fr. Pyotr in Exile (Letters)

Over the course of five years, we learned nothing about Fr. Pyotr. Finally, we managed to learn his address, and I wrote him a letter. Fr. Pyotr's response is quoted below:

> The Grace of God and His blessing be with you. I thank you from the depths of my soul for your heartfelt letter, and I ineffably rejoice that you still remember and sustain good feelings for me. For me, life in the world with its vanity, disturbances, and anxieties ended five years ago. Since then, I have lived as if in crowded conditions, where I bear my penance, and now am located in a quiet little wilderness, in the most majestic temple of nature, silently lifting up continual praise to the Creator, where I spend time in humble obedience given to me.
>
> In the situation I found myself in, on December 25, the past stopped for me. Constantly, both in my thoughts and before my eyes, the radiant faces of people near to me in body and soul appear before me. I continue to see them, converse with them, and pray with them. I rejoice in their joys and thank God for them, grieve for their sorrows and woes, and mourn and sympathize with them. My real life consists in these memories, for which I thank God from the bottom of my heart. For the time being, I am saddened and mourn only that I am devoid of the comfort of the sacraments, but I remember the ancient hermits, and in them, I find comfort.
>
> All around here peace and quiet and the undisturbed beauty and majesty of nature rule. Huge pine trees and larches rise majestically and powerfully into the sky, as candles before the Lord, and the snow-white trunks of birch trees with their fragrant branches please the eye, reminding us of our shortcomings, drawing us downward.
>
> Below, the eye is attracted to a wonderful carpet made of various flowers: lilies, tulips, irises, carnations, violets, and other kinds—all of them impossible to count. Among the grasses is the red color of wild strawberries, which are on the point of ripening, and which, they say, may be collected by the bucketful in July. The song of the feathered world enlivened the air, but now, after St. Peter's Day, they also have fallen silent here. Among all of this, one does not feel oneself alone, and one merges together with everything, as though one unintentionally participates in their common hymn of praise to the Creator.
>
> In answer to your letter about the children, I will say: At present, it is difficult for the youth to protect himself or herself from all kinds of temptations and seductions and to preserve one's soul, but I hope and

believe that the Lord, through the protection of our common protector St. Sergii and the request of their Godfather, will give them the possibility to overcome all obstacles.

What concerns you personally, you are right: unfortunately, now we all are devoid of those spiritual leaders, whose living word would help us direct our internal ship to a life-saving harbor. We have remaining above all the eternal "Book of Books," and, after that, the works of the ancient fathers, and later, Bishop Feofan Zatvornik, Bishop Ignatius Brianchaninov. The works of the first of these are such pearls, in which you will find all necessary instructions on how to build the internal storeroom of the soul for salvation, you will find concluding resolutions to all doubts, questions, and vacillations, inevitably emerging in practical life. To them, I also direct to your attention: Bishop Feofan, with whom you, with your spiritual baggage, will fully consult and find satisfaction; Bishop Ignatius, to us ordinary mortals, is closer and more understandable, but also one who gives great and very helpful advice.

Our own reasoning and philosophizing are as weak and bland before these powerhouses of spiritual thought and action, as all our words, speeches, and pronouncements are paltry and shallow, in comparison, for example, with the resounding word of the sacred John Chrysostom in Easter week.

I would personally add still one more thing—live more simply, a not especially complicated life, carry in good humor that living Cross, which the Lord entrusted to us, as the easiest and life-saving thing for you. Try to exhibit in your situation and present time only the maximum kindness to people, and then calmness, peace, and joy will reign in your soul, and you will then perceptibly begin to anticipate the rudiments of bliss. I myself say that I feel immeasurably better than I did five years ago, and more and more I am convinced that the Lord really gives us precisely what is needed and required for salvation.

There is neither anxiety, nor agitation, the future doesn't frighten, and for the present, I give thanks to God.

In a letter in 1950, Fr. Pyotr told us how he, as a night watchman in a kolkhoz barn, served the Sacred Easter service with difficulty, at the time when all around swirled a snowstorm and a penetrating wind:

Thank God, in this year, comparatively quietly, I was able to give way to precious memories and feelings that provided comfort and tenderness. Easter night I spent alone. Everyone slept in a peaceful dream, and nothing interfered with my absorption and concentration. As is the custom, I finished my "memories" at three o'clock at night and went to my place of duty; a snowstorm swirled outside. With difficulty of falling any minute, I crossed the low-lying area and thankfully fell into my sentry box. In the morning, the frost intensified. Penetrating gusts of wind froze the watery mass into ice.

I send to everyone passionate Easter greetings with prayerful good wishes of joy and comfort. Distresses, annoying small things, natural in our world of sadness and tears, the evil one shoves them on us during moments of the most sublime and lucid transformation, but let them not penetrate into the very depths of the soul, and let the heart not become entirely cool to love, and may the peace of God not leave us completely feeble.

From these letters, we see how Fr. Pyotr related to arrest and exile, and how he accepted his isolation and separation from the church and those close to him.

Everything difficult that he had to bear in no way darkened his spirit. Under no circumstances did love and spiritual joy abandon him. A great distance from the church that he so loved, with all his soul, he immersed himself in the "majestic church of nature and silently offered unceasing praise to the Creator."

Having parted from those closest to him, he not only remembered them and prayed for them. He wrote, "I continue to see them, converse with them, and pray with them. I rejoice in their joys and weep with their sorrows." There was no place for depression, melancholy, and the feeling of loneliness. Even forced labor for him was only "humble obedience," and the camp was a crowded settlement. After his return from exile, in neither his letters nor personal conversations did Fr. Pyotr recall those horrors, rudeness, cruelties, and violence that he lived through and that again passed before his eyes.

When you think about Fr. Pyotr, the verses of A. S. Khomiakov come to mind: "A heroic deed has wings, / And you fly away on them / Without labor, without effort / Above the earthly darkness."[10]

He carried out, perhaps, the supreme heroic deed in this terrible world, because he fulfilled the words of the apostle: "Always rejoice!"

The love of Fr. Pyotr for people, with all their weaknesses and incapacities, was derived from his unquestionable confidence in God's compassion and indulgence. For him, God was above all *Deus caritatis*,[11] about which Fr. Pyotr spoke in his farewell talk. He did not make great demands of people.

"Sincere afflictions, mistakes," he said, "are unavoidable in our world of sadness and tears." Fr. Pyotr only warned us against depression, against the darkness, and said, "If only they didn't penetrate into the very depths of the soul, and God's peace didn't completely forsake us weaklings."

Return from Exile

Fr. Pyotr returned ill from exile: while still in the camp, he became sick with a serious illness, which local doctors diagnosed as skin cancer. However, he wanted to be assigned a parish, and he was appointed director of a church in the town of Borovsk in the Kaluga diocese.[12]

In Borovsk, a new period of his life began. Fr. Pyotr lived in the home of the church *starosta*, an elderly woman. She occupied two large rooms on the second floor. On the first floor, her children and grandchildren lived. The room in which Fr. Pyotr resided was so small that one could put nothing in it except a narrow bed, on which he slept, a small table, and a shelf with books. Fr. Pyotr dined and received visitors in the *starosta*'s room. All this made his life very difficult. He did not have the chance to talk with anyone privately; the landlady overheard everything that was discussed and often inserted her comments. This very much distressed Fr. Pyotr. He was lonely and, with great cordiality, received all who came to see him. He so much wanted to spend private time with his guests and talk about everything. If a visitor expressed the desire to make confession, Fr. Pyotr took him to his tiny cell.

The goal, the center of his life, was the liturgy. He arose before dawn to prepare for the service and prayed in his small cell up to the moment when he had to go to the church. In the church, in the liturgical service, he truly lived.

During the liturgy, he was transformed. It was as though age, fatigue, and sickness departed from him. His [Fr. Pyotr's] voice became cheerful and clear. It was full of strength and energy and carried through the whole church, rapturous and happy. The parishioners spoke about him as "a heavenly father!" In this, there was no exultation. It was the triumph of the soul, "the feast of faith," in the words of John Chrysostom.

Fr. Pyotr always celebrated alone. His relationship to the liturgy excluded the possibility of a simultaneous service with those who did not feel themselves united with him. I recall an occasion when Fr. Pyotr resolutely refused to serve together with one of the priests of a neighboring church.

Once to Fr. Pyotr came a deacon, who wanted to be assigned a place in the church. Talking with him, Fr. Pyotr confirmed that, in his family relationships, the person had everything right. It turned out, however, that he was married for the third time. This deception agitated and exasperated Fr. Pyotr for a long time, and he could not set his mind at rest.

In his relationships with people, Fr. Pyotr was simple and cordial. They loved him and appreciated everything. I remember him on the street of Borovsk, surrounded by children, who always greeted him, and whom he blessed to go mushroom picking. In those instances when a matter concerned the Sacraments of the Church, he was strict. Thus during a great holiday, when parents brought many children from the villages for baptism, Fr. Pyotr immediately noticed a lighthearted mood among those young godparents who came. Fr. Pyotr loudly said, "Unbelieving godparents leave; let the one believing godmother stay."

Each day, Fr. Pyotr had the habit of remembering not only his spiritual children but also those who had come to him in the church even once with a request for a memorial. Each deceased became his own, and he kept the prayerful memory about him all his life.

If there were even a small possibility, he considered it his duty to read the burial service and conduct the last rights of those about whom he constantly prayed. While already very ill, lying in bed, he became distressed when he learned that someone else had replaced him. Because of his humility, Fr. Pyotr turned down leadership as an elder, although he had all the right qualities for it. For this same reason, he also avoided theology (in the narrow sense of this word).

I was fortunate to spend two successive years on leave in Borovsk (1957 and 1958). Fr. Pyotr gave me books for reading. He had the complete collection of the works of John Chrysostom, which he loved very much and always recommended for reading. There I read the tenth and eleventh volumes. Fr. Pyotr had very little free time for conversation, but I wanted to assemble what little I managed to grasp about his thoughts on a number of issues. Above all, his sincere, personal, wide relationship to questions of spiritual life instilled joy. Thus, for example, understanding the liturgy as something unifying, he acknowledged that, in people's souls, it was interpreted in diverse ways. "Grace produces everything good," he said. "Grace is one, as the liturgy is one, but in what different ways it acts in human souls, for everyone their own measure, as much as one can take."

"And in nature, there is grace, and the singing of the birds in the forest is the liturgy. Orthodoxy is not the Old Belief, it is all-embracing."

Fr. Pyotr's understanding of Orthodoxy had almost no trace of sectarianism, which we frequently encountered. There were still people who recoiled from Western Christianity as something foreign and even inimical. There were also those who thought that an Orthodox priest must not engage with the "secular" sciences or take an interest in art. Fr. Pyotr was alien to these prejudices. "The Church is one body," he said. "In each liturgy, we pray for the unity of all. And Catholics have grace. They have many serious shortcomings, but we have them, too. 'The Savior would not recognize us as His disciples' (the verses of Maikov).[13] A person should read and study everything, whatever one is able to do, and in every place one can act as a Christian."

The view of Fr. Pyotr on the issue of the individuality of the soul and his understanding of eternal life was interesting. "Each soul," he said, "can grow in keeping with its uniqueness. Eternal life is the continuation of earthly life, and the growth of each soul will continue there."

Fr. Pyotr always warned against gloominess, depression, despair, and the feeling of hopelessness. "The sense of hopelessness happens," he said. "But, as you know, even in classical antiquity there existed not only an understanding of fate but also an understanding of catharsis, of purification through suffering."

He knew how to dispel darkness in the soul of a person. "Sometimes," he said, "sickness seems to get worse, and one looks, and the sick person gets better. It is a blessing that he who does not doubt what he chooses to do will not encounter ambivalence. And never despair about sins, but cry and ask for help."

Once, I told Fr. Pyotr about one fact, which we observed with Pavlik, when we were in Glinskaia Pustyn'. With a young monk, early one morning, Pavlik walked in the hayfield (the monastery at the time had its meadows and cows, and all young people were recruited to help in agricultural work). Pavlik directed the attention of his companion to the clouds, colored by the rising sun. The young monk did not even raise his eyes. "I did not enter the monastery in order to admire beauty, but to weep for sins," he said. After listening to this story, Fr. Pyotr said, "It is not correct that, if one wishes to cry about one's sins, one must never admire the heavens. On the contrary, when one is moved by one's emotions and delight from the beauty of God's creation, then one's sins also will be felt more keenly." In his internal life, Fr. Pyotr always advised one to go along an even path, to aspire to use one's talents, and not to be in a hurry. "Over everything place the shield of faith, which can extinguish the arrows of evil." "Without love, it is impossible to do anything, but love will be, when one thinks of the other person first, then peace will reign in families."

Fr. Pyotr was always active, cheerful, and quick in his movements. He always walked to the church with such a quick step that it was difficult to walk beside him.

Once, I want to Borovsk on the holiday of Ignatius Bogonosets.[14] There was not a night service in the church on this day. I wanted to make confession in the evening and to receive communion during the liturgy in the church in the morning. Fr. Pyotr heard my confession in his small cell. Unexpectedly, during confession, I had a sharp spasm of the blood vessels of the brain. I lay down immediately on the bed in the large room of the owner of the house. Fr. Pyotr tried to do what he could to help. On the next day, before going to the church, he said matins in his house, and during this, opened the door to the room where I lay, so that I could see and hear him. Fr. Pyotr loved Ignatius Bogonosets and, in this unusual situation, served with such inspiration and concentration that this morning would never pass from my memory. After lunch, I went home and, as soon as I was better, I wrote Fr. Pyotr a letter.

In response, I received a letter in which he wrote:

> I was endlessly glad to receive your news about your health. I worried a lot, and in each liturgy prayed especially about you. Thanks be to God that you have gotten stronger, but do not be abused by work and with all manner of puzzling questions. I mourn about Glinskaia Pustyn' and the Kievan elders.[15] I thought to look for you in Moscow, but decided that this may not be entirely appropriate. I have not been able to make it to Mother [Mariia]—always matters and seasonal religious rites intervene. My health for an old man is tolerable. To all heartfelt greeting and blessing.
>
> May you have good health and be under God's care.
>
> January 1958

In the last year of his life, Fr. Pyotr began and finished a huge project: the external and internal repair of the church. He devoted days and nights to this matter. He took on himself the accounting and bookkeeping part of the work (now his knowledge of bookkeeping came in handy). He had to conduct business with many people of different professions to implement all the repair work. With everyone, he had to come to an understanding, to maintain control over many things, to follow different aspects of the work, and to plan them. Many difficulties emerged. He had to deal with the representatives of the local authority. The funds for repair of the church were insufficient. Fr. Pyotr invested his personal funds in the repair.

Meanwhile, the illnesses that he brought from the camp were coming back. A hidden sickness crossed over into a sickness of the blood. Fr. Pyotr sacrificed his sleep and his rest for work. He hastened to finish the repair of the church. What joy the completion of the repair was for him! The church was unrecognizable. It became the jewel of the town.

I want to pass on here a letter, sent by Fr. Pyotr from Borovsk in response to my congratulations on the holiday of the Birth of Christ:

> "Our Savior on High visited us today, from the East, and existing in the darkness and the vestibule, protected by the truth, because from a

Virgin was born the Lord" (light of matins). The peace and blessing of God be with you.

I received your note of congratulations, and, in turn, welcome you with the coming Great holidays of Christmas and the Epiphany. I send prayerful wishes to you for them and convey joy and peace, in such a great spirit, with which fulfills and breathes the miraculous holiday service in all its beautiful and sublime prayers and singing.

Having begun to make notes, to stop is difficult: all that is good and wise for that which summons us to the sacred Church! I limit myself only to the praising "And today" in the same matins: "Christ in Bethlehem is born of a Virgin: the beginning is without a beginning, and the Word is fulfilled; the heavenly powers rejoice, and the earth of man is merry; the Lord's gifts have come; the shepherds marvel at the birth. We incessantly shout out: glory to God on high, peace on earth, and good will to men."

In each liturgy, and I celebrate it very often, at least every week, I prayerfully remember you and all my near ones, together with my other spiritual children, and I myself consider that for us this is most important that I only can do for all who are in sorrow and have burdens, and seeking God's mercy and help. "Wash away, Lord, the sins of the deceased through Your Saintly Blood, through your sacred prayers," says the priest at the end of the liturgy, submerged in the elements of the chalice, which connects the healthy and the dead. What may be more effective than this?

You put difficult questions to me. What can I say, immersed in this very vanity, which you so well note, in describing our general spiritual state? In childhood and adolescence, I was attracted to the monastery myself, but somehow the high level of the monastic vows frightened and held me back. How could I, useless and weak, be a worthy and genuine monk? In the monastery, I wanted to be then and now, in my years as an elderly person, in the declining years of my life. To the strict monastery, with its secluded regulation, I would go live with such joy, because I see in monasticism the most desired fulfillment of my life. Meanwhile, to take monastic vows and remain in the world, to remain immersed in earthly vanity from which a monk must flee, I feared still more and, probably, never could resolve. Monasticism as an ideal, as the very highest goal of all my life, will stand before me, even if I were not dressed in cloak material, although in my affairs I aspired to fulfill the vows of a monk.

In one of the journals of the Patriarchate, there was a good article about Bishop Feofan Zatvornik, with an excerpt from one of his works:

"One must not enter the monastery when one wishes, but when a person feels it is essential, that one cannot, must not, remain any longer, without taking the vows." I still did not feel this.

One of my spiritual daughters, complaining of her spiritual poverty and emptiness, in spite of her acceptance into monasticism, dissatisfied with her situation, almost accused me because she, through me, became acquainted with the person through whom she received a cassock and proved in her affairs to be a very poor nun, because she did not completely accept and comply with monasticism.

In my opinion, you have taken an entirely correct path: you are waiting for blessing and are prepared to receive it as obedience to a person of the highest spiritual disposition and having a great ascetic experience, which I entirely do not have. I only think whether it is necessary to hurry with taking monastic vows should you begin, without them now, learning under the guidance of an experienced and most respectable person, who could put you on a straight and true road of asceticism, resolving all your doubts and questions that inevitably will arise? Will your life's circumstances allow you to peacefully take up the "science of all the sciences"? You will not be relying on your personal reason but will be following the fundamental monastic vow of obedience to the Mother Superior, the elder, the person who you will be entrusted for guidance or who will give direction for study of the alphabet of spiritual life. It seems to me that you will fulfill the words, quoted by you, of Jesus the Savior, because you will follow Him, having taken your cross. You will find comfort and peace.

Alik passed on to me your work; with joy, I will become acquainted with it, only when I find a little time; I am very tired from my physical work and in such a condition my head works poorly and to read serious things is difficult. When it arrived, I was very glad, because for a long time I heard nothing about you.

If there is still time, before you concern yourself with the "alphabet," in my opinion, your serious works should not be left behind.

To all my acquaintances, I send warm greeting and blessing. Forgive my poverty, if I have written something inexact or incorrectly expressed myself. May you be in good health and protected by God. May the Lord grant you salvation.

Illness and the Final Days in the Life of Fr. Pyotr

Fr. Pyotr himself did not want to acknowledge his illness. In the mornings, he continued to go to the church. He already could not celebrate, and once they drove him home in an automobile because he could not walk. He collapsed and spent some time in bed in the room of the *starosta*, under the observation of Borovsk doctors. The condition of the sick priest worsened with each day.

This time, when Fr. Pyotr lay at home, he could not reconcile himself with the fact that it was impossible for him to serve, and he was torn with desire to go to the church. A doctor from the Borovsk hospital, who came to visit him, was surprised with his upsurge of energy and exclaimed: "You so love the Lord God?" The former *starosta* added, "Fr. Pyotr wishes to comfort the people."

The doctors of the Borovsk hospital refused to admit him, under the pretext that they had no blood for a transfusion, and the doctor who did transfusions had departed. Subsequently, it became clear that they had decided not to assume the responsibility, out of the consideration that the patient was too weak and might not withstand a blood transfusion. One of the parishioners recommended that we appeal to the head doctor, Z. L., of the Ermolino hospital, whom she knew as a good doctor and a compassionate person. But not immediately did they manage to convince her to take our sick patient, since it put her in a very difficult situation, and, what is more, the sick person lived in Borovsk and came under the observation of the Borovsk physicians. We tried to catch her everywhere, and, waiting for hours for her departure from the executive committee meeting in Borovsk, we stationed ourselves by the door of the Ermolino hospital. The doctor had a sincere desire to help the sick man, but circumstances hampered its implementation: the hospital was undergoing repair, the sick lay in the corridors. The main obstacle consisted of the necessity of securing an agreement with the Borovsk doctor: Professor Egorov had approved the medical treatment prescribed for him.[16]

Finally, the Borovsk doctor sent Professor Egorov a telegram with the information that, in the Borovsk hospital, it was impossible to perform the blood transfusion. The doctor in the Ermolino hospital sent a telegram, offering to put the sick priest in the Ermolino hospital, if both the Borovsk doctor and Professor Egorov agreed. Then I went with the telegram to Egorov. All these negotiations dragged on, and, in the meantime, the sick priest's hemoglobin fell to 12 percent, so that a blood transfusion turned out to be useless. Finally, the doctors convened a "conference," and they came to a common agreement. Then the question emerged of how to obtain the blood or, still better, a mass of red corpuscles. This was almost impossible. Unexpectedly, a general acquaintance, I. [I. is identified here as her general acquaintance] volunteered to go with me to the Institute of Blood Transfusion. After all this, our negotiations failed. By chance, I encountered an acquaintance of his in the institute, who, in filling Professor Egorov's prescription, helped us order six ampoules of hemoglobin. I took on myself the delivery of these ampoules, one at a time, and every day of the week I went to the Institute of Blood Transfusion and from there to the Ermolino hospital. The first blood transfusion Fr. Pyotr endured with great difficulty. More truthfully, the transfusion itself he endured well, but after an hour, a fever, a chill, and vomiting began. The second transfusion went somewhat more easily. His condition continued to remain grave; the patient was so weak that he could hardly talk, would forget the words, and did not understand anything we said to him. An infection of the kidney and ear added to his sickness.

The head doctor, Z. L., did everything possible to create the best conditions for the patient. She gave him a separate room and sent for an ear, nose, and throat specialist. She asked us, apart from the medical personnel, for someone close to the patient to be with him at all times; she herself dropped in on him several times each day. We summoned the brother of Fr. Pyotr from Moscow. We kept watch in turns. I spent the twenty-four hours on the eve of Pentecost in the hospital. At night, the patient was delirious, tried to tear the compress from his head, and was very agitated.

Outside, a strong thunderstorm had come up; in the morning, water so covered the road that it was impassable. The Egorovs, who came to Ermolino in a large ZIM automobile, were forced to return, since the automobile got stuck. On the Day of the Holy Spirit, the nun Tat′iana came. On Tuesday, the patient improved. His hemoglobin want up from 12 percent to 18 percent, his general condition improved, and for the first time during his stay, he ate a bowl of semolina kasha. On Wednesday, the twenty-fourth, his twenty-four-hour condition became better still. Fr. Pyotr awakened alert and cheerful, crossed himself, and said, "Lord! How good it is to live in Your world!" He rejoiced at his return to life. With great feeling, he talked a lot about love, joy, and God's compassion.

Then, unexpectedly, he turned to everyone present with these words: "To you everything is easy, you can do kind acts, but with what will the priest manage to vindicate himself?" In response to the retort that the priest can still do much good, Fr. Pyotr replied, "There are those who do, but there are those of whom I am afraid even to think. One person wrote to his children: 'Even the first Christians sinned, and did not stop, but renounced their sins, moved forward to their goals, to the Lord, and that is why they were saints—that is, people who please God, saints.'" Fr. Pyotr said with tears in his eyes, "In Dostoevsky's [tale], remember, Marmeladov says: '. . . There go the drunkards, there go the weak . . . and he judges and forgives everyone, both the good and the evil, the wise and the submissive . . . Then we will understand everything! . . . Everyone will understand.'"

From the Letters of V. Ia. Vasilevskaia to N. V. Trapani[17]

July 6, 1959

Dear Nina!

After such a good day on Wednesday, the twenty-fourth, which I wrote about in my last letter to you, when Fr. Pyotr so well and vigorously conversed with us, and, it seemed, he was on the road to good recovery, but again weakness set in, a cough began, and his temperature went up. They decided not to do a fourth blood transfusion, and his hemoglobin fell from 18 percent to 14 percent. On Monday, the twenty-ninth, one could still talk with him, he remembered everyone, and asked about everyone. On Tuesday, a further decline set in. On Wednesday, the thirtieth, Fr. Pyotr ceased to talk and to breathe with difficulty. Emphysema began. On Thursday, July 2, Fr. Pyotr died at three o'clock in the morning. Only Tania (the nun from Roshcha) was with him. The burial service was very celebratory: nine priests came, the majority from the Kaluga region, and several people came from Moscow. From Zagorsk came one L. F. She and I spent the night in the church and took turns reading the Gospels at Fr. Pyotr's coffin. At five o'clock in the morning, people from the town began to arrive; they came continuously, as if he were a relative. Mothers brought their children. The guardian of the church of Nachaiannaia Radost' (Unexpected Joy) in Moscow came. He knew Fr. Pyotr from the day of his ordination (in 1921). At the funeral, he talked about the rare purity of the life and service of Fr. Pyotr, about how sacrificially he gave himself to the Church in everything, giving up not only his personal life, but also all kinds of personal interests. He talked about that uncommon joy, which seized Fr. Pyotr's whole being during his celebration of the liturgy. Someone else talked about Fr. Pyotr as about the ear of corn that ripened for harvest.

The entire town literally turned out for the burial of Fr. Pyotr. His coffin was carried on the main streets of the town, behind it came a religious procession with the choir and then the people. From time to time, the priests stopped the procession, and served the *panikhida* for the departed.[18] The songs "Holy God" and "Helper and Protector" did not cease for the length of the entire route.

They had dug the grave in a very picturesque place on a high hill next to the river by the chapel where, according to legend, the parents of St.

Paphnutius were buried.[19] They say that Fr. Pyotr himself chose this place beforehand for his grave.

It was comforting to see and to listen to the reactions of very diverse people, characterizing their relationship to Fr. Pyotr, and to be convinced that people were able to feel and value the beauty of his soul. I wanted to thank God for the opportunity to be by Fr. Pyotr's side in his last days and weeks of his life and to see him off on his final journey.

Now they have all gone, but they have left us a rich legacy. I ask only that I might be allowed to preserve a little, that I might at least fulfill a small piece [of this legacy] before the light of this world has died out in us.

Part III

My Journey

Elena Semenovna Men

In the very early years of my life, I felt God's presence. My mama was a believer, and imperceptibly instilled in my heart an understanding about God—as the Creator of the whole universe, who loves all people. When, for the first time, I heard words about the fear of God, in bewilderment, I asked Mama: "Since we love God, how can we be afraid of Him?" Mama responded to me, "We must be afraid to bring Him distress, by some kind of evil action." This answer completely satisfied me.

My grandmother, even more deeply, was a believer. I observed how, each morning, she prayed, fervently and sincerely, and her prayers overflowed into me. The need to pray took root in me. I do not remember what I prayed about, but I always prayed before the cross of the Church of the Sacred Nicholas, which was visible from our window and marvelously glowed before sunset. This seemed miraculous to me. It seemed that, in addition to the natural light, it also radiated with some kind of otherworldly Light . . .

At eight years of age, I matriculated in the private gymnasium, in the upper preparatory class.

I studied willingly; to me, school was easy. They taught us, of course, the Scriptures. In the elementary classes, the priest explained the foundations of the Orthodox faith and offered to teach the prayers.

In the first grade, they taught the Old Testament, and in the second, the New Testament. During this time, several people of non-Orthodox confessions could leave the class and walk in the corridor or go downstairs into the hall, where they held dance lessons. But for the most part, I stayed behind and listened attentively to what the priest explained. Once, he talked about how God is one but in three persons: the Father, the Son, and the Holy Spirit. I interpreted this as axiomatic; everything simply and clearly lodged in my heart.

All the lessons began and ended with prayer. Of course, I soon learned these prayers.

At Christmas, in school, we had a Christmas tree. They assigned several of us a poem related to the holiday. They assigned me the poem "Carolers." I was happy that they gave me precisely this poem at the same time that they gave other girls poetry unrelated to the holiday of the Birth of Christ. This poem was from the collection "Reflections" by Popov.

Carolers

Under the cover of the starry night
Sleeps the Russian village.
All roads, all paths
Are blanketed with white snow.
Here and there in the windows lights,
Like stars, shine.
To the light a throng of children
With the star runs like a snowdrift.
Under the windows they knock,
"You are Born," they sing.
"Carolers, carolers!"
It resounds there and here.
And in the discordant children's choir
So mysteriously pure,
So pleasing is the sacred news
About the birth of Christ.[1]

In the first grade, I listened, with great interest, to the lessons of the Old Testament. Often I borrowed a textbook from the other girls and read the assignment.

At this time, my mama gave French and German lessons, and our home was busy with remedial students. It was wartime, and Papa was at the front. Mama had to think about feeding my brother, grandmother, herself, and me. Grandmother took care of the household and helped Mama a great deal. Morally, thanks to her firm faith, she strongly supported Mama in the most difficult wartime years. Not without reason, in 1890, Fr. John of Kronstadt found it possible to heal her.[2] At that time, after the death of her husband, she was left with a large family on her hands: she had seven children, among whom the oldest was eighteen years of age, and the youngest was three. Grandmother's stomach began to swell. No kind of medicine, doctors, or professors could help her.

Here in Khar'kov, where she then lived, Fr. John of Kronstadt came.[3] A neighbor woman persuaded Grandmother to go to him and ask for healing. People filled the church and square in front of them, but the neighbor woman managed to lead Grandmother through the whole crowd, and she appeared before Fr. John. He cast a glance at Grandmother and said, "I know that you are Jewish, but I see in you deep faith in God. Let us pray to the Lord, and he will heal you from your illness. In a month, you will be well." He blessed her, and the swelling began gradually to recede, and a month later it was all gone.

Grandmother did not teach me anything, but her example and her love for me acted more powerfully than any kind of moral instruction. I always marveled at why Grandmother loved me so, more strongly than all her own children and grandchildren. She had a premonition that I would always remember her, both up to and especially after her death. Mama loved my older brother Leonid more, and Papa loved the younger Volodia and me more.

Once, one of Mama's students left a text of the New Testament at our house and went away to the countryside for the summer holidays. I began to read this text (the New Testament, by the account of the priest Vinogradov), and the more I read the more I was overcome by its spirit and the more love for Christ flared up in me. When I came to the Crucifixion and heard the words "Father, forgive them because they know not what they do," something in me shuttered, a shock came over me, which had never happened either before or after that moment. I would seal myself up in some secluded small place and for hours would not take my eyes off the Crucifixion, and kissed and showered Him with tears.

I made myself a promise, without fail, to be baptized. But I did not know how to do this. Mama had a first cousin, Inna L'vovna; she was baptized out of love for a Russian youth, whom she then married. But at the time, I thought that it was possible to be baptized only from love for Christ. I resolved to confide my secret in her. Once, she came to visit us. I had grown into a shy young girl, and it was very difficult to force myself to tell her that I intended to be baptized. She responded, "And have you thought whether you are worthy of this?" These words embarrassed me, but Mama and Grandmother then entered, and it was impossible to continue the conversation.

Finally, I decided to talk to Mama about it. My words produced the impression of a bomb exploding on her. She was struck with horror, began to yell at me, and then started to beat me. Frightened, in order to distract her attention, Brother broke out a windowpane. In the end, she threw me into the corner toward the stove. But the whole time I continued to repeat, "I don't care, I will accept baptism." I was nine years old. Soon Papa returned from the front, and Mama told him about my desire. Papa tried to dissuade me with kindness and love, but I firmly said that it made no difference; I would fulfill my intention.

I did not talk about this subject any more with my parents. Once, Mama's pupil gave me *Fabiola*, a chronicle about the first centuries of Christianity.[4] I began to read it, but Mama, after seeing my book, seized and hid it. Soon I found it on top of the wardrobe closet and read it all the way to the end. In the library, I checked out *Quo Vadis* (Kamo griadeshi), by G. Senkevich, and, in ecstasy, read and submerged myself in the life of the first Christians, in the first century of our era. I also read Farrar's *The Dawn of Christianity* (Na rassvete khristianstva)—at that time, such books could be checked out of the library.[5]

I was still a child and played a great deal. The content of the books I had read filled all my games. Even in the school choir, we sang such songs as "Baby Jesus Had a Garden." This song had an unusually profound effect on me. I imagined myself among the Jewish children who wove a prickly crown of thorns for Christ.

In 1924, I finished the seven-year school and went to Moscow to visit Grandmother, who since 1920 had gone to live with her son, whose wife had died. The son, my uncle Iasha, had two children: a son Venia and daughter Verochka.[6] With great love, all of them accepted me. Vera immediately became attached to me, and I to her. We felt that our souls had some kind of special closeness to each other, although our personalities sharply differed: Verochka was reserved, for the most part melancholy. She still could not reconcile herself to the death of her mother, whom she and her brother tenderly loved. In his diary entries, the brother called her "my saint," and although he was twenty-one years of age when his mother died, he mourned over her for many years, often saw her in his dreams, and constantly felt her presence nearby.

I was full of *joie de vivre*, a cheerful girl, and I had just turned sixteen years old. I rejoiced in life, rejoiced that they surrounded me with love and care. When they invited me to remain in Moscow and take the exams for the eight-year class, I willingly agreed. Mama and Papa also permitted me to remain in Moscow. The fact is that Khar'kov, where we lived during this time, had no nine-year schools and had only vocational schools. Since I still could

FIGURE 6. Elena Tsuperfein (Men) and Vera Vasilevskaia, in the 1920s.

not choose my occupation, then I preferred to go to a nine-year school and receive a full secondary education. But in the ninth grade, I already began a specialization. We had a drawing and design class for construction specialization with two divisions: engineering-construction and machine design and construction. I was placed in the engineering-construction division. Drafting came easily to me: I completed all the assignments. We had eighteen subjects, general and specialist.

Toward the end of the school year, for three months, I fell ill with paratyphoid, pleurisy, and pneumonia. When I regained a little of my strength, I began to get up from the bed and draw the required blueprints. In 1926, among the drawing plates that served as models for architectural blueprints, churches and chapels still remained. I made a blueprint of a hospital church, having enlarged it by four times, I drew one stone chapel (a bit reminiscent of the Tarasovka church) and one wooden chapel; the latter I drew with an especial mystical feeling. In some way, it reminded me of the chapel in Nesterov's painting *The Youth of St. Sergii*, which so impressed me, when I was in the Tretiakov Gallery for the first time.[7]

These three months of illness had a beneficial effect on me. Some internal matters came together, which were difficult to achieve in the noise and bustle of daily life. Since I had a high temperature, the doctor did not allow me to read. Verochka sat for hours by my bedside and read aloud *War and Peace*.

FIGURE 7. Elena Tsuperfein (Men), Veniamin, and Vera Vasilevskaia, September 14, 1924.

I got better, went to the director of studies, and asked permission not to take specialization exams, only general education ones. But he responded to me, "You are capable and can pass everything." These words inspired me, and I really did pass everything. After finishing school, Mama summoned me to Khar'kov, and I had to go.

During the two years I spent in Moscow, I only rarely went to church. Much was not understandable to me, and the Church Slavonic language was unfamiliar. I wanted to understand everything, each word. Because of my youth and ignorance, I did not understand that not everything came immediately. Over the years of constantly going to church and listening to the liturgy, a person became accustomed to the language and the incomprehensible Church Slavonic turns of phrases but, most importantly, [managed] to enter into the very spirit of the divine service.

Once, not long before the end of school, by the Petrovskie Gates, I saw a sign with the inscription, "Community of Christian-Baptists."[8] On the doors was a leaflet on which was written, "The community is organized according to the model of the Christian community of the first centuries of Christianity." Since the first centuries were especially dear to me, I went in there to the meeting. The most appealing aspect that drew me in was that the whole time they spoke in Russian, clearly and intelligibly. I regularly began to attend their meetings. Once, I invited Vera to go, but she did not like it; it seemed to her simple and on a low level. But I wanted to hear about Christ, always think about Him, and pray to Him.

When I returned to Khar'kov, I first found a community of Baptists and, to my parents' great horror, I began to visit it.

In the autumn, I sat for the exams in the Khar'kov Construction Technical College, but I did not matriculate. During this time, in both institutions of higher education and technical colleges, they primarily accepted children of workers and peasants, and my papa was a chemical engineer. I next found a job as a drawing copyist and on Sundays visited the Baptist meetings. I became acquainted with several people, and they even aspired to baptize me.

Once, I observed a baptism service of the Baptists. This was in 1927. An entire procession moved along the streets of Khar'kov toward the river. Those preparing for baptism and other members of the community sang spiritual songs. A whole crowd of curious people gathered around them and converged with the arrival of a large group of people. Two elders stood up to their waists in the water. Women in white clothing, with their arms crossed across their chests, walked toward them on one side, and men came up on the other side. The elders submerged them three times in the water, baptizing them in the name of the Father, the Son, and the Holy Ghost. This made a very strong impression on everyone standing around them.

At home, this time Mama struck me hard. My parents took up arms against me even more. Once, I came home late in the evening, and they caused a great scandal. Papa began to tear down all the pictures that hung over my bed (the *Madonna* of Kaulbach and *Christ in the Wilderness* by Khramskoi), and flung around my books and journals.⁹ By some miracle, the Gospels remained intact, since I had hidden it under a mattress. In a frenzy, Mama began to beat me. All this ended when I fled from home and lived for several days at the home of a sister-Baptist. On my cheek, a scar remained, and I was ashamed to go to work. When fellow workers asked me about this, I tried in every way possible to make a joke, but everyone saw my unusual condition.

During this time, Mama wrote a letter to Verochka, telling her that I had run away from home to the Baptists. Immediately, Verochka came to Khar'kov, searched for me, and on the next day took me away to Moscow. At work, I took a discharge, and before my departure I reconciled with my parents.

In Moscow, I arranged to work as a drafting-copyist and, afterwards, they transferred me to the office of drafting-detail work, then I became a drafting-designer, and finally, a mechanical artist. Simultaneously, I studied in the school of drafting and design on Sretenka [Street].

I stopped going to see the Baptists. They closed the community at the Petrovskie Gates, and I did not begin to search for a new one. Something had alienated me from them. Work, studies, and household duties filled my days. On Sundays, a strange melancholy overcame me. My soul was starving.

From 1929 on, I began to go to church a little. I liked the Church of the Trinity in the Leaves (Troitskaia tserkov' na Listakh) on Sretenka [Street], but I went also to other churches.¹⁰ Gradually, I became accustomed to the Old Slavonic language. I began to discover the beauty of the church service in front of me. Several canticles I learned by heart; separate concluding sounds and words sank deeply into my soul. The first things that deeply moved me were the words of the priest, "Glory to You, who has shown us the Light!" Immediately, I learned "The Resurrection of Christ is visible . . ." I very much loved the Song of the Virgin, "My Soul Glorifies the Lord."

Verochka and I lived in harmony. She introduced me to all her friends. But none of them attracted me to themselves as Tonia did. Tonia was a young woman of deep belief—and all of her actions and words reflected this. I knew that she had a spiritual father—an elder. Once, I read *The Brothers Karamazov*. This book made a very strong impression on me. Everything said about the elder Zosima in it affected me. Dostoevsky said about the elder: "This is a person who takes your soul in his soul and your will in his will." I paused on these words and thought, "How good it would be for me to have such an elder!" Alyosha Karamazov became my beloved literary hero, and Dostoevsky—my beloved writer.

I loved to read, and I read a great deal. At this time, it was possible to find books of spiritual content in secondhand bookstores. Thus I bought the drama *The King of the Jews* by Konstantin Romanov—the uncle of the tsar—which I loved very much, and several verses from it I repeated instead of prayers (among prayers in that time, I knew only "Our Father").[11] For example, I loved the "Prayer of Jesus's Disciples":

Allow me not to be faint-hearted,
Give me a humble soul
To be a devoted servant
To Your Will be a follower.
Give me in the hours of trial
Courage, strength in the struggle!
Give me in the moments of suffering
Faith to remain in You.
The sun with its rays illuminating
My mortal eyes,
Give me, of the one who has loved the people,
Incessant love!
[. . .]
With the first rays of the sun
Scattering the fog of night,
Give us pure hearts
To sing Your Name
[. . .]

From the library of their teacher, who had gone abroad, Verochka acquired *The Confessions* of the Blessed Augustine.

This was the first serious spiritual book that I read. I read it with great interest. In a present from my cousin Venichka, I received Khitrov's book *St. Eustace* (Evstafii Plakida).[12] This was the lives of saints, depicted in artistic form. In an oil lamp shop, my brother bartered several newspapers for this book, which were intended for wrapping soap. Out of all the poets, I loved A. K. Tolstoy the most.[13] His poems "John of Damascus" and "Sinner" I learned, in part, by heart, as I did also "Christian [Woman]" by S. Ia. Nadson.[14] In all the poets and in all the literary works, I searched for Christian motifs close to my heart. I very much loved to sing "The Angel" and "In a Difficult Minute of Life," by M. Iu. Lermontov and "Now Our Sea . . . Come to Ground" (Neliudimo nashe more) by N. M. Iazykov.[15]

At that time, we had no acquaintances who could give us spiritual books. Tonia was very careful and afraid to disturb the slow progress along a spiritual road that had only begun to take shape in us. Tonia lived outside the city (Verochka had been at her home earlier). When I went into her room, the décor affected me. Icons covered all the walls. I experienced trembling and reverence, which happens when you enter a church. I do not remember what we talked about. I remained silent almost the whole time.

Tonia introduced me to her relatives. When we were leaving, Valentina (I do not remember her patronymic), Mother Mariia's sister-in-law, said, pointing at me, "Tonechka, are you really not going to take such a good young lady to Fr. Serafim, so that he might bless her?" I was very embarrassed. Tonia, apparently like me, said nothing and left. As it turned out, the woman referred to Fr. Serafim.

Several years later, Tonia asked me for a photograph of Verochka and me. I gave her the photo where we sat together in a boat, and in Bykov, in 1920, an amateur photographer took a picture of us. On my next visit, Tonia said that she had shown the photograph to Fr. Serafim, and he said, "They have traveled halfway along the road." "And what the second half will be, we do not know," Tonia added. I understood that there was a person who followed our spiritual growth and prayed for us.

Until 1931, I worked and studied. In 1931, I completed the coursework for drafting and design and continued to work in the Leather Project (*Kozhproekt*) office. When I received a new task—drafting or some other kind of work—I mentally solicited God's blessing on this work and thanked God when I completed the task. No one taught me how to do this; it was my internal need. Sometimes I very much wanted to pray. Then I went out onto the flat roof of our establishment (a large house by the Ust'inskii Bridge, which we had designed ourselves) and there found a place where no one would see.[16] None of my fellow workers, except for my close friends Ana[17] and Lina, suspected my beliefs. Only once, at Easter, one of our engineers, as if it were a joke, turned to me with a holiday greeting: "Christ is risen, Elena Semenovna!" When I responded to him, "Risen, indeed!" he stepped back with an open mouth.

On another occasion, I went to a demonstration. At the time, in this regard, people were very strict about missing a demonstration and considered it anti-Soviet behavior. In the 1930s, antireligious propaganda was very strong. During the demonstration, people constantly sang antireligious songs and chants. Once, they started to sing one of the godless songs. I, of course, did not begin to sing. What showed on my face, I do not know, but one young woman approached me and whispered in my ear, "I also believe in God."

Once, Verochka went on vacation with her father to Optina Pustyn'. She had many interesting things to tell me about it, and I wanted to go there.

FIGURE 8. Elena Tsuperfein (Men), beginning of the 1930s.

In 1933, I booked a place in the resort "Optina Pustyn'." Eight women lived in my suite. I was very overwrought during that time and did not try to make friends with anyone. After breakfast, I took my satchel with the Gospels and went into the forest. Along the path, here and there, I came to a field where wild strawberries grew in abundance. I gathered them in a small birchbark container. Finally, I found a picturesque clearing among thick trees and decided to stop here and read the Gospels. But the strawberries did not give me peace; everywhere the red berries peeped out at me, and I wanted to pick and pick them. I understood that this was a temptation. Then I took the container and threw away all the berries I had gathered. After this, I sat on a log and peacefully began to read the Gospels. The berries no longer attracted my attention.

Toward lunch, we gathered in the large refectory of the monastery. Gazing at the beautifully executed gospel subjects around me, my soul relaxed. The holidaymakers responded in various ways. One of them addressed the gathering and announced that it was necessary to take two barrels of paint and paint over all these "gods." This was not done, however, in my presence.

In Optina, among all the dense Briansk forests, I rested well and, internally, pulled myself together.[18] In our room, one of the women engaged in fortunetelling. She told the fortunes of all of us. She told me that I would soon marry, that I would have two children, and that I had no predisposition for the technical sciences. The last observation surprised me: "How strange, since I work as a technical designer and builder, and I very much love my occupation." "Nevertheless, this is so," the fortuneteller responded. From this point on, I never again had my fortune told. I thought that the Lord hid the future from us, that this was for our own benefit, and we absolutely must not attempt to learn it.

The forecasts of the fortuneteller came true. After several months, in April 1934, I actually married. I very much wanted to marry a believing man, but this did not happen. If I found out that a person was a believer, it turned out that he already loved someone else. But most of the young men I met were nonbelievers. Since at that time to be a believer was almost the same as being an enemy of the people, several simply hid their faith.

One of my acquaintances, Vladimir, was an engineer-technologist, a specialist in a field of the textile industry. I became acquainted with him in 1927. I was then eighteen years old. He worked in Orekhovo-Zuev, together with my cousin Venichka, an electrical engineer.[19] On Sundays, they both came to Moscow, and Vladimir Grigor'evich (as I called him, since he was six years older than I) was often at our home. He usually bought tickets to the theater or movies and invited me. I went with him everywhere, to friends' and acquaintances', even to his deputy director's. But during this time, I did not want very much to get married. At that time, I had other thoughts and aspirations.

The years passed, and Grandmother began to insist that I had to make a decision at last. "All the time you look at Vera, and you wish, as does she, to complete the term of a Nikolaevan soldier." This is what people said about girls who remained unmarried by the age of twenty-five.[20] In her letters, Mama also hinted that it was time to get married. These discussions very much distressed me. Vladimir Grigor'evich not once proposed to me, and I always avoided such talk. On one occasion, he was gone from Moscow for a long time. When he returned, he settled in a company apartment at the First Cotton Print Factory, where he worked, and again we began to date. The year 1933 approached its end. He invited me to go with him to his company's party for New Year's. At first, I consented. But in church they announced that at midnight there would be a New Year's prayer service. Then I said to Vladimir Grigor'evich that I could not be with him on New Year's and would not be able to do anything with anyone. He went alone, having invited no one else. Suddenly, on this night, he decided to stop smoking. He knew that I did not like it when people smoked, since smoking made a person a slave of cigarettes. He stopped smoking forever. I was overcome. I knew that since I preferred prayer to New Year's entertainments, the Lord laid on the heart of Vladimir Grigor'evich to do some good deed.

One time, he directly put the question to me: Why did I not want to marry him? I did not answer immediately, but I understood that to remain silent any longer was impossible. I said to him, "Because I confess a Christian faith." Least of all did he expect such an answer. For a long time, we walked in silence. Finally, he said, "You have become still higher in my eyes. For some reason, I thought that you loved somebody else." With this, our date ended. The next time he said to me, "That you are a believer will not impede us in our life as a family. You can go to church and listen to some archbishop, and I will go to lectures, and then we will share what we found interesting."

Suddenly, I felt it to be God's will that I should marry Vladimir Grigor'evich, and I gave him my consent.

"When will the wedding take place?" he asked.

"In two months."

Krasnaia Gorka, St. Thomas Sunday, fell in exactly two months.[21] On this day, weddings after the Great Lent period usually took place.

This Great Lent I felt stronger than ever. I limited myself in dress, in words, and in desires, refusing anything superfluous. The only thing I did not understand was that I should limit myself in food choices. I lived in the family of Uncle Iasha, and I could not allow myself to restrict my food intake in various ways. If I had known that it was necessary to eat other kinds of food, then I would have found a way out of the situation. But I simply did not know that.

During Lent, I felt as though the spiritual world had seized my soul, and suddenly the question about my forthcoming marriage turned everything upside down. Doubt came over me. Should I go through with the marriage? Several times, it seemed to me that, when the doorbell rang, I would open the door and see before me a nun with a lighted candle in her hands, who would beckon me to a distant monastery.

I asked my friend Ania whether I should marry. She suggested that I try it, and if I did not like it, I should divorce. "But no," I thought, "I am not going to do this. The Savior said that one must not divorce." These words were the law to me.

I asked Uncle Iasha the same thing. He said, "If you love him, marry him." I could not then make sense of my feelings, and I was in a state of confusion. Then Verochka told me that she was certain that I should marry Vladimir Grigor'evich.

Thus, on April 15, 1934, both of us took leave from work and went to the Marriage Bureau (ZAGS, Zapis' aktov grazhdanskogo sostoianiia). The process of registration was short and cold. Although the young woman who registered us in parting wished us, "Be happy!" Volodia said that this was her standard phrase, and she said the same thing to everyone. Both of us were so dismayed that we went the wrong way. At work, everyone began to congratulate me (the chief engineer proclaimed from the rooftops to everyone that I had married), and that evening the six associates of our sector sent a huge bouquet of lilacs from the flower shop.

We spent our wedding evening at Uncle Iasha's. I had invited three associates from work; the remaining people were relatives. In all, twenty people gathered there. On the eighteenth, I moved to Volodia's nine-meter room in Kozhevniki, on Derbenevskaia Street, right across from my work.[22] Thus began my family life.

Verochka missed me, came every day for the next two weeks, and cried. Soon it turned out that I was pregnant. I expected a child at the end of January, and I even hoped it would be born on Epiphany.

Volodia told my brother that I had become more religious. Volodia then tried to assure him, "This is from her pregnancy. Afterwards, all of this will pass."

I read the Gospels constantly, although not every day. Several passages acted on me with great power. But the most powerful of all the words that shook me were: "His Blood is on us and on our children!" When I read this passage, I almost fainted. Verochka often came to see me and treated me with special care. All of us felt that it would be a boy, and I had chosen his name ahead of time—Aleksandr. In her letters, Mama called him Alik long before his birth. I went on leave of absence a month and a half before the birth of the child, and Mama came to Moscow a month before the birth.

On January 22, I gave birth to my firstborn—Aleksandr. The birth was difficult, long, and stretched out almost twenty-four hours. But when they first brought me the defenseless little one to breastfeed, I was happy. On his little hand was a bracelet, with the inscription: "Men Elena Semenovna. Boy."

On the tenth day, the maternity ward discharged me. Volodia, Mama, and Verochka came to pick me up.

With the arrival of my first son, a new life began in our home. Alik stood at the center of our family. I again almost resettled at Verochka's home, since she had a large apartment. Verochka's father, Uncle Iasha, willingly accepted us in his home and treated Volodia, little Alik, and me with love. Verochka would sit for hours by the cradle of the child and compose inspiring verses. From the verses, she put together a collection, titled "Ten Songs about a Little Boy."

At the beginning of summer, we went to the dacha in Tomilino.[23] One day, Tonia came to us and asked whether we wanted to baptize Alik. I said that I very much wanted to baptize him, but I did not know how to do this. Tonia offered to help. Then she asked whether I also wanted to be baptized. Suddenly, some kind of fear came over me, and I refused. "This means we will baptize Alik alone," Tonia said. She conversed a little more with me and left for home. I walked with her. On my return trip, a powerful upsurge of thoughts and feelings seized me. From the time I was nine years old, I had intended to be baptized. Eighteen years had passed, and when this question was put in earnest before me, I became frightened, weak-spirited, and refused. Why? How could this be? I sat down immediately to write Tonia a letter, asking forgiveness and, of course, said that I would accept baptism with joy.

After some time had passed, Tonia again came to see me. She had shown my letter to her elder, and he said that when my husband left for a holiday, I could come immediately to him with Alik and Tonia. On September 2, Volodia had to be in the Caucasus. I also planned that day for Tonia to go to Verochka's place in Moscow, and Alik and I would go there from Tomilino.

On this day, Grandmother treated me gently, and, before our departure, she embraced and kissed me for a long time. At that moment, Tonia softly said to me, "Say goodbye, say goodbye to Grandmother—you will come back a different person." These words lodged painfully in my heart.

Verochka was terribly worried, not knowing where we were going with the child, although I had told her the goal of our journey. Tonia invited her to go with us, but Verochka declined. I took along a handbag with swaddling clothes. On the way, Tonia bought two fish and five buns, and we went to the Northern Station. So many times, I asked Tonia where we were going, but she did not answer. Only when we stepped out of the train car did I understand that we were in Zagorsk. I had been there on an excursion in 1929.

Tonia took Alik in her arms, and I carried the bags. Powerful anxiety came over me. I knew that I was going to Tonia's elder, and I knew why I was going there. All the while, I worried more and more. The bags with the swaddling clothes and the buns became excessively burdensome. Tonia quickly walked along with Alik in her arms. (Later she confessed that she worried that I would change my mind and turn around.)

Alik was calm, as if he anticipated the significance of what had to be accomplished, although he was only seven-and-a-half months old. I began to gasp for breath and implored Tonia to stop. But she hurried ahead. Finally, in complete exhaustion, I sat down on some kind of bench. Tonia sat down beside me. "Well, tell me a little about what he looks like," I said. "You know that I have not even conversed with Fr. Serafim." Tonia said that he had gray hair and sky-blue eyes. "These eyes can see straight through you," she added.

Then we got up and went on our way, and soon we arrived at his house. Tonia rang the bell, and a middle-aged woman, very welcoming and dressed in nun's clothing, opened the door. She led us into a room, clean, lighted, everything covered with icons. There, apparently, they awaited us. Fr. Serafim himself was not there, and for a long time he did not appear. I understood that before he received us he prayed. Finally, he came in to us. Tonia, carrying Alik, went up to him for his blessing, and I followed behind them. I, not knowing, placed my left hand over my right. Fr. Serafim immediately noticed and rearranged my hands. Then he proposed, "Sit down." If he had not said this, from anxiety and exertion, I would have collapsed onto the floor. For some time, we sat in silence.

At last, Fr. Serafim asked me, "Do you know Russian literature?" This question surprised me, but, having recalled *The Brothers Karamazov* and the elder Zosima, I understood why he asked me about this. He put several questions about life to me. Then we sat down to supper. The food was Lenten, and Fr. Serafim underlined that this had a direct relationship to our baptism.

After this, the woman who opened the door took Alik in her arms. Alik remained quiet and calm, as though understanding the entire seriousness of what took place. Fr. Serafim led me into another room and asked me to tell him all about my life. I told him, as much as I could. Then we lay down to sleep. Alik slept soundly, but I did not sleep the entire night and, as I could, prayed.

In the morning, the sacrament of baptism took place.

The baptism was accomplished by immersion. Each time Fr. Serafim immersed me, I felt that I was dying. After Fr. Serafim baptized me, he baptized Alik. Tonia was our godmother. On the previous evening, Fr. Serafim had showed me three crosses. One, the large silver one, with the words "Let God arise, let his enemies be scattered," he intended for Tonia; the second one—smaller, gold—he intended for me, and the third one, silver with blue enamel and the Crucifixion with the words "Save and protect," was for Alik.

My heart, however, pulled me toward the cross with the Crucifixion of the Savior. Suddenly, by mistake, Fr. Serafim placed this cross on me. He saw the will of God in this, and so the cross remained there. He placed the gold cross on Alik. I was very joyous to have the cross I wanted.

After this, Fr. Serafim began to hear my whole life's confession. Soon the liturgy began. They sang in a low voice, in order not to be heard on the street. The godmother sang very well, from her soul, although her voice was soft and weak. When the time came for communion, she presented Alik to me, and I moved forward behind her.

In my heart rang out the words, "He who eats my flesh and drinks my blood abides in Me, and I in him." After the completion of the service, everyone came forward to congratulate us. The entire day I remained in a white embroidered baptismal shirt (which reached down to the floor and had long wide sleeves), and on top Fr. Serafim told me to put on a white voile dress without sleeves.

After the meal, Fr. Serafim summoned me to his room and gave me a series of instructions.

First, he gave me a notebook with morning and evening prayers, and he said that I should learn them by heart. "Then they will always be in you," Fr. Serafim added.

Second, when you breastfeed Alik, he said to repeat three times "Our Father," three times "To Mary, Mother of God," and one time, "I believe."

Interestingly, when Vladimir Grigor'evich returned from the Caucasus, he brought me a photograph, taken with the cave of Simon the Canaanite in the background.[24] On the second day, right before the day of our baptism, he had a dream: a large group of people walked by, and they carried in front of them a large linen sheet on which was a depiction of Christ.

When we left Fr. Serafim, he devoutly blessed us with the words, "God's blessings on you." The stress was on the word "God." After returning to Moscow, I dropped in on my friend Ania, since it was urgently necessary to change the baby's clothes. When Ania saw the golden cross on Alik's breast, she gasped and threw up her hands.

Verochka awaited me at home. I spent the night in Moscow and, in the morning, went to Tomilino. At home, I tried to fulfill all the instructions of Fr. Serafim. It was especially difficult to memorize the morning and evening prayers. I had a good memory, and I quickly memorized poems and everything assigned in school. But here I met an unexpected obstacle: someone clearly prevented me from memorizing the prayers. The difficulty was not the Slavic language, which I, of course, had insufficiently assimilated. I quickly learned any language, but in this case, something strange and inexplicable impeded me. At that time, I did not have any understanding of dark forces. Finally, with great difficulty, I memorized everything and began to recite by memory.

At the beginning of the following year, the household worker Katia came to work for us. She was a devout believer, a spiritually tempered young woman. She helped me a great deal in becoming acquainted with the Orthodox faith. Lent arrived. Fr. Serafim said to me that I should fast on the first and fourth, and on Holy Week, and not to give Alik any meat. I continued to prepare meat for my husband.

Katia and I often went to church, sometimes individually, sometimes together, leaving Alik with Verochka. The beauty of the church service gradually opened itself up to me. The Lenten service was especially good. Bishop Afanasii wrote that through the power of its influence on the soul of a person, a service during Lent had no equivalent in the entire world.

They gave me the Lenten verses and the book containing the liturgy from Easter to All-Saint's Day, and each day I read them. Katia and I together sometimes read the morning and evening prayers. Most often, this took place at Verochka's home, since she had a separate room, and no one bothered us. Even more, Verochka herself came nearer to her moment of baptism. In January 1936, she went to Fr. Serafim's for the first time. Afterwards, Fr. Serafim told me about this first session: "When she stood before me, the enemy enveloped her so much that even I was surprised." Fr. Serafim completely freed her from these fetters of the enemy, and in the future their relationship became still deeper and closer.

I went to see him each month, sometimes with Alik, sometimes without him. Once, Alik and I took communion at Fr. Serafim's house and went to

FIGURE 9. Elena Semenovna Men, June 27, 1938.

Verochka's apartment at 1 Koptel'skii Lane. Alik was nearly eleven months old. Verochka greeted us with much love, embraced and kissed us. Suddenly, Alik, sitting in my arms, attempted to take the cross from me. I saw that he wanted to do something, and I helped him with this. Unexpectedly, he placed the cross on Verochka. Verochka was shocked. She crossed herself and with reverence kissed the cross.

In the summer of that year, we lived in Tarasovka, in a dacha.[25] Suddenly, Tonia came and said that, presently, but only temporarily, Fr. Serafim resided at their place in Bolshevo and wanted to see us. Katia and I took the little cart, sat Alik in it, and we went on foot. I was very glad to see Fr. Serafim, especially at Tonia's home. Alik and Katia remained in the courtyard. Fr. Serafim summoned me to the window and, pointing to Alik, who was then a year and a half old, said, "He will be a great man." Later, he told me: "In him, all our aspirations will be fulfilled." After staying a short while, we went home by train.

The summer ended, and we again moved to Moscow. Verochka more often communicated with Fr. Serafim, and although the road to baptism was long and difficult, all the same, it drew her near to the end. Fr. Serafim responded to all of her questions, and finally she gave her agreement for baptism. In her last letter to him, she wrote, "How good to be conquered, when you know Christ is the conqueror." The day of her baptism had already been set—November 18.

Verochka went there on the eve of her baptism. I could not do the same because of Volodia, but on the following day, I went on the early morning train. Since everything took place very early, when I got there, everything had been resolved. It gave me comfort to see my Verochka in a condition of complete sinlessness. She had on a pale blue dress, and her eyes gleamed with some kind of uncommon light. It was as if it were the same Verochka and, at the same time, someone else entirely. It was as though something new had permeated her being.

Thus yet another member enriched our Christian family. Verochka, Katia, and I lived in the bosom of the Orthodox Church, and Uncle Iasha, Venichka, and Volodia remained nonbelievers. In the summer of 1937, we settled in Losinka, where Fr. Ieraks lived.[26] We could often be at the worship service, although Volodia and visitors (his sister, my mother, and others) did not even suspect this. In 1938, I was expecting my second child. After I had the influenza, I had a complication—an invasive tubercular growth in my right lung. The doctor insisted on aborting the pregnancy, but I refused, no matter how much the doctor tried to convince me, scared me that I would infect my older son and husband, even suspected me of being a Tolstoyan, and insisted on the application of pneumothorax, which was incompatible with pregnancy, I did not agree to this.[27] My husband then called for a concilium, and the doctors decided that I had to be sent to the village, increase my eating, and every month be x-rayed. Verochka herself became terribly thin. After a month, the x-ray showed that the growth had declined, and after still another month, everything healed. I became very well, and on December 1, I gave birth to a completely healthy child.[28] The professor and the doctors studied my x-rays and were surprised. They looked upon this as a miracle.

In the autumn, when I came to Fr. Serafim, he approved of my behavior.

In the maternity ward, they placed me in the tuberculosis section, and under the care of a professor-gynecologist. During this time, Alik stayed with my mama, but he had no connection with her. We were made much differently. Once, Alik proclaimed to her: "Thank you, Grandmother, for giving birth to my Mama, and that is all I have to say." This made a strong impression on Mama.

When we brought Pavlik [diminutive of Pavel] home, Alik looked at him for a long time, and asked, "Does he have thoughts?" I was distressed that my second child was a boy. I had wanted a girl. Volodia said, "Two sons? Not bad, not bad!" This calmed me. But we could not come to an agreement about a name. Volodia wanted to name him Leonid, but I wanted Sergei, in

FIGURE 10. Vladimir and Elena Men with their sons, 1939.

honor of St. Sergii. Verochka said how she loved the apostle Paul, and she proposed to name the child Pavel [Paul]. I immediately agreed, and Volodia, to my surprise, agreed. We baptized him in 1939 on the Day of the Annunciation.[29] Unexpectedly, it turned out that we could not go to Fr. Serafim, and not wanting to postpone such an important event, we went to Fr. Ieraks's. Verochka was the godmother, and the godfather, by default, was Fr. Serafim.

To educate the children in such a complex environment and in such a difficult time was not easy. I could not be the educator. At that time, I appealed to Mary, Mother of God, with the request that She educate my children. She heard my prayer. Now, after several decades, I see that my children carry the fire of faith through all their ordeals. In this, I see the special kindness of Mary, Mother of God.

In 1938, Volodia received a strip of land by the Kazan' road at the Repose Station. I did not want to build a dacha and be responsible for its ownership, but Fr. Serafim blessed it, and I agreed. In 1939 and 1940, we already lived there, although many parts of it remained uncompleted. The workers continued to construct it under my supervision (I understood a little of construction art). My Katia left for the village, and Pavlik had another nanny, Olia, whom I loved like my own daughter. She was a believer, although not like Katia. From her first days, she loved all our family, but she especially became attached to Pavlik. To the present day, she relates to all of us with love. Living at our house, she completed the seventh grade and courses in dressmaking and needlework. During the war, she married, and everything had prepared her for family life.

When Alik turned four, I enrolled him in a preschool French group. In early childhood, children easily learn a foreign language, and I especially loved the French language; therefore, I enrolled him in the French group. The little collective was less stressful on the nervous system than a large group. Alik spent two years in the group. The director was a pleasant, cultured woman, and there were in all six children in her group. Alik found out that three of the children were believers, and three were nonbelievers. Once, Alik said to a nonbelieving girl, "Who, in your opinion, created the world?" "Nature," the girl answered. "But what is this nature? What about the fir trees and chickens? How were they created?" The girl was at a loss. "No, God created everything, and He governs the entire world."

The supervising teacher loved Alik very much. "Never have I met such a talented child," she said one time. "He will always be the soul of society." Her forecast came true. I understood that this was a gift of God, and I did not allow myself to take pride in it.

In the beginning of 1941, Volodia was arrested. As the technical director of the factory, he had the right to sign on a level with the director, and he allegedly signed a document that allowed someone to put money in his pocket. In the middle of January, a search took place at our home. This made the most painful impression on me. I appealed to the Lord, and suddenly I heard some kind of internal voice: "What I am doing, you do not know now, but will comprehend afterwards." This calmed me, the more so because, under the mattress, I had put a large prayer book. They did not see it, did not even search there, and they opened the cabinet with the icons and instantly closed it, and so the neighbor-witness to the search did not see anything. They took Volodia, and the very same day released him, but two weeks later, they imprisoned him. I was afraid to go to Fr. Serafim, in order not to lead them to him. In my place, Verochka went to him.

Fr. Serafim directed me to write a prayer, to the "Victorious Leader" (*Vzbrannaia Voevoda*) and present it to Volodia.[30] I did as he said. To my delight, Volodia received the prayer, read it, and kept it for himself. Several months later, in a dream, I saw that they allowed me to have a meeting with Volodia. In the room, there were many people, and I needed to speak in private with him. I asked him, "Did you throw away the prayer?" "No," Volodia said, "I kept it." With this, I woke up. Fr. Serafim said that this dream was sent to comfort me. He especially blessed me to pray for Volodia, and the children, too, had to offer short prayers for him. He imposed a strict fast on the children during the Great Lent.

When I was at the investigator's office, I saw half a room filled with documents from the factory where Volodia worked.

Our life abruptly changed. I worked from home and made embroidered curtains. I placed the children in a small daycare [center] and embroidered from morning to evening. I had never done needlework, but since I, as in my youth, took blessing for every kind of work, everything turned out successfully, and there was not any waste whatsoever.

In June, war suddenly burst upon us. Fr. Serafim communicated through Verochka that I had to leave Moscow quickly and attempt to rent a dacha near Zagorsk. I immediately traveled to Zagorsk and from there to Glinkovo,[31] where our friends lived.

I managed to rent a room. On this same evening, I returned and packed our things, took the children, Verochka, Olia, and Katia (unexpectedly, she turned out to be in Moscow), and again left for Glinkovo. I will not talk about those hardships that we endured in Glinkovo during the first year of the war, but Fr. Serafim was beside us, 4.5–5 kilometers from our house. It was always possible to go to him for advice, and this calmed me.

Verochka traveled to us every Saturday and left on Sunday. She brought me provisions, various things that I exchanged at the Zagorsk market. One time, her brother Venichka came to see me, and together we went to the market. All the horrors of the war terribly traumatized him, and he was surprised that I remained so calm. The whole atmosphere was calming, unlike that in Moscow. I carried a sled, in order to exchange something for potatoes. On this sled, we came down the hill on the road. He was happy as a child, and I felt as though his soul relaxed. Suddenly, he said, "If the war ends and Easter comes, I will accept Orthodoxy." When I related this to Fr. Serafim, he said, "Perhaps he will be saved by these words." I did not see Venichka again. He died in 1942, on the labor front. A problem with his intestine had begun, and he passed away on the operating table.

In the beginning of the war, they moved Volodia to Tula. There the food was in shorter supply than in Moscow, and his legs began to swell. On December 18, on the eve of St. Nicholas's Day, the court convened.[32] The signature by which they had incarcerated Volodia turned out to be false (they photographed and magnified it, and it turned out to be a forgery). Immediately, after the court session, they released Volodia, but they did not permit him to live in Moscow and offered him any other city. He chose Sverdlovsk, where his parents and his married sister lived.

When I received the telegram about Volodia's release, I rushed to Fr. Serafim. He took the telegram from me and cried. How he had prayed to Mary, Mother of God, and how he thanked Her! I felt that precisely because of his prayers, they had freed Volodia. "You see," said Fr. Serafim, "it was half a room of documents, and Mary, Mother of God, closed it down."

In 1942, the hunger began. The Germans advanced, and the situation became dangerous. All the while, it became more difficult to obtain provisions. Volodia summoned me to Sverdlovsk. I, of course, went to Fr. Serafim to resolve this important issue. This time, he did not give a definite answer and left it to me to decide for myself. "Sorrow will be there also, but the sorrow there will be longer," Fr. Serafim said. Volodia bombarded me with letters and telegrams, even wrote Alik (although he was only seven years old). The Germans were very close, and they, of course, would have no mercy on us. I even cried, but decided to keep everything as it was.

Soon Fr. Serafim became ill. His life was nearing its end. When I came to see him the next time, he was very weak and almost did not rise from his bed. "The Lord is in charge of me and will lead me somewhere. Perhaps toward death," Fr. Serafim said in a quiet voice.

Not long before his death, he said to me, "You will have a good life, but let there never be even a shadow of a complaint." Once, during the night, in a dream, I saw Fr. Serafim very distinctly. He suggested that I read the Gospel of Luke. I looked up this Gospel.

He said, "No, this is not it. You need to look up the Gospel in the Slavic language." When I awakened, I told Alik my dream and that I had decided to go to Zagorsk. M. A. met me. To my question, "How is the health of Fr. Serafim?" she answered, "Right now he is well; now he is very well."

I understood and wept. To comfort me, she gave me Volodia's letter, but I did not even want to look at it. I also felt that Fr. Serafim did not permit me to cry about him. From a neighboring room resounded the reading of the Gospels. "Now you will read," someone said to me.

I entered the room where Fr. Serafim lay covered with a shroud. His face was also covered. They suggested that I read the Gospels. The first chapter of the Gospel of Luke lay open before me. I remembered my dream, and a quiver came over me. I read the first ten chapters. Then Kseniia Ivanovna came up to me, and pulled back the covering over the face. "How like relics," K. I. said. She said that the funeral would be at night. I wanted to come, but K. I. said it was not necessary. "I comforted you, as I could, and showed you his face." I decided to obey, although I was very bitter. It was good that I did not go. At the funeral services, a woman appeared who informed on everyone in attendance. Almost all of them were later arrested.

When I returned home and told Alik about the death of Fr. Serafim, he responded, "I knew it. He died, went to the Heavenly Kingdom, and this is not frightening at all." During the next several days, Alik declined to play any kind of game.

They buried Fr. Serafim underground, under the place where the altar was located.

During our visits to Zagorsk, we always descended below, to pray at his grave. The internal connection with Fr. Serafim continued.

After the death of Fr. Serafim, Fr. Pyotr became our spiritual guide. He was a spry, joyful man of fifty-two. He worked as a bookkeeper, but in his free time, he served and conducted occasional religious rites in the home. At the time, he was married, but his beautiful wife could not endure the ascetic kind of life and left him.

A spiritual disposition shone in his face, and I immediately felt a liking for and complete trust in him. We attended his services, but to walk ten kilometers in both directions was impossible with the children, since Pavlik was only three years old.

Obtaining food became more and more difficult. In the rural areas, they did not issue ration cards at all, only bread to those on the list. While he was still alive, Fr. Serafim said to someone close to him that it was necessary for me to resettle in Zagorsk. The opportunity soon presented itself. The large family of one of Fr. Serafim's spiritual sons was gradually dying from tuberculosis. At that time, his father had also died, and one young girl, Nadia, aged nine, was left. They asked me to move there, so that she would not be left alone. I gladly agreed, and on March 1, 1942, I resettled in Zagorsk (I moved when the deceased father was still at home, and for the first time, almost the whole night, I read the Psalter over the deceased).

They registered me immediately and gave all of us ration cards. I, however, did not get to live there for long. Relatives of Nadia arrived; they treated me with suspicion, and therefore, I hastened to get away from them. My friends (a husband and wife) invited me to move in with them, on the other side of the line.[33] They worked in Moscow, but their household worker, the nun Savel'evna, remained at home. She got along very well with my boys and me. When I asked her, "Why?" she responded, "The Lord commands me to get along well with you."

Alas, I did not manage to live there for long. Someone from the family needed the room, and I moved again to this side of the line, into the room of friends, who were Nadia's neighbors. The landlady slept on a bed with her two children; I slept in the same room on a bed with my two children.

During this time, I became acquainted with Mother Superior Mariia. I began to go to her for the resolution of all questions, since I saw Fr. Pyotr only rarely. When I brought Alik to her for the first time, he was seven years old. She asked him, "Alik, what do you wish to be?" Alik replied, "A zoologist." What after that? "A paleontologist." "And after that?" "An artist." "And after that?" "A writer." "And after that?" "A priest," Alik softly answered. Gradually, all his wishes were fulfilled . . .

Soon I also had to leave this flat. It was terribly difficult to change flats so often, each time to look for something new, and to scurry about over all of Zagorsk with my children and things. I went to the home of Fr. Serafim, stood before the icon of the Iverskaia Mother of God (in this wonderful icon, Mary, Mother of God, is so alive), and burst into tears. Suddenly, I saw that on the floor, on the carpet, my tears lay in the form of a cross. This so astounded me that I took it as an answer to my prayer: "This is your cross," as if Mary, Mother of God, had said it to me.

This time, Fr. Pyotr found a room for me, and I moved to Ovrazhnyi Lane. To live there, I had to provide firewood. For half a year, I bought the landlady six cartloads of firewood, and, by some kind of miracle, I obtained all of them. If the firewood was in scant supply, then we walked with the landlady into the woods and carried the bundles by ourselves.

To transport the firewood, I bought a toboggan; Alik and Pavlik were in raptures over it. Once, Alik came up to me with glowing eyes: "Mama, do you know what happened? Pavlik and I rode down the hill on the toboggan. Some boys came up and took our toboggan away from us. I prayed, and suddenly big boys appeared, seized the toboggan from the other boys, and gave it back to me." I was happy that, during this experience, he again had felt the power of prayer.

I tried to get accustomed to do everything with prayer. I had to carry two pails on a yoke up a steep hill—the entire way I said the Jesus prayer. When the landlady and I sawed and cut up huge logs, I always felt the help of God. Everything I did turned out all right, and I did not even get tired. During this time, neither the children nor I fell ill with anything, although food was very scarce. Once, while still in autumn, there was no food at home, and I went to the forest to pick mushrooms. By the side of the road stood a destroyed church, in which there was a workshop, and around the church was a small cemetery. On the outside of the church, a mural was preserved. On one of the walls was a very good representation of the Crucifixion: under the footboard of the Cross, Mary Magdalene embraced the feet of the Savior. I stopped before the Crucifixion and prayed. Afterwards, I went into the forest and found a few mushrooms and sorrel. On the way home, I again approached the Crucifixion and saw a large bundle of beet leaves at the footboard of the Cross. I picked it up, clasped it in my arms, and carried it home, as a gift from Heaven. At home, on the Russian stove, I cooked *shchi* made from beet leaves, mushrooms, and sorrel. It seemed to me to be the tastiest food I had ever eaten.

One day, after receiving communion, friends proposed that I go with them to pick mushrooms in the woods. I went home to change clothes, and when I came back, no one was there. I was a little chagrined, but Kseniia Ivanovna suggested, "If you walk along this road, perhaps you will meet them. They left for the Annunciation Church." I walked along and, after a half hour, it was as if I flew on wings. I walked a long distance but met no one. On the road, asking the rare passersby whether I was going in the right direction for the Annunciation Church, I came finally to a small cluster of trees, where it appeared there were many white mushrooms. After filling my basket comparatively quickly, I walked back, fully grateful to the Lord for sending me this miracle. The landlady's eyes opened wide at them: "Where did you find so many white mushrooms?" "Behind the Annunciation Church," I answered. "It is seven kilometers to the destination," the landlady exclaimed. "With whom did you walk?" "I went alone," I answered. I boiled and dried these mushrooms and even carried some of them to Moscow.

I could no longer provide firewood for Aunt Niusha, and again I needed to search for lodgings. In my quest, the Lord did not forsake me: because of hunger, the family of a priest's spiritual children had left to live in the village; their house needed watching over, and Kseniia Ivanovna proposed that the children and I serve as the guardians. The landlady agreed.

I again moved closer to the center of Zagorsk. Firewood there was sufficient, but it was very difficult to feed us. Food was sent to us for only one day. Fr. Serafim had said to me that St. Sergii would sustain the children and me in times of hunger. We ate grass, plants, the roots of burdock, bran, and, from them, I boiled kasha in kvas or in a fruit drink. I remember that in ancient times hundreds, even thousands, of people came to St. Sergii, and in the lavra, St. Sergii fed everyone.

Alik learned to read very early. Even before the war, my friend Marusa[34] showed him the letters of the alphabet in the *akathist*, which we read each Friday, and the first phrase that he read was its title: "*Akathist* to the Passion of Christ."

In 1943, Alik turned eight. By this time, he already read well. I remember, with such delight, he said to me how beautiful is the "Song of Hiawatha" (*Pesn' o Gaiavate*). I registered the children in the library and brought them interesting children's books, which Alik read aloud to Pavlik. This helped them not to think about food.

On Saturday evenings, Verochka continued to come and bring us food that she obtained through her ration cards. Sometimes, Uncle Iasha divided part of his ration and asked that it be transferred to the children. He had already fallen ill from malnutrition. Verochka had also begun to suffer from malnutrition. She grew increasingly weak. One day, Uncle Iasha came to me and said, "Lenochka, I have come to say goodbye." I calmed him down but saw that he was very emaciated. The doctor said that he had two months to live. Then Verochka sold the piano and urgently began to feed her papa. He improved somewhat and even went to work. When we talked to the doctor about this, he said, "I am not changing my opinion." Exactly two months later, her papa became worse at work, and they took him to the hospital. In the morning, he died.

At this time, in Moscow, they did not allow a person to enter [the city] without a permit, and I could not even attend the funeral. I prayed for him daily. He was very kind to my children and me, and he gave everything he had to protect the children in the most difficult years of the war.

One day, I went out to get food for the children and left them at the home of Kseniia Ivanovna. When I returned, Fr. Pyotr was there. The children ran to me: "I am hungry, I am hungry, we are hungry!" Fr. Pyotr sat Alik on one knee, Pavlik on the other, and he pulled two pieces of white hardtack from his pocket and gave them to the children. He embraced both of them and, with love, clasped them to himself.

Great Lent began. We kept fairly strictly to our regimen, since food was scarce. On Great Saturday, I exchanged Pavlik's shoes for a half-kilo of cottage cheese (*tvorog*), and I bought one and a half loaves of bread for the two days. From one loaf, I made an Easter cake. On it, I put pastry and toffee (which, on the children's ration card, they gave me in place of sugar) in the shape of X.V. [Christ is risen!]. Unexpectedly, my friend brought me a bone, which an acquaintance obtained at the butcher's, and I cooked a lovely broth. I write about this, because we accept it as a miracle. From the cottage cheese, I made *paskha* and put it next to the Easter cake. The children walked around the table and sighed but did not touch anything.

At night, we went to the Easter vigil at Fr. Serafim's place. Fr. Pyotr performed it. The mood of everyone was especially solemn. Early in the morning, at sunrise, everyone dispersed to their homes. There we broke the period of fasting—we ate the Easter cake and *paskha*—and went to visit N. I. She also spent the entire war in Zagorsk with two of her younger children. They suffered from starvation, although her son worked in a factory shop and received a worker's ration card. We brought them a jug of broth, and they treated us to a soufflé. This was an exceptionally tasty dish, especially in those times. Suddenly, Fr. Pyotr arrived. And they treated him, too, to the broth and soufflé. Fr. Pyotr was moved. "One lady obtained food, another brought them to the children, a third one cooked and brought it to a fourth. A fifth person arrived as a guest, and they fed him a delicious holiday dinner. This is the meaning of love!"

Predicting that they would come and take him away, Fr. Pyotr appealed to Mother Mariia: "Mother, if I am not here, do not abandon my spiritual children!"

I sold or exchanged all my more or less valuable things in the Zagorsk market. My former landlady Aunt Niusha even laughed at me: "You are like a drunk—all your things you haul down to the market." It was important to me to keep the children safe and not to lose strength myself. Such was how many people in Zagorsk lived . . .

Each month, my husband sent me quite a small sum of money, but it was enough for only ten days. At that time, a loaf of bread cost 200–250 rubles. Sometimes, I bought a lump of sugar for ten rubles and divided it into three parts, and each part served the three of us. The children split one-ninth of a part into small pieces, and each piece lasted all day. Sometimes, early in the morning, my girlfriend L. F. knocked on the window and said, "I have placed a pot of boiled vegetable leaves in the window. Feed the children while it is hot." Once she gave me a whole row of very small beetroots. How they came in handy in those times! Kseniia Ivanovna often fed me when I stopped by her place. My good friend E. N. lived at her sister Irina's house. Her two sons and daughter were soldiers and sent some things to their mother. She always shared with me. Thus St. Sergii and good people helped me, and they did not allow me to become completely weak from hunger. In this beneficial atmosphere, blessed by the prayers of St. Sergii, and among good believing people, my children grew. This helped their spiritual growth . . .

In the autumn, the owners of our apartment returned (the owner did not get along with his superior), and again we had to leave. I felt I needed to go now to Moscow. The situation at the front had significantly improved; the Germans had retreated. Many Muscovites were returning to Moscow. On September 8, I packed all of our things, took the children, and went to Moscow. No one occupied our room, and two little nails kept it shut. At one time, an elderly man with his elderly wife lived in it, but they were given another room. They had not disturbed anything in my room. Our neighbors told me that the household administration had come and were surprised that nothing was taken: "This is the single room in our entire jurisdiction that has not been robbed." Not for nothing had Fr. Serafim suggested that we leave the icons in the closet in Moscow and take with us only the most beloved ones. "The Lord will then guard your apartment," said Fr. Serafim. And I had left them.

Soon I got a job in the laboratory at the Department of Deaf Education and Speech Therapy in the Lenin Pedagogical Institute, and I began to receive the ration card of an office worker. How many times did I try to register my room? No one was there, and it was paid for until the end of the year (my husband sending money from Sverdlovsk to the household administration for the apartment), but I was not successful. One day, the police burst in and fined me 200 rubles for living there without a registration certificate. A day later, I went to Zagorsk to redeem bread provisions with my ration card. On the way back, I stopped in Semkhoz, collected brushwood, and with this bundle returned home by eleven in the evening. For heating, my neighbors used two iron trivets, constructed from a half-destroyed Russian stove. There was no stovepipe; smoke often filled the kitchen and blackened the ceiling and walls.

In September, classes at the institute had not yet begun, and I worked in admissions. The institute had a shortage of applicants and no entrance exams. Once, I said to the senior laboratory assistant that I was prepared to enroll in the evening preschool department of our institute. "Why enroll in the preschool, enroll in the Mental and Physical Disabilities' Section of our institute," she said. "Come a half hour before your classes and stay for two and a half hours after them. In addition to this, we will count the intervals between lectures. In all, it will be your one-half of a working day." I agreed to do this. The next day, I brought my high-school diploma and my curriculum vitae and handed in my application. They gave me a summons as a student and registered me at the same time. Thus I was a student! I was always joyful and gay, and now I rejoiced, as if I had passed into my second youth.

We took many interesting subjects: ancient and contemporary literature, Western and Russian; Folklore; Introduction to Linguistics; Old Church Slavonic and Ancient Russian Languages (they were especially interesting to me). The pedagogical subjects included pedagogy and the history of pedagogy. The medical subjects included medical anatomy of the central nervous system and pathology. I studied all kinds of physical education and did well in everything. I felt the help of God, and it was visible, even to others. One of the girls asked me, "Lena, how are you able to do so well? It is as though you have some kind of invisible protector who helps you."

Each day I went past the Nikolo-Khamovnicheskaia Church, memorized the troparion to the Theotokos "Surety of Sinners," and constantly repeated it on the road.[35] The beginning words of the troparion especially inspired me:

All despondency now doth cease
And the sin of despair vanisheth away! . . .

I enrolled Alik in school. At that time, children enrolled in the first grade at the age of eight. I put Pavlik in a kindergarten located across from our home.

On Saturdays, Sundays, and holidays, Verochka, the children, and I went to church. At first, we walked to the Church of the Martyr St. John the Warrior, and later, the children walked alone to a church they liked more. After his afternoon session of classes at school, Pavlik, with a knapsack on his shoulders, most often went to the Mournful Mother of God Church. Alik went to various churches.

We rarely traveled to Zagorsk; approximately once a month, we went there and joined in. Our friends came to see us, and we tried to teach the children the liturgy and, in general, accustom them to life in the church. It was as though we were absorbed in church life, and this gave us enormous joy. From their early years, I had taught the children the religious holiday psalms; they quickly learned the hymns of all Twelve Holiday Feasts, and they knew all the beginning verses of the Christmas canons by heart. Alik was very much drawn to the spiritual life and, on all topics, could turn them into spiritual ones. Pavlik was not far behind. I read the Gospels to him every day.

In 1944, Volodia returned from Sverdlovsk, but I did not change our arrangement. The spiritual life had always occupied a central place in our family, and this continued in the following years. I associated almost exclusively with believing people.

Volodia, of course, wished that the children came more under his influence. More so, that they loved and respected him. He especially worried about the children's observance of fasting. But they were so settled in their beliefs that he could do nothing about it. During all thirty-five years of our life together, only two instances provoked a negative reaction in him. In general, he was very meek and patient, and one of my girlfriends said, "Whether you will enter the Kingdom of Heaven is unknown, but I do not doubt that Vladimir Grigor'evich will be there."

The Lord overcomes all sins because of his great patience!

Combining the responsibilities of a mother, wife, household manager, office worker, and student, I was, of course, very much overloaded. Volodia insisted that I drop out of the institute. But I decided to carry on my work to the end. Sometimes I needed to prepare for a seminar or write an essay on political economy, and then I had Volodia sit beside me, so that he could nudge me in the side when I began to doze off.

After the third year, I had to leave my job, since the practical application part [of my schooling] began, and it became impossible to combine work with study. Once, the exams started in the period of Holy Week. The Lord, however, helped me attend all the services and, at the same time, prepare and pass the exams. When I took the exams, I always asked the children to pray for me; they worried more about my exams than they did about theirs. Thanks to the grace of God, I succeeded in everything I took, and my student girlfriends could not understand the secret of my good marks, especially without cheating. I simply tried to do everything conscientiously, and I prayed a great deal.

One day, the proctor for the history exam wanted to designate me to be among the first five students. I refused, since I had never done this. For a long time, she tried to persuade me, and finally she said, "Well, why do you not want to be among the first five? You will arrive early in the morning, with a clear mind. God will help you." Then, surprisingly, I immediately agreed, because my inner being drew upon the last of her phrases. On the next day, we went to the exam. On the way, I saw on the wall a map and paid attention to the fact that the Ugra River flowed into the Oka. I was among the first five students and took a ticket. The first question dealt with the Baptism of Rus', the second question concerned the period of the NEP [New Economic Policy]. All this I knew well and answered without hesitation. The examiner asked additional questions concerning the NEP; I answered all of them. Then, he asked, when did the last battle with the Tatars take place? I answered, "In 1380." "And when was the final crushing defeat of the Tatars?" "A hundred years later, in 1480." "And what is that event called?" "The stand on the Ugra." "And what is this Ugra?" "A tributary of the Oka." He gave me a five, and I, beaming, flew out into the corridor.

In such a way, throughout my four years of study, the Lord helped me in everything. I finished the institute in 1947. They wanted to introduce me to the sister of Fr. Pavel Florinskii, Iu. A. Florinskaia, so I could work under her direction, but she fell ill and died from a stroke. All my plans collapsed. Volodia also became ill with lobar pneumonia in both lungs, and for two months, he remained in the hospital. In the mornings, I began to go to the church to pray about his health, and during the afternoons, I prepared food and took it to the hospital. When Volodia's condition became very bad, he said, "If I am able to leave the hospital alive, it will mean there is some higher Power."

After leaving the hospital, Volodia spent a month in a rehabilitation center. When he recovered, I came down with rheumatic heart disease, and for

Figure 11. V. S. Tsuperfein, V. Ia. Vasilevskaia, E. S. Men, A. V. Men, and Lenochka Tsuperfein, beginning of the 1950s.

half a year, I had to remain in bed. The attending physician said that I had a heart defect, and if I wanted to live a little longer, I should not go to work and should occupy myself with only light household affairs. In the future, Mother Mariia and my spiritual father[36] did not give me their blessing to go to work.[37]

In 1946, many of my friends were arrested. But we continued to go to Zagorsk to see Mother Mariia, and she guided us until her very death. Verochka, the children, and I put very complex questions to her, and she always gave the right answer, although she was a minimally educated person. Everything emanated from her spiritual experience, love for people, and complete devotion to the will of God. She was ill with some kind of sickness, reminiscent of the illness of Elder Amvrosii of Optina Pustyn′. Sweat constantly covered her entire body, and, several times each twenty-four hours, they changed her shirt and dress. Continual pain from a hernia, then other illnesses, tormented her, but she bore everything without complaint and was always joyous, smiling, and she received everyone with love. "My heart is enlarged," she said to me one time.

I brought my friends and acquaintances to see Mother Mariia, and she gave all of them help and comfort. When I fell ill with the heart condition, Alik lived at her home for some time and received grace, emanating from her and from several of her spiritual children who visited her there. He said to Verochka that he sensed a certain aroma in Mother Mariia's home. Mother Mariia said that he felt the grace of the Holy Spirit. Everyone in the house loved Alik and called him "Father Archimandrite."

With the consent of Mother Mariia, Verochka often traveled to monasteries (she visited nine of them). When Alik was fifteen years old, Verochka took him to Kiev. They stopped at Mother Mariia Agafonika's in the Pokrovskii Monastery.[38] They [the nuns] lived in caves (at that time, the lavra was not closed), where, in one of the rooms, there was a myrrh-dispensing head. If a group of believers arrived, the priest anointed them with the myrrh, but if they were unbelievers, he tried to pass them by. (They told the story that one day the authorities wiped this head with alcohol and hermetically sealed it in a room, where it was found. Next morning, fragrant myrrh filled the whole dish.) In the courtyard, Alik and Verochka met a nun, and she said to Alik, "Do the Lord's work. Many people serve the world, but few serve God."

Verochka took Pavlik with her to Glinskaia Pustyn′. This trip made a great impression on him. When I asked Pavlik what he liked most of all in Glinskaia Pustyn′, he answered, "The worship service. There they pray for many hours, but one does not even get tired from this, and that is good." "And what else?" "The people," said Pavlik, "such people I have never met, they are so inspired and uncommon."

How Volodia let the children go with Verochka, until now I did not understand.

Of course, it was through the prayers and blessing of Mother Mariia.

Appendix

Childhood and Youth

V. Ia. Vasilevskaia

Childhood

I

"And there was evening, and there was morning," we read in the book of Genesis. Happy is the human being, created by God's grace, and who has found peace in the bosom of His Creation. This feeling is naturally innate in a child but, if it is not illuminated by faith, quickly goes out and gives way to excruciating searching, which finds its expression in innumerable childhood questions. Most of these questions remain not only unanswered but also unasked: "Why do flowers wither?" "Why do people die?" "Why does the fierce wind blow the leaves?" "Why is there so much that is terrifying in this evil, incomprehensible world outside of children's stories and games?"

How to communicate these torments of childhood? Torments from the impossibility of appreciating one's impressions, of comprehending, of illuminating with some higher light, of putting them in their places . . .

Echoes of the life of adults seeped through a partially closed door into the children's room and pierced my heart with sharp needles . . .

II

The year 1905 rumbled by. Grownups were rereading and burning some books. The kind girl Esther, who so expertly had made small paper boats for us, was sentenced [by the state] to die as a revolutionary. She managed to escape to Egypt. "How is she faring there, poor one, between the pharaohs and the pyramids?" I thought.

Mama and Aunt, shut up in a room, read aloud the book of Leonard Andreev, *Anathema*.[1] I stood by the door for several hours, not having the strength to leave, understanding little, but shivering from fear.

In the evening, someone talked about Nietzsche, and at night, an *übermensch* walked on the tables and strangled people . . .

Often relatives and acquaintances came to visit Papa and Mama. We, the children, always lay down to sleep on time, but for a long time I could not fall asleep, and I listened to their stories. Each one of them talked about past misfortunes and insults, accusing others in everything and justifying themselves. Unwillingly, in the child's head was born the thought: "And what would happen, if instead of these people who came to visit our house, the people they blamed came; would they also justify themselves and accuse others? Should not everything be the opposite, and would there then be less misfortune and suffering?"

Often the adults talked about death. Lying awake at night, I listened in fear to the breathing of the others around me—had anyone died? Wishing to imagine more clearly my own death, I closed my eyes and ears, and thought, "There will not be the sun, the sky, flowers, sounds, everything will be extinguished, one after the other, nothing will remain. This will be death."

In the evenings, when we went to sleep, Mama often left to go to lectures, and Grandmother sat in the kitchen and read something under her breath. I listened to her whispers and thought: "Grandmother is already old; she will soon die, and I will never hear her voice again, never see her face. Why is this so?"

I wanted to squeeze her hand in mine and keep her for all eternity . . .

III

Grandmother Rebeka Abramovna was a kind, quiet woman with slow, gentle movements. Almost always, she dressed in a long dark skirt and a wide white jacket, and she had a black lace kerchief on her head. She knew how to prepare tasty dishes and bake fluffy challah, but household duties little interested her, and no one could imagine Rebeka Abramovna without a book or newspaper. She read all her life until extreme old age. When her glasses ceased to help her, Grandmother read with the help of a strong magnifying glass. She knew the history of the Jewish people perfectly and simultaneously, but partly, world history. She was always informed about political events and deeply worried about everything relating to the fate of her native people, no matter the country where the events took place. To these events, she often responded in a much more lively way than she did to what took place in her own family and connected to her personal interests. Acquaintances who came to see us gladly conversed with Grandmother, and her memory and curiosity surprised them.

Grandmother gladly read all our children's books with us. I remember how, with Grandmother, we read such books as *On the Floating Pieces of Ice* (Na plavaiushchikh l'dinakh), *The Country of the Long Night* (Strana dolgoi nochi), *School Comrades* (Shkol'nye tovarishchi), and *Don Carlos*.

On the days of major Jewish holidays, Grandmother neither cooked nor read the newspapers. From morning to evening, she closed herself off in her room and read the Psalms and the prayers in Hebrew (this was accessible to few women).

In those days, Grandmother was not to be disturbed. I resolved to acknowledge to no one how agonizingly I wanted to know what was written in Grandmother's large books and what those unfamiliar square letters meant. Under some kind of pretext, I tried to slip into Grandmother's room and, hastening, in a secretive whisper, to ask her to show me "only one letter." "This is 'alef,'" said Grandmother, showing me a strange letter resembling the Latin "N" but in a more correct form. After this, I quickly fled from the room, trying not to reveal my secret to anyone.

On Friday evening, Grandmother lit two large candles and prayed over them. During this time, in her room, some kind of special quietness held sway, and I knew that Grandmother prayed not only for herself or for her grandchildren but also for all the Jewish people, dispersed across the whole world but united by centuries of oppression and sorrow. She felt that in the quiet of Saturday evening, in the soft light of these candles, the spirit of a suffering people rests for a brief moment. In the Jewish religion, there is no "I," only "we." Not "God's slave" but "God's people," standing before God in prayer . . .

"You chose us from all the people and extolled our language over all other languages," Grandmother read in a singsong voice . . .

On the holiday of Hanukkah, Jewish people lit eight small candles in memory of the brothers Maccabee. Papa and Mama did not consider it necessary to perform something from the religious rites. That which was done was done for Grandmother, but always in a warm and good spirit. Thus Papa, wearing a hat at Grandmother's request, lighted the Hanukkah candles. In the room, everything became joyful and festive. The small fires bound together the unbroken threads of centuries; people from the past were revived in their distant descendants.

IV

I was—I must have been—six years old when we went to Balaklava [on the Crimean Peninsula, a city that was independent until 1957, today part of the city of Sevastopol], for the summer. "A small radiant bay with decorated yachts"—this is our childhood, I thought—"a boundless sea, concealed below cliffs—this was that large world that awaits us on the outside."

In Moscow, in the winter, with the coming of evening, endless night worlds opened up; in the sky, distant stars blazed. I was afraid of stars . . . Curtains were lowered, lamps were lighted, beloved games and books were laid out on the table—a small world, similar to the Balaklava Bay—almost deceit . . . For a time, it [the deceit] concealed from my eyes the large terrible world, which was prepared to swallow us up. God, whose existence neither my parents nor I doubted, was as far away as these distant stars. No one taught me to pray. I knew only that God created the world and gave people moral law. This knowledge could not alleviate my sufferings.

V

The only religious day of repentance established by the Jewish people is Yom Kippur. On this day, remembering the sufferings of the Inquisition, the Jewish people weep and pray over their sins.

I had a very vague understanding of what the sins were and why it was necessary to pray about them.

On Yom Kippur, Grandmother was gone the whole day to the synagogue and fasted (that is, she ate nothing from the evening of the preceding day to the evening of the next day). When she felt weak and could not leave the house, she read prayers from morning to evening, shutting herself up in her room. Mama also fasted on Yom Kippur, although she did not go to the synagogue and did not read the prayers but was more melancholy than usual.

Once, in the summer, we sat in the garden. I played at something, and Grandmother conversed with an elderly peasant woman. They talked about how heavily sins weighed on one's soul and the happiness and innocence of children.

In the light of the dying summer day, with all my strength, I suddenly felt the weight and inevitability of the sin awaiting us, and one more shadow lay across our forthcoming life. Something else was also connected with it, ostensibly accidental, but leaving an indelible impression. As always, children played in the courtyard. One naughty child ran up to a small child and, after making a threatening gesture, jokingly cried out, "To live or to die?" "To die," in a serious tone the little one unexpectedly answered. "Why?" in surprise, the children asked. "When a little one dies, he will be an angel," the child replied even more seriously.

VI

We knew very little about the events of biblical history, and, because of this, every kind of miracle was eliminated: Moses was a great scientist. He knew well the laws of nature, and, therefore, many of his teachings were useful for our own times. The crossing of the Red Sea they explained by its ebbs and flows. Everything had to be kept within the confines of cause and effect. Internal feeling resisted that; distrust toward grownups and their tenets took shape.

[The year] 1910: Haley's Comet. For many, this was only one of the interesting phenomena of nature worthy of examination. Among the people, they talked about how the comet could harm the Earth by its tail feathers, and then life on Earth would end. No one in our home attributed the smallest significance to such talk and laughed about it, as over the fantasy of idle and ignorant people. For me, an eight-year old girl, the expectation of the end of the world, contrary to everything, became, as for a medieval person, a real and all-embracing worry. In truth, this thought for me had no connection to any kind of religious belief, and the sense of fear did not predominate. Fundamental was the sense of pity for all—not only because all will suffer an inevitable death, as much as because no one knows, and does not wish to know, about this.

There was a sunny day. I walked together with Papa and Venichka alongside the Chistye [Clean] Ponds and clearly felt as if all the reality of the external world, everything customary and known, was going to collapse, like a house of cards.[2] In an hour or two, everything would be destroyed.

I wished to cry out, to tell everyone, but it was necessary to be quiet: no one would understand, no one would believe me . . .

We returned home. The day moved toward evening. Everything remained as before; the comet did not strike the Earth. "Are you ill?" Mama asked, after looking at me. I did not have the strength to answer, and I burst into tears.

VII

A wave of pogroms and antisemitism, which arose at the outset of the [political] reaction, swept through Russia. We read about this weekly in newspapers and journals, and we heard it from people coming from the south and west. Among those who suffered were relatives and acquaintances. Yesterday's friends and neighbors pillaged and killed old people and children. The thought of pogroms hurt the heart. Perhaps the most frightening [element] was, as they said, pogroms always began with a religious procession and the singing of prayers. People blasphemously attempted to consecrate a malicious affair and with prayer committed a crime. "Are they not pagans, indeed?" unwittingly flashed through my head. Antisemitism penetrated Moscow, where the Jewish population in this time made up an insignificant minority. There were days when we could not go outside to play, because our usual comrades at play met us with malicious words and insults. For a long time, I thought about how to soften the hearts of my little persecutors, and once, going outside into the courtyard, I began to prepare my speech in advance. "We are children," I said, "and the differences between nationalities does not have any significance for us." I did not know whether many understood my speech, but for a short time, this helped, and our friendship was renewed.

With the approach of Easter, antisemitism always became stronger. Once, when I went out into the courtyard, girls met me with unusual hostility, and one of them defiantly said, "You are a Jew, and Jews crucified Christ!" "This cannot be," I thought. "Jews, the most enlightened and noble people of antiquity, could not carry out anything cruel and unjust." I ran to Grandmother for an explanation. Grandmother sat in her usual place by the window and read. "Grandmother," I said excitedly, "is it true that Jews crucified Christ?" "No," Grandmother quietly responded, not taking her eyes from the book, "not Jews, but Romans."

VIII

I grew up together with my brother, and we were inseparable. Venichka was older than I by three years, and his interests took another direction. In his ninth year, he conducted some kind of experiments in botany, and he resolved questions about the connections between electricity and magnetism. By his character, he was gentler than I, and defenseless. We worried about each other more strongly than either of us did about ourselves. Only Venichka's, and not my own, insults and derisions seemed to me deserving of serious attention. In the gymnasium and in the university, I worried only before his exams, not before my own. When the doctors forbade him to eat salt, I asked Mama for permission also not to eat it, in order that it would be easier for him to endure this deprivation. Venichka was just as affectionate toward me. His relationship to Mama reached an unhealthy state. He often called Mama "my saint," although Mama did not like this very much.

Once, at night, Venichka suffered a nervous attack. No one went to bed that night until morning. Mama was desperate and blamed herself for everything. In vain, Papa tried to calm her. For me, this was the first major sorrow. The attacks were repeated. Professor Rossolimo advised us to remove Venichka from the gymnasium for a year and not permit him to travel in the summer to the south, recommending instead a nearby Moscow village.

From this time on, Mama and I protected Venichka as we could; for two years, he recovered from the attacks, and then the attacks completely stopped. During these years, I not once saw Mama joyous, and she, it seemed, forgot how to laugh.

From the time when Venichka fell ill, we never slept in the darkness: at night, tiny lamps burned, "phenolic lamps," with colored caps. Their light did not calm us; it seemed like an alarming signal in the dark night. I knew that Mama now slept always dressed and did not allow herself to fall asleep soundly, so as not to miss the moment that her "poor little one" (this is how she now called Venichka, when he could not hear her) might become ill.

IX

In the summer, in the village, we lived a freer and more peaceful life, merging with the surrounding nature and peasant families, experiencing with them many moments of their lives: the return of the flocks, hay mowing, the harvesting of grain, and so forth. Peasants treated us well and warmly. From childhood, we were taught to congratulate those around us on their holidays. In the village, where we lived, the patron saint's day [feast day] was on St. Elijah's Day.[3] For three days, the neighboring peasants ceased all work, rested, and, with their entire families, went to visit each other. In the evenings, they performed round dances, arranged dances, and sang songs.

We, the children, loved these days. Once, I walked up to a group of familiar peasants settled under a tree to rest and greeted them with the usual: "Happy holidays to you!" "And to you, joy for the holiday," they answered affectionately. In this response, there was something good, friendly, something that brought many together.

In the village, little phenolic lamps were unnecessary. The peasants in whose house we lived had icons. Before them, icon lamps often burned at night. Some kind of marvelously peaceful light flowed from these icon lamps or, perhaps, from the unfamiliar meek faces over them. It seemed that quiet angels filled the entire house. We knew nothing about angels. The Old Testament religion knew living angels, messengers of God, but the memory of the civilized descendants in Europe preserved only the outline of rationalistic monotheism. The peace that enveloped the soul in these nights was perceptible but incomprehensible, almost illicit . . .

How We Studied

Our Grammar School

"Our grammar school," "at our grammar school"—these words I constantly used in all my conversations long before I began to study. While I was still a little girl, I already knew that I would study only at this school. When my brother Venichka began at the grammar school, Mama and I walked each day to meet him. The teachers affectionately greeted us and said to Mama, "Verochka will also be ours." I knew that in our grammar school there were many enemies. Some of them did not imagine school without marks, awards, and punishments. Others considered the program of the male classical grammar school too difficult for a girl. Finally, a third group supposed that a girl could not study with young boys without harm to her character, manners, and behavior.

The government also looked askance at our school, which fulfilled its goals in close unity with the family.

This struggle with "enemies" closed ranks and unified the children, parents, and teachers; everyone wished to prove that the school could stand firm and flourish by virtue of its love for learning, hard work, and each other.

The Beginning of the Lessons

The corner of Znamenkii and Krestovozdvizhenskii Lane. The welcoming bell could be heard from afar when you ran from the tramcar, and the knapsack on your back merrily bounced up and down. The wide yard. The friendly faces of the teachers and the motley crowd of children, in which it was so good to lose oneself, and to lose the "I" in "Our": "our class," "our school."

In the classroom, it was comfortable. There were flowers in the windows, an aquarium with goldfish, and on the walls were beautiful pictures and charts.

Seated in place, the children did not immediately stop their conversations and laughter. Avgusta Germanovna had already been in the classroom a long time. She asked the children to quiet down. The noise gradually died down, and A. G. invited the person on duty to read the prayer. For me, this was new and unfamiliar. I did not even know if I should stand up together with the others. A. G. had already detected my confusion; she came up to me and, in a whisper, explained to me that it was necessary to stand up. How grateful I was to her for this tactfulness, and now I knew that she would always understand and help me. The common prayer in the classroom blessed everything that took place here and instilled good spirits. Only one part did I not understand: "For the benefit of the church and the fatherland . . ." When I became a little older, I substituted for myself these words: "for the benefit of my native people and all mankind."

The French Language Class

The first class was French. A. G. commanded the attention of the whole class. She talked to us about her trip to France for the holidays. French children were very interested in our school, she said; they questioned her about it, expressed envy that we were such good students and freely studied, and invited us to come visit. Then she distributed among us new textbooks sent from Paris, and she said that, if we would study well, then in the fourth grade, we would organize a trip to Paris. (When we entered the fourth grade, the First World War broke out, and A. G. did not manage to fulfill her intention.) After this, A. G. hung on the wall a large painting and began to tell us a story about this painting. My knowledge of the French language was far from sufficient, but the story was so fascinating that it was impossible not to remember whole phrases and fragments. Until now, I have in my memory the wolf who hunted for children and said, "I wish to eat a rosy little one, the smallest boy, rosy and pure." After listening to the story, we sang a song: "If I were a small brook." I liked the song very much. A. G. stopped for no one, no one did she reprimand. Only from time to time did she say, "Three hours a week of paying attention, and you will know the language."

Toward the end of the lesson, A. G. proposed to us to give a surprise to Liubova Sergeevna, the young teacher from the youngest preparatory class. "When L. S. enters our classroom, all of you stand up and together say to her, 'Bonjour, Mademoiselle.' She will be very happy." We eagerly agreed, and when L. S. entered, we loudly exclaimed, "Bonjour Mademoiselle." "Bonjour, mes enfants," responded L. S., blushing with pleasure. I understood even more that here everyone tried to do something pleasant for each other.

In the German Language Class

The German lesson was an hour of lively games and dramatizations, during which we sang joyful and funny songs, like "Eule, Eule, Eule, was siehst du mich so an?" ("What are you doing, owl, are you looking at me?"), or "Hop, hop, hop, Pferdchen lauf gallop" ("Gallop forward, little horse"). In the intervals, we learned to count in the form of gymnastic exercises: "Eins, zwei, drei" (one, two, three). We almost never sat at our desks.

Comparative Description

Mariia Vasil′evna, the teacher of Russian language, fell ill, and the same L. S. to whom we had said "Bonjour, Mademoiselle" took her place. L. S. was a very young, inexperienced teacher, very kind and affable. She began the lesson completely unexpectedly for us. "Children," she said, "I have just been in the seventh-grade class; there we wrote about the comparative description of Lenskii and Onegin." That beginning got us very interested. We had already heard about Lenskii and Onegin, but we did not know what "comparative description" meant.[4] In language accessible to the whole class, L. S. explained what it meant, and she offered to write the comparative characteristics of a cat and a dog together. Two halves divided the classroom blackboard. On one half, she wrote the particular features of a cat; on the other, a dog. The whole class enthusiastically went to work. Then the similar and distinguishing features of both were combined, and on this foundation the comparative characteristics were established. This interesting work occupied two lessons and provided rich nourishment for the development of our observation and thinking.

Natural History

The class in natural history took place in the open air. All of us took positions on a bench around the teacher, and we discussed the question of how we would build our class museum. Each person told what he had of interest at home and what he might bring for the museum. There were various animals and plants, collections, herbaria, and a series of pictures. I also decided to bring a sea horse, preserved in alcohol, and a sawfish, which we caught in the summer at the Balaklava Bay.

M. V. talked to us about how to organize the museum, about what kinds of sections there should be, and what one might do in each of them. Then we went out into the garden to dig beds for the planting. I had never been engaged in such matters, and I soon hurt my hand. But was it worth paying attention to this, while everything all around was so fun and interesting that you were afraid to tear yourself away, for even a moment?

The Singing Class

The singing class took place in the "small hall," which was what we called it. We formed a semicircle around the piano. The teacher checked the voice of each person, and explained to us how to organize our sound-producing "orchestra." Each person had to build some kind of musical instrument for this orchestra. The teacher gave me the assignment of making a toy violin, which I made with the help of a teacher of manual labor. In addition, the teacher proposed that we compose the text of a song or a play. The teacher composed together with us, and the musical piece was derived from the life of nature, in which trees, birds, butterflies, and small animals participated and made their entrance in a very amusing way. I represented a birch tree in a white-green costume. We, the trees, had to stand, swinging with the wind and sing:

> Sun, golden sun,
> In the sky, in the pale blue sky
> You rise, rise quickly,
> Shine on us and warm us.

Before the Christmas Holidays

Blue twilights. Starlit evenings. Patterned hoar frosts, branches of trees hanging down with snow, the aroma of pine needles—this tale about Someone, beloved and radiant, but entirely unfamiliar—about a Little One, in the silence of a winter's night, in the whiteness of the snows, in the radiance of the stars, in the ringing of the bells. "Le ciel est noir et la terre est blanche" (The sky is dark and the earth is white). The dark starlit sky and the bright earth, clean in its snow-white dress, as a bride. For whom had she dressed so? For whom was she waiting? Who was calling on her? About whom was this song, tender as the song of angels, whom we sang about in the class: "Stille Nacht! Heilige Nacht" ("Silent night, Holy night"). Perhaps I ought not to have even sung these songs. Perhaps they were not "for us"? But this was the class, and I had to participate.

The bewilderment penetrated my soul, and I did not know whether I should have rejoiced with the others or shrunk into a little ball and not have allowed this joy. The ringing children's voices sang the incomprehensible but excited words:

Welt ging verloren.
Christ ist geboren!

(The world perished.
Christ is born!)

The Grammar School in Danger

The existence of our grammar school did not give a person peace: the inspector from the educational district came to us, and we quickly, in half an hour, received instruction in the art of the curtsey, about which we did not have the faintest idea. Well-meaning reporters from the newspapers came to us and photographed our activities in diverse aspects. During a game, at recess, a boy accidentally pushed a girl, and "the guardians of morality" demanded the closure of this "dangerous" institution. All the parents met together more often and discussed how to save our school. They did not tell us everything, but we were worried and wanted to know everything. They renamed the grammar school and selected a new director. But when someone named Kasso became minister of education, this did not help. He demanded that girls no longer be admitted into the first grade, but the rest were allowed to finish the course.[5]

Girls in the preparatory class were confronted with a dilemma: either to leave the grammar school or "to skip over" into the second class.

To give up our positions and transfer into the female grammar school seemed to me impossible, and I decided to work in parallel with the activities in the class, with Mama's help, on the program of the first grade.

Sometimes it seemed agonizing to comprehend the mystery of subtracting multidigit numbers, or to understand why gases constitute the air, how the change from day to night takes place, and to learn how to locate various seas and islands on the map. Not just once did I cry, knowing my inability, but then with new energy I got to work, and asked Mama ten times to explain to me what I did not understand. If I did not overcome all of this, I would have to leave our grammar school.

The Second Half-year

With this work, the days flew by. Soon, all the activities fell into place, and it turned out that there was still time left over. In my free time, I rewrote almost all the German textbook and read many good books; among them, I especially remember Avenarius's book, *The Childhood Years of Mozart*, and a wonderful book on the history of Egypt, *The Miracle of the Pyramids of Ancient Countries*.

On Friday, we had a club day. After three lessons, we stayed in the grammar school, and each person took up what he or she most liked: they sang songs, drew pictures, sawed wood, told stories, or prepared shows or exhibitions.

The winter cast off its enchanting dress: snows turned gray, sunsets turned pink, bells rang more slowly and sadly. Each morning in class, instead of the usual prayer, they read a different, entirely incomprehensible prayer. Everything took place at the same time as what is called Lent.

Children often caught cold, and when it was impossible to go out into the courtyard, they spent recess in the hall. If disorder prevailed in the hall, one of the teachers sat down at the piano. Music involuntarily organized and quieted down everyone, and when the bell rang, everyone, to the sounds of the march, dispersed in an orderly fashion into the classes.

The Spring Holidays

Once, for Easter, M. V. proposed that we occupy ourselves preparing presents for poor people in places that had suffered a lean harvest. With pleasure, we took up this activity: from home, we brought books, games, drawings, and painted eggs, and we packed small parcels. Each one of us wanted to do something nice for children we did not know. On Palm Saturday, they dismissed us for two weeks. "Are you going to the 'Palm' [Sunday]?" we asked each other. To go to the "Palm" meant to go to Red Square on Palm Sunday. On this day, the streets and squares of Moscow took on an entirely unusual appearance. In different voices, all sang, rang, and chattered. Everything was vivid, gay, and motley. Multicolored butterflies made from scraps of many-colored fabrics adorned the children's costumes and headdresses. What unusual and funny things were sold at the Palm Saturday bazaar: goldfish; puppets jumping up and down in long tubes, which they named sea creatures; and clumsy, colorful rattles, which carried the satirical name "the language of Purishkevich," and many other things.[6] The rays of the springtime sun gently warmed and opened the buds of trees; children ran freely about on the holidays, and the goldfish and the gray sparrows on the road seemed like our old and dear friends.

The End of the School Year

After Easter, it had already become warm, and, during the break, we ran out into the courtyard without a coat. New worries made their appearance. April 20 is the Day of the White Daisy, the international day of the struggle with tuberculosis. We had somehow to help in this matter, since in our grammar school there were weak children, and not all parents could provide them with the essential provisions. We drew white daisies on programs for the evenings that students of the older classes organized to help tubercular children, made appliqués, and helped with donations.

Soon came the summer holidays, and for four whole months, we left the grammar school to live beyond the boundaries of the city walls and spend life among the flowers and clouds, the birds and trees. Both in school and in the forest, we did one and the same thing: we tried to get to know the world and our place in it. To advance to the next grade, did it not signify some kind of growth, to go higher up the hill to see the neighborhood?

Splitting the Atom

"A remarkable event, yes, my good sirs, an event of the greatest importance," excitedly repeated the geography teacher Vladimir Ivanovich, pacing up and down the class and rubbing his small white hands. The children were making noise and were pleased that V. I. would tell us about something and, consequently, would not ask about monsoons and trade winds, which were so easy to confuse. V. I. did not notice the noise; he, it seemed, even forgot that before him were children in the second grade, who were not in the position to understand the whole significance of the event that so excited him. "Lord Rutherford discovered the splitting of the atom, which was always considered the last indivisible unity of all matter," announced V. I. and, having made a sketch on the blackboard, animatedly began to explain the nature of Rutherford's experiments. I sat in the first row and, with all my strength, tried to understand what had so powerfully struck the good-natured, usually phlegmatic V. I. But the experiments of Lord Rutherford were definitely beyond the comprehension of a ten-year-old child, unfamiliar with the basics of physics and chemistry. "Are you listening to me, serious little one?" V. I. asked. He always addressed me in such a way; I was the youngest of everyone in the class and had passed directly from

MY CHILDHOOD AND YOUTH

the preparatory class. I felt sorry for V. I., and I willingly believed that the discovery about which he spoke would have significance for the future of all humanity, but I could not repeat the explanation of the experiments. To the rescue came one child—A. Shura, who volunteered to answer and beautifully repeated the explanation of the experiments. Subsequently, Shura became a professor of physics.

The experiments of Rutherford were forgotten, but the lesson was not in vain. We felt that science was not some kind of abstraction, that scientific discoveries could be exciting events of life. The future showed that V. I. was right in his evaluation of the significance of the discovery of the structure of the atom.

The War with Fractions

I quickly became familiar with the requirements of the second grade. Fractions were the only thing that I could not conquer. I was ready to do everything in order to master them. I filled up entire notebooks; I asked Mama repeatedly to explain what I did not understand. Finally, having finally grasped the explanation, I went out to my papa's room, and there repeated the explanation aloud, forcing imaginary pupils to answer my questions and resolve problems, as though the other girls were sitting there before me. Our teacher of arithmetic soon left us to give birth. For a long time, I did not understand what had happened to Ol'ga Nikolaevna, and it seemed to me that her condition had somehow inexplicably to do with fractions.

Two years later, I met her on the street with a child. "Do you now understand fractions well?" she asked.

As a replacement for O. N. came a new teacher. Viktor Ernestovich brought much love, passion, and enthusiasm into his work. He managed to captivate us not only by the subject but also by the joy of labor. "I do not know uninteresting work," he said, "except for work as a garbage collector." The children did not agree: a garbage collector's work also was not of little interest, because you found different things in the garbage!

"School, the class, must be sacred for us," said V. E., "because here we work together, we bring here all the best that we have." Once, one of the students, not managing to complete a task, copied from her friend. V. E. was very distressed. "Each time, when you want to do something dishonest," he said, "think about those people who suffer for truth, not sparing their lives, and who perish in distant Siberia."

V. E. was very attentive to the students. With his own eyes, he saw those who did not understand an explanation and patiently repeated it as many times as necessary. In his lessons, we forgot that arithmetic was difficult and for some also a disliked subject.

Why Was This Book Written?

We had several exercise books on the Russian language: for composition, dictation, copying, and grammatical exercises. Our most beloved was the notebook on which it was written on the cover: "My thoughts about the books I have read." This notebook satisfied the requirement not to part company with the books one had read, but to strengthen one's connection to them, to give them a fixed place in one's life, and to measure one's personal growth by them. Zinaida Apollonovna gave us several questions that we had to answer: Who among the active characters did you like most of all and why? What places in the book did you like most of all, and so forth? But especially difficult was the question: Why did the author write this book? Several students answered the question simply: "So that everyone would read it," but for the rest of us, this question forced one to think. The habit gradually formed to find moral or social meaning in each book we read, to draw from it our own conclusions. Reading always took place in the last lesson. We were forewarned that the collection *Our World* was not to be read at home, because it had to be a new experience in the class. Reading this or that story in turn, we were then, without noticing it, drawn into conversation, and Z. A. managed to pose questions such that all were active not only externally but also internally.

In my memory, two conversations were imprinted especially clearly: "Does one have to obey one's parents?" and "What do you dream about?" The first question emerged from reading the story "In the Storm." If a girl, the hero of the story, had thought most of all not to distress her parents, she would not have accomplished her self-sacrificing deed. Obviously, there were moments in life when a higher, moral duty directed one's actions. Not many talked about their dreams, but I remember that the eccentric Misha S. raised his hand and said that his dream consisted of discovering a living protein.

All the Class!

Our class became the very noisiest in the grammar school and caused the teachers much worry. A growing feeling of comradeship sometimes took ridiculous forms, which compelled students to conceal any mischief or outburst by a comrade, even if no one approved of it. To the teacher's question, "Who shouted or whistled or let the 'pigeon' out?" during the lesson, and so forth, it was necessary, without fail, "for the whole class" to answer. K. G., the teacher of the German language, more than once cried and left the classroom; the geographer V. I. treated the naughty ones always with the identical question, "What is it, my good ladies and gentlemen?" and the mathematician V. E. indignantly demanded from the more thoughtful part of the class: "Lead our comrades to the common denominator!" If the worn-out teacher asked the disrupter of order to leave the class, one might hear from the departed a tune from the opera *Carmen*: "Toreador, go more quickly into the corridor!" Naturally, the class could not contain its laughter. Z. A. often asked these students questions such as "Who brought you up?" or "Why do you like to display the nasty side of yourself?" These questions did not always penetrate one's consciousness. The noise and mischief in the class, on one hand, were wearisome, but, on the other hand, they provided some relief from the intellectual tension, which the complex and multifaceted program of the classical grammar school demanded. The general atmosphere of a friendly and attentive attitude evened everything out.

Orbis Pictus Romanus[7]

In the third grade, we began new subjects: history, algebra, and the Latin language. Therefore, I impatiently awaited the beginning of the lessons, and as early as August 1, I began to prepare notebooks and count the days until the lessons began.

Papa long ago talked to me about how in algebra, in place of numbers, letters were added and subtracted, and that if it was written $a + b$, then from this one might get something entirely unexpected. History was for me something already familiar and desired, since how good it was, while reading books, to imagine oneself on the banks of the Nile River or hiding inside the huge Trojan horse.

Latin attracted me most of all. Latin was not in the imagination only but practically engaged us in the life of the ancient world and enriched our inner world, making each of us an interlocutor of Cicero and Julius Caesar. And was it not pleasant to know by heart all five Latin declensions, which not one of the girls finishing the female preparatory school knew!

In the store Collaborator of the School on Zalesskaia Street, new exercise books were purchased. Small notebooks for words were like toys. Now I needed four of them. In addition to French and German words, I would write down Latin words and, in algebra, the primary definitions.

In the third-grade class, the first days of classes were festive occasions. In the small notebook, on the first page, was written what the "coefficient" was, and to me it seemed that a door opened up onto some new, still unfamiliar world, and in the booklet with the representation of the Roman forum was imprinted the inscription "Orbis pictus romanus." Now this was my little book, and all these incomprehensible inscriptions and sayings soon would become mine.

Under the Circular

The efforts of the teachers and parents in our grammar school created such a condition that we almost did not feel the political oppression of the regime then existing in the country. Sometimes the teachers talked openly about how the police-monarchical structure served injustice and that there would come a time, when in Russia there would be, if not a democratic republic, then, at least, a responsible ministry. The words "state grammar school," for us, signified something very dreary, and we very much pitied those children who found themselves there. Our history teacher, Vasilii Nikolaevich, also taught at the state grammar school. Therefore, he was the only one among our teachers to dress in full uniform.

Once, one of the students complained about the difficulty of Wipper's textbook on ancient history, adding that nowhere did they study this text, since a circular of the Ministry of Education prevented it.[8] V. N. flared into a rage. "Good," he said, "in that case, let us live according to the circular." In vivid colors, he described to us what would change in our instruction and what our whole school would turn into, if we began to live "according to the circular." The picture proved to be sufficiently convincing. From that time on, no one spoke about the difficulties of prohibited textbooks.

The Coming of War

Préparons-nous pour la guerre!
Préparons-nous pour la paix!

Let us prepare for war!
Let us prepare for peace!

Each summer, A. G. traveled to Paris and, while there, bought for us French textbooks and readers. In the third grade, for the last time, we received textbooks from Paris; in 1914, they came to us only from Switzerland. These books had a special attraction. The artistic images, near to the heart of a child, made one forget that the stories were written in a foreign language. The inclination toward powerful feelings and heroism was so strong, when one stood on the threshold of adolescence! Could one ever forget the little drummer or that little hero from the Great French Revolution, whose life members of the Vendeé promised to spare if he shouted out "Vive le Roi!" ("Long live the King!"), and who preferred to die with the cry "Vive la République!" (Long live the Republic!).

"Which one of you would act like this boy?" A. G. asked. A long silence set in. It seemed that each of us was assessing his or her own moral strength and did not dare reach a conclusion. "I," two or three voices timidly responded. Many stories and verses were devoted to the time of the Franco-Prussian War. The poets advised us:

Préparons-nous pour la guerre!
Préparons-nous pour la paix!
L'avenir obscure naguère
Souleve son voil épais.

Let us prepare for war!
Let us prepare for peace!
The future is dark
It lifts its thick covering.

The future lifted its thick cover; the First World War drew near.

War Is Declared

In the village, where we spent each summer, hussars were stationed. They were billeted two to three people in each hut. They were, for the most part, young peasants from Ukraine. We liked them for their adroitness, gaiety, and openheartedness. We loved their beautiful, slender horses and the melodious, inviting sounds of the bugle that we heard several times a day, but it was most pleasant of all to hear their choral singing in the evenings. Somehow, we grew accustomed to their way of life and the way of life in our village.

At eight o'clock in the evening, the hussars gathered by a well on the edge of the village, sang the evening prayers in chorus, and then long into the night the air resounded alternately with the sad and the joyful sounds of Ukrainian songs. Already in bed, we, the children, listened to their singing, in which, it seemed, poured out everything that had accumulated in the souls of each of the singers, and which so harmonized with the coming of the summer night.

In the village, from time to time, a meat trader appeared. He rode along the main street in a small, old wagon and, inviting buyers, slowly cried out:

"I am leaving, and I am not coming back!" These words left an incomprehensible footprint on the soul and seemed like a dark foretelling. Soon the butcher was taken into the army and killed at the front. Venichka remembered these words to the end of his life. He was destined to leave and not return . . .

It was the summer of 1914. Rumors of war ever so persistently set in. On July 19, the mobilization was announced.

It seemed that everything changed from that day on. The war became a reality, a part of daily life. Our friends, the hussars, left for the front. Not many of them survived. By day and night, trains passed by us: going to the front with the mobilized, from the front with the wounded.

At night, we heard the alarming whistles of locomotives, and in the clatter of the wheels resounded the ominous words: "I am leaving, and I am not coming back!"

Unforgettable Verses

The war changed everything. It was as if everyone grew up and drew closer to each other. The country breathed with heroism. The heart grew and expanded beyond the boundaries of the narrow circle of family and friends. Mothers and children of soldiers going to the front seemed like relatives. Our grammar school organized its field hospital. We helped look after the wounded, read to them, wrote letters for them, rolled bandages, collected presents for the front. With trepidation, each morning we opened the newspapers and waited for news from the theater of military operations. We searched for echoes of awakened feelings in art and literature. In the first days of the war, I remember that I heard a song in a concert, words that struck me and compelled me to think:

> A heroic deed is in battle,
> A heroic deed is in the struggle;
> The highest heroic deed is in patience,
> Love, and supplication.[9]

Everything connected with the war was especially worrisome. One time in the French anthology, I read verses that literally shook me deeply with the depth of the feelings described in them. They spoke about a young woman, joyous and cheerful. She lived in a peaceful and carefree way and had a husband, whom she loved very much. Then war was declared. Her homeland was in danger. The bridegroom left for the front. The young woman cried for him, but she also did not stop laughing.

Elle mit sa robe noire
Et ferma son piano.

She put on a black dress
And closed the piano.

She left for the front as a nurse. There she learned that her bridegroom had been killed. She did not give in to despair, but with more diligence, she continued to fulfill the duty of a nurse. Once, they brought a dying captive into her tent. She selflessly looked after him. In the evening, examining the papers of the sick man, in horror she learned that this was the very enemy soldier who had killed her bridegroom.

Repressing her own suffering in the name of a Higher Love, all night she continued to look after the wounded enemy. In the morning, the doctor came in. The wounded soldier was already out of danger, but the head of the young woman had become entirely gray.

Thus is it, war! Thus is it, life!
Courage, denial of the self, love to the enemies!

I did not notice that this accidental poetry reading became for me the first homily of Christianity.

Beloved Teacher

In the fifth grade, a new teacher joined us. Sergei Nikolaevich was to be our homeroom teacher and teach the Russian and Latin languages. We had S. N. for two years. I cannot remember him without a feeling of deepest gratitude.

These years were difficult: war, government disorder, and two revolutions dragged down social life . . . The complex and excruciating transition from adolescence to youth troubled personal life.

S. N. was sharply distinguished from the rest of our teachers: he had none of the complexity characteristic of all the intelligentsia of that time, which beneath great cultural wealth left a feeling of vagueness and uncertainty. In S. N., a wholeness, a deep sense of integrity, and an adherence to principle were based on an unshakable foundation that we did not feel among other teachers, "who fluctuated with the wind." Precisely this healthy core of his personality, this "high order of the soul," the clarity of his view of life, the certainty and simplicity about everything were such beneficial and positive influences on those searching souls of youth. Even his manner of behaving, which flowed from inside, from his personality, had great significance. I still remember how S. N. entered the class, took out his books, and began the lesson. In my memories of this, I always imagine a clear winter morning, the classroom flooded by sunlight, and intact snowflakes on S. N.'s mustache and beard. He instilled a kind of cheerfulness, peacefulness, and desire to work. Whatever we studied in the lesson, whether it was the monuments of ancient literature, the poetry of Ovid, or Latin declensions, with him, everything became interesting, understandable, and essential. S. N. taught us to work.

Composition in Russian was always assigned a month in advance, but on the same day it was assigned, we had to begin to work on it. S. N. looked over the plan of each composition, the rough draft, and those parts of the work accomplished in the course of the week; he wanted to see and feel the movement of thought of each one. How this helped put in order not only my work but also my inner world!

In the hands of S. N., each subject acquired an indisputable meaning that made his lessons impossible to forget. Now, after some forty years have passed, I have forgotten much, but the historical or artistic images that S. N. instilled have remained in my memory all my life: Vladimir Monomakh, Iuliana Lazarevskaia, Niobe, Philemon and Baucis, and many others.[10]

In connection with everything we saw and experienced, innumerable questions emerged from each of us. At the breaks, everyone clustered around S. N.; and each one was fervently proving something. Once a week, we convened in the evenings. S. N. attentively listened to everyone; on no one did he force his convictions. One time, they asked S. N. how he related to the teachings of L. N. Tolstoy. "While still a student," S. N. told us, "I went to Yasnaya Polyana.[11] Lev Nikolaevich talked with me for a long time, but he could not convince me of the truth of his teaching." Another time, someone asked S. N. about Marxism. S. N. briefly answered, "Study Marxism. I studied it but did not accept it."

Several pupils considered themselves supporters of this or that political party. S. N. said, "It is not important whether you are Social Revolutionaries, Bolsheviks, or monarchists; most important of all is whether you are honest Social Revolutionaries, monarchists, or Bolsheviks."

Each word spoken by S. N. came from deep internal conviction and, therefore, was authentic and unforgettable.

On Fridays, after the lessons, we assembled to roll bandages for soldiers at the front. Once, on the eve of a geography exam, the majority of us did not appear to participate in this work. The next day, congratulating everyone as they turned in their exams, S. N. especially enthusiastically congratulated those who, even on the eve of the exam, found the time to participate in the work to help our wounded soldiers. "Remember," he said, "a social matter must always come first and a personal matter second."

Once, we were assigned a topic about the war. Everyone wrote in a common patriotic spirit, and only Katia G. (the daughter of a Tolstoyan) and Slava D. (the son of a Bolshevik) wrote something entirely in opposition. Returning the notebooks, S. N. turned to them and said, "I do not agree with both of you, but I am glad that you decided to express your convictions against everyone. That is how an honest person must always act."

With clear consciousness of his social responsibility, S. N. was incapable either of compromises or betrayals of conscience, He said, "I can fight against some kind of proposal that seems to me inexpedient, but when it becomes a law, I am obligated to obey it. I am obligated to obey the society and the government in everything, excluding that which is opposed to either my moral or my religious convictions. In such cases, I will not submit to any secular power."

How many times did I remember these words of S. N.!

S. N. managed to instill in the girls and boys such trust that they willingly told him about their personal affairs and first passions. S. N. was unusually sensitive to these childhood feelings, and he allowed no one to speak about them in a joking tone. One time, S. N. also told us about his first love, and leaving to go to the front, he left for our class [his] memory of the *Madonna*, by an Italian artist, which his beloved young woman had once given to him as a gift.

Indelibly imprinted in our memory was a conversation about the meaning of life, to which one of our evening gatherings was devoted. Each person hastened to reveal everything that he had in his soul. What did we not tell that evening! S. N. patiently listened to everyone and did not object to anyone. Only after everyone had spoken and asked him to expound on his own thoughts did he quietly answer, "You may consider me stupid or backward, as you wish, but for me the meaning of life is found in the words of the Gospel: 'Be perfect as our Heavenly Father is perfect.'"

During the spring holidays (Holy and Easter Weeks), we were much occupied with social work (sorting letters in the post office, etc.). We rarely saw S. N. We knew that he spent these days in the church.

On his own free will, S. N. left to go to the front. For us, his departure was not entirely unexpected. We knew that his sympathetic conscience suffered because, at a time when his brothers shed their blood, he remained in safety and did not share their sufferings. This could not continue for a long time.

After the departure of S. N., they divided our class into two parts. One transferred to the grammar school S., where mostly politics and playing parliament occupied them. We (fifteen persons) remained in our grammar school and, with more zealousness, began working on study of the sciences, taught, in part, by a university type. Not long before the end of the course, we received a long-expected letter from S. N. The front at that time had already taken on a distinctive character—civil war had begun. During this time, S. N. found himself in horrible conditions and suffered greatly through everything taking place.

"The single thing that sustains me," he wrote, "is religion. May God give each of you such steadfastness and firm support in your life."

S. N. addressed these last words to us. We heard nothing more about him, and soon we, too, left forever our beloved school.

Viktor Germanovich

> *Blessed are those who search out His testimonies;*
> *They shall search for Him with their whole heart.*
> —Psalms 118:2, Kathisma 17

Everyone in our family loved Viktor Germanovich. One generation passed on tales about him to another. The oldest members called him simply Vitia Rikman.

V. G. had been a friend of Papa's since childhood. Together they studied in the modern (nonclassical) school in Poltava, together entered and together finished the technological institute in Khar'kov, and remained friends until the end of their lives.

I saw V. G. for the first time when I was fifteen years old and, after that, met him four or five times, at great intervals, in various periods of my life, but each meeting left an indelible mark on my soul.

By nationality, V. G. was German, by faith and upbringing Lutheran.

From his childhood, as people who knew him well at that time related to me, he stood out among his comrades and persons of the same age by his remarkable spiritual purity and the force of his personality. "Such people as Vitia Rikman no longer exist," they said in Poltava. V. G. treated everyone equally and good-naturedly, and to each it seemed that in his presence a person became better, purer, and more trusting.

When he was alone, he always had a thoughtful look. Bushy, overarching eyebrows created, it seemed, protection from the surrounding outside world. Someone had only to approach him, however, and his face instantly lit up with a welcoming smile. It seemed that he was especially glad to see this person and was prepared to do everything for him.

Sometimes, when he unexpectedly came out of his reverie, he seemed to be embarrassed and somewhat confused. But he quickly regained possession of himself, and he recaptured an expression of peacefulness and his usual intensity of thought returned.

He willingly expressed his thoughts aloud, when there was an appropriate listener, but he rarely talked about his own experiences.

Once, V. G. recounted the following incident from his childhood. In his school years, he loved to pray often and at length. At the same time, in the

FIGURE 12. Viktor Germanovich Rikman.

modern school, he earnestly engaged in studying mathematics. And it often happened that, during his prayers, into his consciousness was revealed the resolution to this or another problem that earlier he could not resolve. The child considered these resolutions the suggestions of a so-called enemy, who tried to distract him from prayer, and sometimes he did not use them.

As a result, he came to class with unsolved problems and received poor marks. His parents had a hard time dealing with the poor progress of their son, the causes of which they could not understand, knowing his good capacities and diligence in his preparation of the lessons, and he suffered from the fact that he caused grief for his parents and from knowledge of his "sinfulness."

After several years went by, he met an elderly religious person, to whom he told everything and who explained to him his mistake. After this, to the surprise of everyone, he immediately began to study well and successfully completed the modern school.

From his youth, V. G. tried to lead his associates to God. This was the central idea of his life. At the same time, in his conversations with people he displayed not a shadow of the "teaching authority," which was often characteristic of Protestant preachers, especially. He thought, searched, and suffered together with those who found themselves in the position of his listeners, not showing off his learning or convictions but [acting] as though he forgot about himself, and he was sincere and truthful to the end.

Upon completing the modern school, V. G. wanted to become a pastor, but his father demanded that he enter the technological institute and become an engineer.

V. G. told us about this moment in his life: "I began a kind of double life," he said, "I diligently prepared for the exams at the institute and no less diligently prayed to fail the exams and to become a pastor." He passed the exams and entered the institute. Afterwards, V. G. did not regret what had happened and was even glad of it. "If I had spoken to people about God as a pastor, many would not have listened to me, thinking that I was doing this as my duty. But when I talk with them as a chemical engineer, they listen with interest," he said.

In his student years, V. G. often withdrew from his colleagues, and no one knew how he spent his free time. By the way, his comrades accidently learned that often, in the evenings, on the streets and boulevards, he looked for women who, by virtue of their living conditions, were forced to take the path of vice, and he tried to return them to an honest life, giving them support, both morally and materially.

Conversing with nonreligious people or those who doubted, V. G. always attentively listened to their opinions, in order to help them sort out the questions that troubled them. Pursuing this same goal after graduating from the institute, he went abroad and for a long time lived in Switzerland, Sweden, and other countries, where he became acquainted with the latest achievements in science and various philosophical systems. He compared skulls in the museums of anthropology to clarify the question of the origin of man; he spent nights pouring over the books of Drews and those similar to him.[12] He conversed equally with the young and the old, with people educated in philosophy and with people who were not educated at all.

In this activity, he fulfilled the call of the apostle Paul: "To all people I have become everything, so that I will save a few."[13]

Wherever V. G. went during his travels, he became good friends with the people around him, so that each time it was difficult to part with them. With especial warmth, he remembered his time in Switzerland, where by his own testimony he met many good people.

I saw V. G. for the first time in the summer of 1917. I had then begun my last grade in the school [gymnasium]. During this time, we had as guests R. and Ia. I., who came from Finland, and many people gathered at our home.

Everyone was glad to see V. G.

Many of those present had not seen each other for a number of years, so there was a great deal of talk: they spoke about the past and the present, about the unending war and the yet uncompleted revolution. However, when they spoke in the presence of V. G., the talk always ended up as a conversation about God and eternal life.

This seemed to happen naturally; no one was surprised and no one felt burdened, although if someone else had attempted to conduct a conversation on this question, it would have seemed to many strange and out of place. In the beginning, I did not pay attention to the words of V. G., but I keenly felt the amazing, unusual atmosphere that the presence of this man created. In some kind of miraculous manner, he united everyone around the most important matters that people rarely talked about among themselves and, therefore, remained distant from and alien to each other, despite their superficial closeness.

V. G. began to talk about the eternal soul. He said that just as the body left the womb and began a new independent life, so also the soul, departing the body, was reborn for a new life. He compared the body of the person to a complex musical instrument, from which the musician-soul could extract

FIGURE 13. V. Ia. Vasilevskaia with her father, Iakov Veniaminovich, and her brother Veniamin.

various beautiful melodies, but which, by itself, did not possess the capacity to create music . . .

V. G. needed to hurry to catch his train, but no one wanted to see him go, each person had a great deal to say to him. In everyone, a radiant feeling remained from this unusually enchanting evening . . .

Several years went by . . . March 6, 1921. Outside, it was night, darkness, in which shots resounded—echoes of civil war and internal disorder. In the house, it was cold and partially dark. Everyone had gathered around the table—each with his or her own troubles, thoughts, and melancholy. Exactly one year had passed since the day of Mama's death, but after all this time, no one was able to speak aloud about her; no one said her name. Now, everyone was silent, silent about one thing . . .

Suddenly, the doorbell rang. Strange! We were not expecting anyone. In this gloomy year of general distrust and fear, no one came to visit.

"Vitia!" Papa cried out with joyful emotion in his voice, opening the door. "Where have you come from?"

V. G. was no less glad than Papa. He had come to Moscow on behalf of his wife's brother, who had been arrested. He had supposed that he would not find anyone he knew in Moscow.

"And here I am again in the circle of friends," he said. He was excited. Papa told him which anniversary we were marking. Everyone remained silent. V. G. did not talk with us about anything this evening . . . He asked, "Would it be hard on you today to listen to music?" We requested that he play. He sat at the piano. He played for a long time. It seemed that everything we bore, everything we had lived through in these difficult years, poured itself out in these sounds. It seemed that something entirely unexpected, dispatched mysteriously from somewhere, purposely entered our life on this evening.

V. G. calmed down, but weary and, sitting at the table, recited an unpretentious German quatrain:

Where they are singing,
Sit down quickly close by—
Evil people
Have no songs.

On the following morning, V. G. left to go about his business, and in the evening, we gathered and began to talk. V. G. asked me about the subject of my university studies. I said that I was studying philosophy. We began to talk about ancient philosophy, about Plato; then we switched to Leibnitz and Kant.

When we switched to Kant, V. G. quoted his words, which he especially loved: "Two things are capable of calling forth the feeling of sublimity: the starry heavens above us and the moral law inside us."

Being fairly well acquainted with philosophy, V. G. valued in it not so much the settlement of theoretical problems as the desire to facilitate for the mind the human road to God, a desire that could be found in every conscientious philosopher. I knew about nearly all the books that V. G. discussed, except one—the Gospels, which I had never held in my hands. Meanwhile, V. G., more often than anything else, turned to it in his conversations and discussions. The Gospels were central to all his searches, all his diverse studies and interests. It was his passion, his life, the living concrete connection between God and man.

V. G. often talked about the Old Testament and the prophets. I was somewhat acquainted with the prophets and even knew from memory separate excerpts in the original, but I knew them only as fruit of the poetic inspiration of man. When V. G. talked about the divine inspiration of the Sacred Writings, it was for me something entirely new and unexpected. V. G spent more than a week at our house.

Every evening, when we all gathered in the room where, for the past year, such emptiness and discomfort had set in, our conversations resumed as if between us there had been no break and ended long after midnight. We forgot about everything: about the surrounding environment, the hunger, the war, the unending anxiety, enduring internally, even our grief. More truthfully, we did not forget about anything but began to feel everything anew.

"Well then, is it possible?" I said to myself, returning home from the university. "For what reason is it impossible? Who and by what right negates the living sources of the life of the soul?"

Once, in the evening, during one of our conversations, a neighbor, L. N., from another building, entered through the door. She came to ask for some kind of medicine for her gravely ill husband. V. G. was the first to respond to her request and, although he saw her for the first time, asked her to allow him to sit at night by the bedside of her sick husband.

This seemed to me strange at first. "V. G. is entirely unacquainted with Ivan Ivanovich," I thought. "In addition, he is not a doctor. What gives him the right to volunteer to look after the sick man?" I wondered.

V. G. did not see anything awkward in this, for him it was something entirely natural and even on its own terms understandable.

Everything that V. G. said about sin, about the damage to a person's essence, was entirely incomprehensible to me. Some of his words especially startled me with their unexpectedness and, at the same time, their deep internal truth, which it was impossible not to feel. "If until now, I have not killed a person, then it is only by the grace of God," he once said.

I did not understand then the significance of these words, but how many times they came back to me! Not all that was incomprehensible passed by us, as they often thought, but much left a deep mark on the soul and became comprehensible, even many years later.

It astounded me still more when V. G., with such genuine love for every person, said, "To love a person is possible only through Christ."

These words sank deeply into my heart, but I did not immediately understand their meaning, as I did not then understand that the love that the Tolstoyans and humanists of various understandings had taught us since childhood was not true love.

I did not want us to part with V. G. and did not want him to leave us. "It is always difficult for me to leave," he said. "Your soul gets so closely linked to people that one does not want to separate from them."

Before his departure, V. G. extracted from our old family album his student photograph, which for a long time had been preserved in Papa's memory, and wrote on it a new inscription: "To Dear V. Iak. And Ven. Iak., in memory of the evenings and conversations we shared together in Moscow, 1921."

On the day following V. G.'s departure, after leaving the university and before making my way home, I dropped into the Church of Christ the Savior. Never before had I been in the church, and I somehow felt ill at ease. To buy the Gospels in a red binding, with difficulty I forced myself to approach the candle box. Having bought the book, I went out on the street. My head was spinning. I felt sick. When my aunt asked me why I was later than usual, I told her where I had been and presented the book to her. "What is the matter with you?" asked the woman in surprise. "I do not know," I answered, lying down on the bed.

The illness turned out to be serious, and for the first time in my life, I was sent to the hospital. Over the course of two weeks, contact with those around me was interrupted because I could not speak. I prepared for an operation. My soul was peaceful as never before. What difference did it make, to live or to die, if the same Light shone on this or on the other side of life?

After my release from the hospital, I wrote V. G. a letter. He did not answer (perhaps he did not receive it, since at that time Ukraine was cut off from Moscow), and there was no need to answer it.

The next time we saw V. G. was four years later, and then for only a short time. He came through Moscow for several hours on a trip to Leningrad, where he traveled with a group of students. At the time, he was giving lectures at one of the institutes in Khar'kov.

During the day, we did not have the opportunity to meet, and we went directly to the station. I wanted to talk with V. G. and ask him many questions. I could not arrange a talk, but a rendezvous with V. G. could not go for naught. There were people for whom everything they did reflected their inner life so that, on many questions, one received an unspoken answer.

In 1929, Papa traveled to Kislovodsk for medical treatment. Unexpectedly, by telegram, they sent for me to come to Khar'kov. It turned out that Papa had become ill on the road and was hospitalized.

When Papa began to recover, I asked Uncle Nisa to help me search for and meet with V. G. Uncle willingly responded to my request, because he, like everyone in the family, loved and respected V. G.

It turned out that V. G. lived on the outskirts of the city, and it was not easy to reach him. We managed to visit V. G. only on the eve of my departure from Khar'kov.

The house in which V. G. lived with his family was small and stood right by the train tracks, so that when the express train flew by on the line, everything in the house shook. When we arrived, V. G. and his wife, Mariia Mikhailovna, were at home. M. M. respected her husband's convictions, but she did not understand his aspirations.

We did not stay at their house for long. We conversed about Papa's health, about the marriage of their daughter Verochka, and so forth. V. G. and M. M. expressed the desire to accompany us to the tram. It was a long walk. I wished, not losing time, to talk with him about "the most important thing." In all the years that had passed since our last meeting, I had not lost interest in books and systems of philosophy, but they had ceased to be my "daily bread."

This time, V. G. did not wait before questioning my point of view but addressed me with a question: "Do you believe that the Lord guides each person?" I did not expect this question, and it forced me to look into the very depths of my soul.

Did I believe? I did not know. I could not answer. I did not have then that clear consciousness of God's leadership, which appeared later, especially after baptism. How could I not believe this! "I hope that it is so," I answered. With V. G., it was easy to talk, thanks to his wonderful sincerity. He did not preach, he lived, and the dearest things in the life he lived he willingly passed on to anyone who had the ears to listen.

What he said contained neither a shadow of philosophizing nor passion; recalling the apostle Paul, he always inserted his "I" in last place: "So neither the one who plants nor the one who waters is anything, but only God who gives the growth" (I Corinthians 3:7).

We went out into the field. All around was quiet. Innumerable stars dotted the dark southern sky.

I wanted to put a question to V. G., a question that agitated me and that I would not have asked anyone but him: "How should we understand the Mystery of the Eucharist?" I asked. "Literally or symbolically?"

"Christ said," V. G. began, and, after a period of silence, continued, "You will excuse me if I give the translation in German, because I am accustomed to read the Gospels in this language. Christ said, 'Das ist Mein Leib!' (This is my body!)."

He pronounced this phrase with special power, giving stress to the words "Das ist" (This is) . . .

It seemed that the Ukrainian night, with its myriad stars, echoed his words!

Never again did such a question arise in me.

The next day, when I went to see Papa in the hospital, I found V. G. there. I did not know what they talked about, but apparently their talk dealt with religion. "You will not manage to convince me, Vitia," Papa said. "For my whole life no one could convince me of this, as no one could convince me of the opposite." "Thank God that no one, at least, could convince you of the opposite," V. G. said.

The next time we saw V. G. seven years had passed. It would be our last meeting. By then, V. G. was already seriously ill. He suffered from attacks of asthma and could sleep only sitting up in an armchair and, then, not for long.

In August 1936, V. G. went to Leningrad to collect material for his dissertation. According to the nature of his work, he could not refuse the defense. This weighed him down.

"I don't have left much time to live now," he said. "I want to devote the remaining time to help people come to God, and not to scientific studies."

V. G. traveled with his wife and grandson. Little Igor' was a very nervous child, required constant attention, and became calm only when someone read aloud to him.

For me, the arrival of V. G., unexpected as always, this time had exceptional significance and was one of many visible proofs of God's help. I was preparing to accept baptism and somehow, for me in that moment, the most difficult thing was the separation of one's inner life from the life outside. I felt and understood that the changes that lay ahead for me could not be restricted to the sphere of subjective experiences but touched all of life. Therefore, I had an excessive need to build a bridge between my outer and inner [being] and to take those events that related to my inner life and make them entirely real.

Meanwhile, I did not have the chance to talk about everything with any of the people who knew me previously, who knew the life of our family. V. G. was precisely such a person. I decided I had to have the chance to talk privately with him.

In the daytime, V. G. and his family were at Lena's dacha. Grandmother and Grandfather spent the entire time with their grandson. The conditions for conversation were not suitable. Toward evening, they left for Moscow. I went with them. In the train car, M. M. read aloud to Igor' to keep him in his seat. I immediately turned to V. G.

"I have a large request of you. It is essential for me to talk with you today about a matter that is, for me, an extremely important question." I myself was surprised at my audacity, but I could not act otherwise. V. G. seemed confused and agitated. Because of his exceptional modesty, he never offered advice and did not take upon himself the resolution of difficult questions.

"What am I? What can I do?" [he said,] as if he excused himself.

"I don't need anything," I said, trying to calm him. "I need only to know your perspective."

All the same, V. G. could not calm down, and when we were in the Moscow apartment, he asked me the field to which the question was related that I wanted to talk with him about.

"The field of religion," I said.

"You have some kind of doubt?" he asked.

"No," I answered, "on the contrary."

With this, the discussion broke off.

In the evening, relatives and acquaintances gathered, everyone wanted to talk with V. G.

I said to Papa that I needed to talk with V. G. in private. Papa, as always, did not ask for any details. When everyone dispersed, I immediately turned to V. G., trying to state everything as briefly as possible: "Over the course of twenty years of occasional meetings with you, we carried out conversations on one and the same theme. I have passed through many stages during this time, and now I have before me the possibility, and perhaps the necessity, to accept baptism. I would very much like to know your opinion on this question," I said.

V. G. fell to thinking. His thick eyebrows moved still closer together. It seemed to me that he took a long time to reply . . .

"I am very glad," he said finally. "As a Christian, I am very glad. I supposed it, especially today, when I read this book you have (he had in mind *The Confessions* of the Blessed Augustine). Only how will Iasha take this? To him it will be painful." (V. G. very much loved Papa.)

"For now, we must keep it a secret," I said, "but afterwards Papa will understand."

"In earlier times," said V. G., "several people accepted baptism in order to acquire worldly advantages, but now . . ."

"Now it is possible to lose everything," I finished.

"Precisely so," V. G. agreed.

V. G. again fell to thinking and then began to speak, as if continuing his thoughts.

"If you so believe in Christ, then you want to join His Church . . ."

I was very happy that V. G. brought up the question about the Church not as a Protestant, but as a Christian. (Still earlier, he once said to me, "In many ways, I do not agree with Luther.")

V. G. said many things to me that evening. He spoke about what he considered the most important things in Christianity: about the Cross of the Savior and about atonement. He also said never to postpone repentance.

M. M. entered the room.

V. G. rose and began to excuse himself. It was three o'clock in the morning.

Several years later, we heard that V. G. had died in prison.

When M. M. heard the news of his death, they also said to her that those who brought an accusation against him had not been able to corroborate it, and he was not guilty of anything.

Everyone who was with him in prison, both the prison guards and the incarcerated, were left with the most radiant memories of him.

Notes

Editor's Introduction and Preface

1. Pavel Vol'fovich Men, interview with author, Moscow, September 12, 2016.
2. Vera Iakovlevna Vasilevskaia, *Katakomby XX veka: Vospominaniia* (Moscow: Fond imeni Aleksandra Menia, 2001).
3. James H. Billington, *The Icon and the Axe: An Interpretive History of Russian Culture* (New York: Random House, Vintage Books, 1970), 570–83.
4. Christel Lane, *Christian Religion in the Soviet Union: A Sociological Study* (London: G. Allen and Unwin, 1978).
5. Julie deGraffenreid, "Combating God and Grandma: The Soviet Antireligious Campaigns and the Battle for Childhood," in *The Dangerous God: Christianity and the Soviet Experiment*, ed. Dominic Erdozain (DeKalb: Northern Illinois University Press, 2017), 32–50.
6. See, for example, Nicholas V. Riasanovsky and Mark D. Steinberg, *A History of Russia*, 9th ed. (New York: Oxford University Press, 2018); and Ronald Grigor Suny, *The Structure of Soviet History: Essays and Documents*, 2nd ed. (New York: Oxford University Press, 2013). See Fr. Aleksandr Men's statement on this shortcoming, in his preface to the present volume.
7. Vladimir Il'ich Lenin, "O znachenii voinstvuiushchego materializma," in *Polnoe sobranie sochineniia*, vol. 45 (Moscow: Izd-vo politicheskoi literatury, 1964), 28.
8. Mikhail Vital'evich Shkarovskii, *Russkaia Pravoslavnaia Tserkov' v XX veke* (Moscow: Veche, Lepta, 2010), 241; François Furet, *The French Revolution, 1770–1814*, trans. Antonina Nevill (Oxford: Blackwell, 1992), 81–85, 91–92.
9. "Poslanie Patriarkha Tikhona ob anafematstvovanii tvoriashchikh bezzakoniia i gonitelei very i Tserkvi Pravoslavnoi," in *Sledstvennoe delo Patriarkha Tikhona: Sbornik dokumentov*, ed. Protoierei Vladimir Vorob'ev (Moscow: Izd-vo Pamiati istoricheskoi mysli, 2000), 813–14.
10. Irina Ivanovna Osipova, *"O, Premiloserdyi . . . Budi s nami Neotstupno . . .": Vospominaniia veruiushchikh Istinno-Pravoslavnoi (Katakombnoi) Tserkvi. Konets 1920-kh–nachalo 1970-kh godov* (St. Petersburg: Kifa, 2011), 12.
11. Philip Walters, "A Survey of Soviet Religious Policy," in *Religious Policy in the Soviet Union*, ed. Sabrina Petra Ramet (Cambridge: Cambridge University Press, 1993), 8.
12. Osipova, *"O, Premiloserdyi,"* 12–13; Natal'ia Aleksandrovna Krivova, *Vlast' i tserkov' v 1922–1925 gg.: Politbiuro i GPU v bor'be za tserkovnye tsennosti i politicheskoe podchinenie dukhovenstva* (Moscow: AIRO-XX, 1997), 31–34.
13. Walters, "Survey of Soviet Religious Policy," 9–10.
14. Ibid., 10. Awaiting trial, Patriarch Tikhon was confined to his patriarchal quarters in the Danilov Monastery in Moscow.

15. Krasnitskii had long advocated reform in the Orthodox Church, and he then had the opportunity to enact it. Earlier, in a letter to the Soviet Commissariat of Justice, he had proposed to the Soviet government that it should forge an alliance with the Orthodox Church to achieve its revolutionary goals. See Edward E. Roslov, *Red Priests: Renovationism, Russian Orthodoxy, and Revolution, 1905–1946* (Bloomington: Indiana University Press, 2002), 31, 53–55.

16. Shkarovskii, *Russkaia Pravoslavnaia Tserkov'*, 241.

17. Shkarovskii specifically mentions the Kirsanovskii, Morshanskii, and Borisoglebskii districts.

18. Ibid., 363–64.

19. Nikita A. Struve, *Christians in Contemporary Russia*, trans. Lancelot Sheppard and A. Manson, 2nd rev. ed. (New York: Scribner, 1967), 44. According to Struve, most Orthodox clergy understood why Metropolitan Sergii had signed the declaration, interpreting it as an unavoidable effort to prevent the Church from an all-out assault and wanting to preserve church unity as a supreme need in the face of such intense political pressure. While Metropolitan Sergii's pledge is most often interpreted as the cause of the church schism, Hegumen Innokentii, reexamining the language in the "Declaration of Loyalty," finds the major reasons for the schism lay elsewhere. First, Metropolitan Sergii did not possess the authority to make binding decisions on the Russian Orthodox Church; as *locum tenens*, he had only the right to conduct the day-to-day affairs of the Church. Second, and most important, Hegumen Innokentii argues that Metropolitan Sergii did not betray the Church. Looking at the full text of the "Declaration," Hegumen Innokentii maintains that Metropolitan Sergii held fast to the principle that the Church had to maintain its inner freedom, its own "truth and life." Political events, however, conspired to undermine this sacred principle (Hegumen Innokentii, "Deklaratsiia mitropolita Sergii i sovremennaia tserkov'," *Nezavisimaia gazeta* [July 29, 1992], 5. For an English translation, see "Metropolitan Sergii's Declaration and Today's Church: Before Saying Goodbye to the Past, We Must Recognize It for What It Was," *Russian Studies in History* 32, no. 2 [1993]: 82–88).

20. Osipova, *"O, Premiloserdyi,"* 19. The higher-order clergy in Metropolitan Agafangel's group of supporters included Bishop Evgenii (Kobranov), Archpriest Varlaam (Riashentsev), and Archpriest Serafim (Samoilovich).

21. Dimitry Pospielovsky, *The Russian Church: The Soviet Regime, 1917–1982*, vol. 1 (Crestwood, NY: St. Vladimir's Seminary Press, 1984), 153–54; Lev Regelson, *Tragediia russkoi tserkvi, 1917–1945* (Paris: YMCA-Press, 1977), 134–35.

22. Shkarovskii, *Russkaia Pravoslavnaia Tserkov'*, 243–44. Members of the IPKh strongly opposed the Renovationists, whom they viewed as heretics. They also declined to take part in any of the government's social organizations, refused to pay taxes, and interpreted the state's collective farms as Antichrist institutions. "They were primarily monarchists, although they were extremely critical of what they called the tsar's repeated lies." See the detailed description and analysis in Z. A. Nikol'skaia, "K kharakeristike techeniia tak nazyvaemykh istinno-pravoslavnykh khristian," in *Voprosy istorii religii i ateizma*, no. 9 (1961): 161–88; and Mikhail Vital'evich Shkarovskii, "The Russian Orthodox Church versus the State: The Josephite Movement, 1927–1940," *Slavic Review* 54, no. 2 (1995): 365–84.

23. Osipova, *"O, Premiloserdyi,"* 22–23.

24. Ibid., 23n36.

25. Vasilii Osipovich Kliuchevskii, "Znachenie prep. Sergiia dlia russkogo naroda i gosudarstva," in *O nravstvennosti i russkoi kul'ture* (Moscow: Institut rossiskoi istorii RAN, 1998), 108.

26. The Trinity-Sergiev Lavra later played a major part in the revival of monasticism. The monastery's growth owed a great deal to several renowned Orthodox leaders, beginning with Metropolitan Filaret (Vasilii Drozdov, 1792–1867), who, in 1821, became archimandrite of the monastery. Early in his church career, Metropolitan Filaret formed close relationships with leading church officials, as well as with Tsar Alexander I. In 1831, Metropolitan Filaret selected Archimandrite Antonii (Andrei Medvedev, 1792–1877) to serve as prior of the monastery, and under Archimandrite Antonii's leadership, the Trinity-Sergiev Lavra became one of Russia's most prominent spiritual centers. The lavra's economic foundation flourished, and it, too, became a major charitable institution. There contemplative spirituality combined with active service to the community. As the historians Scott Kenworthy and David Miller have admirably shown, the Trinity-Sergiev Lavra provided a connecting link between it, the people, and Russian history, which shaped the national consciousness of the Russian people. See Scott M. Kenworthy, *The Heart of Russia: Trinity-Sergius, Monasticism, and Society after 1825* (New York: Oxford University Press, 2010); and David B. Miller, *Saint Sergius of Radonezh, His Trinity Monastery, and the Formation of the Russian Identity, 1392–1605* (DeKalb: Northern Illinois University Press, 2010).

27. Fr. Serafim's background is elaborated in Fr. Viktor Grigorenko, "Zhiznennyi put' Arkhimandrita Serafima (Bitiukova)," in *Tserkovnaia zhizn' XX veka: Protoierei Aleksandr Men' i ego dukhovnye nastavniki. Sbornik materialov Pervoi nauchnoi konferentsii "Menevskie chteniia" (9–11 sentiabria 2006 g.)*, ed. M. V. Grigorenko (Sergiev Posad: Izdanie prikhoda Sergievskoi tserkvi v Semkhoze, 2007), 110–12.

28. In the nineteenth and early twentieth centuries, the Diveevo Monastery was a well-known women's monastery that originally began as a monastic community that attracted peasant girls to the service of the Church. Founded by the wealthy widow Agafiia Semenovna Mel'gunova (d. 1789), who moved there from Vladimir and began monastic life under the name of Aleksandra, the monastery was located in the proximity of Nizhnii Novgorod, some 250 miles east of Moscow. Diveevo was once a mining settlement, a rough, unruly community. Under Mel'gunova's leadership, the whole area underwent a transformation. She developed a close relationship with St. Serafim and the nearby monastery at Sarov. Pilgrims going to Sarov often stopped and rested at the Diveevo Monastery before moving on to Sarov. See Donald Nicholl, *Triumphs of the Spirit in Russia* (London: Darton, Longman and Todd, 1997), 19–20; and "History of the Diveyevo Monastery," https://diveevo-monastyr.ru/en/chronicle/istorija-diveevskogo-monastyrja.

29. Sergei Iosifovich Fudel' was the son of the Orthodox priest Iosif Fudel', whose spiritual writings were widely read by religious believers.

30. Aleksei Viacheslavovich Rufimskii, "'Skhiigumeniia Mariia i 'pustynnaia tserkov" Episkopa Nikolaia (Parfenova)," in *Tserkovnaia zhizn' XX veka: Protoierei Aleksandr Men' i ego dukhovnye nastavniki. Sbornik materialov Pervoi nauchnoi konferentsii "Menevskie chteniia" (9–11 sentiabria 2006 g.)*, ed. M. V. Grigorenko (Sergiev Posad: Izdanie prikhoda Sergievskoi tserkvi v Semkhoze, 2007), 86–87.

31. Monakhinia Dosifeia (Verzhblovskaia), "O matushke Marii," in Vera Iakovlevna Vasilevskaia, *Katakomby XX veka: Vospominaniia*, ed. Rosa Adamiants et al.,

comp. Nataliia Grigorenko and Pavel Men' (Moscow: Fond imeni Aleksandra Menia, 2001), 279–306.

32. Ibid., 284.

33. Aleksandr Men', "Pis'mo k E. N.," in *"AEQUINOX": Sbornik pamiati o Aleksandra Menia*, ed. I. G. Vishnevetskii and E. G. Rabinovich (Moscow: Carte Blanche, 1991), 185.

34. Optina Pustyn' adopted its name from a legendary brigand named Opta, who took the monastic name of Makarii after his conversion to Christianity; after him, the monastery's identity signified transformation, in which the physical and spiritual were integrated. The formal name of the monastery is Opta's Hermitage of the Presentation of the Mother of God at Kozel'sk (Kozel'skaia vvedenskaia Optina Pustyn'). See Leonard J. Stanton, *The Optina Pustyn Monastery in the Russian Literary Imagination: Iconic Vision in Works by Dostoevsky, Gogol, Tolstoy, and Others*, Middlebury Studies in Russian Language and Literature, no. 3, ed. Thomas R. Beyer, Jr. (New York: Peter Lang, 1995), 53.

35. Ibid., 46–47.

36. Sergii Chetverikov, *Optina Pustyn*, 2nd ed. (1926; repr., Paris: YMCA-Press, 1988), 84–85; O. N. Ordina, *Fenomen starchestva v russkoi dukhovnoi kul'ture XIX veka* (Kirov: Viatskii sotsial'no-ekonomicheskii institut, 2003), 61–62; Ann Shukman, "Introduction," *Christianity for the Twenty-first Century: The Life and Work of Alexander Men*, ed. Elizabeth Roberts and Ann Shukman (London: SCM Press, 1996), 4; Stanton, *Optina Pustyn' Monastery*, 92–93.

37. Irina Paert, *Spiritual Elders: Charisma and Tradition in Russian Orthodoxy* (DeKalb: Northern Illinois University Press, 2010), 4, 214.

38. Larisa Nikolaevna Slavgorodskaia, *Pravoslavnye startsy: Zhizneopisanie, mudrost', molitva* (Moscow: Eksmo, 2016), 13; Sergei Sergeevich Khoruzhii, "Fenomen russkogo starchestva v ego dukhovnykh i antropologicheskikh osnovaniia," *Tserkov' i vremia* 21, no. 2 (2002): 211–13.

39. Slavgorodskaia, *Pravoslavnye startsy*, 13.

40. Anna Grigor'evna Snitkina Dostoevsky writes movingly about her husband's trip in her *Dostoevsky: Reminiscences*, trans. and ed. Beatrice Stillman, with an introduction by Helen Muchnic (New York: Liveright, 1975), 294.

41. Fyodor Dostoevsky, *The Brothers Karamazov*, trans. and annotated Richard Pevear and Larissa Volokhonsky (New York: Farrar, Straus, and Giroux, 1990), book 1, chapter 5, and book 6, chapter 3.

42. Rowan Williams, *Dostoevsky: Language, Faith, and Fiction* (Waco, TX: Baylor University Press, 2011), 201.

43. A. Gorelov, "Misticheskii soiuz liubvi," in *Optina pustyn': Russkaia pravoslavnaia dukhovnost'*, comp. A. Gorelov (Moscow: Kanon+, 1997), 405.

44. Joseph Frank, *Dostoevsky: The Mantle of the Prophet, 1871–1881* (Princeton, NJ: Princeton University Press, 2002), 627–28; Dostoevsky, *Brothers Karamazov*, book 6, chapter 2(d).

45. Aleksandr Men', *O sebe: Vospominaniia, interv'iu, besedy, i pis'ma* (Moscow: Izd-vo Zhizn' s Bogom, 2007), 27–29; Monakhinia Dosifeia, "O matushke Marii," 288–90, 292–93; Pavel Vol'fovich Men, interview by author, Moscow, June 2, 2006.

46. Men', "Pis'mo k E. N.," 185; Slavgorodskaia, *Pravoslavnye startsy*, 33.

47. Ibid., 185. Men's emphasis on the importance of dialogue with different religious traditions is further explored in my book, *Russia's Uncommon Prophet: Father Aleksandr Men and His Times* (DeKalb: Northern Illinois University Press, 2016), 214–16, 223, and chapter 12.

48. Fr. Viktor Grigorenko, interview with author, Semkhoz, July 4, 2013.

49. Ibid.

50. Pavel Vol'fovich Men, interview with author, Moscow, June 2, 2006.

51. Ibid.

52. Ibid.

53. As Igal Halfin and Jochen Hellbeck, the chief analysts of the autobiographies, have maintained, Soviet citizens consciously or otherwise internalized the state's value systems. Such collaboration enabled individuals to achieve a sense of security and self-worth in a time of rapid social transformation. See Igal Halfin, *Terror in My Soul: Communist Autobiographies on Trial* (Cambridge, MA: Harvard University Press, 2003); and Jochen Hellbeck, *Revolution on My Mind: Writing a Diary under Stalin* (Cambridge, MA: Harvard University Press, 2006).

54. Mariia Vital'evna Tepnina, "Iz vospominanii-interv'iu," in Vera Iakovlevna Vasilevskaia, *Katakomby XX veka: Vospominaniia* (Moscow: Fond imeni Aleksandra Menia, 2002), 267.

55. E. B.—In the Duma, several priests even voted with the Social Democrats.

56. All-Russian Sobor: Preceded by several assemblies of the clergy, the All-Russian Sobor (Council) opened in August 1917, five months after the fall of the tsarist government. Operating in new conditions of freedom, the Sobor was the most representative national meeting of the Church in Russian history. The Sobor's most significant accomplishment was the election of a new patriarch, Metropolitan Tikhon (Bellavin) of Moscow to serve in an office that had remained vacant since 1711. The Sobor also recognized the Church's administrative structure and reformulated parish administration, bringing the clergy and laity closer to a bishop, placed in each diocese of the country. The Church intended to convene an All-Russian Sobor every three years. Because of the Bolshevik's accession to power in November 1917, the latter act never came to fruition, leading later to many church leaders, looking back on the 1917–1918 meeting, to see it as the last legitimate church council during the Soviet period. See Aleksandr Bogolepov, *Church Reforms in Russia, 1905–1918* (New York: Russian Orthodox Church in America, 1966); Anton Vladimirovich Kartashev, *Tserkov', istoriia, Rossiia: Stat'i i vystupleniia* (Moscow: Probel, 1996); James W. Cunningham, *The Gates of Hell: The Great Sobor of the Russian Orthodox Church, 1917–1918* (Minneapolis: University of Minnesota Press, 2002); and Sviashchennik Iakinf Desvitel', *Pomestnyi sobor Rossiiskoi Pravoslavnoi Tserkvi 1917–1918 gg. i printsip sobornosti* (Moscow: Izd. Krutitskogo podvor'ia, 2008).

57. The "Renovationist Schism" took place after a group of church reformers, in 1922–1923, spearheaded a revolt within the Russian Orthodox Church. The Renovationists, members of the so-called Living Church, seeking the "renovation of the church," demanded that Patriarch Tikhon give them authority over church affairs. Convinced that the Orthodox Church was dying, they believed the only hope lay in renovating it, and they advocated radical changes in the Church's internal structure and the liturgy, as well as rapprochement with the Bolshevik government. They maintained that the Orthodox Church had either to accommodate itself to the Soviet

government or face extinction. The Renovationists failed to overcome the suspicions of the Orthodox laity and to generate much popular support for their reforms. The majority of Orthodox believers viewed the reforms as heretical, and those who advocated them as traitors to the Orthodox faith. See Gregory L. Freeze, "Counterreformation in Russian Orthodoxy: Popular Response to Religious Innovation, 1922–1925," *Slavic Review* 54, no. 2 (1995): 305–39; and Edward E. Roslof, *Red Priests: Renovationism, Russian Orthodoxy, and Revolution, 1905–1946* (Bloomington: Indiana University Press, 2002).

58. E. B.—The history of the Renovation movement is elaborated in the work of A. Krasnov-Levitin and V. Sharov, *Ocherki po istorii russkoi tserkovnoi smuti*. The authors show that the reformism of the Renovationists from the very beginning concealed servility and denunciation (Moscow: Krutitskoe podvor'e, 1996).

59. After Patriarch Tikhon's arrest in April 1923, the Renovationists summoned a council (*sobor*), which met in Moscow from April 29 to May 9. At this national council, attended by nearly five hundred delegates, the Renovationists had the largest number of representatives, although other groups within the Church, including supporters of Patriarch Tikhon, participated. The government, however, heavily controlled the selection process, and the GPU had a large hand in the proceedings. The council passed a series of resolutions condemning Patriarch Tikhon, voicing political support for the Soviet government, proposing liturgical reforms, calling for church unity behind the Renovationists, castigating all forms of capitalist economics, and giving canonical authority to a newly formed Higher Ecclesiastical Administration (VTsU), which the Renovationists controlled (Roslof, *Red Priests*, 103–6; Anatolii Emmanuilovich Krasnov-Levitin, *Likhie gody, 1925–1941* [Paris: YMCA-Press, 1977], 149–51).

60. Patriarch Tikhon left a will naming three church leaders as his possible successors. By the time of his death, the first two of them were in internal exile, leaving only the third, Metropolitan Pyotr (Polianskii) of Krutitsy and Kolomna as a viable candidate. A hastily called ad hoc meeting of bishops confirmed Metropolitan Pyotr as the patriarchal *locum tenens* in the interim, until a church sobor could duly elect a new patriarch. But in December 1925, the police arrested Metropolitan Pyotr, falsely accusing him of conspiring with émigré forces to overthrow the Soviet government. Before his arrest, he, too, had written a will, in which he named Sergii (Stragorodskii), metropolitan of Vladimir and Shuia, his successor as provisional occupant of the patriarchal throne.

61. E. B.—The original text of the declaration of Metropolitan Sergii was written in much more restrained tones, but they [government officials] forced him to change it.

62. E. B.—The publication of these documents dated to 1927, when the interim patriarch, Metropolitan Pyotr (Polianskii) was in exile. Hieromartyr Pyotr, metropolitan of Krutitsk (Polianskii, 1862–1937), was canonized in 1997.

63. E. B.—See A. A. Shishkin, *Syshchnost' i proiskhozhdenie obnovlencheskogo raskola v Russkoi pravoslavnoi tserkvi* (Kazan', 1970).

64. Within the Russian Orthodox Church, members of the church hierarchy and priests who sympathized with Metropolitan Sergii's decision to compromise with the Soviet government agreed to sign the pledge of loyalty, which the government required in 1927–1928. They followed the so-called Sergianskaia line, as opposed to those who refused to make accommodations with the atheist power.

65. In an effort to serve his political agenda, in September 1943, Joseph Stalin allowed the Orthodox Church to rebuild its internal structure and regain its footing. He hastily convened a sobor of nineteen bishops, who elected Metropolitan Sergii as patriarch. The elderly and ailing Patriarch Sergii lasted only a short time; he died on May 15, 1944.

66. In Stalin's deliberations over the revival of the Orthodox Church, the question arose about the Church's administrative structure and how much independence it would be allowed. Among several competing proposals about which party agencies would have jurisdiction, Stalin created the Council for Russian Church Affairs, to be chaired by Georgii Georgievich Karpov. The Church came under the direct control of the state, as it had earlier when Metropolitan Sergii served as a guardian of the vacant patriarchal throne. For Karpov's leadership and relationship with the Church, see Tatiana A. Chumachenko, *Church and State in Soviet Russia: Russian Orthodoxy from World War II to the Khrushchev Years*, ed. and trans. Edward E. Roslof (Armonk, NY: M. E. Sharpe, 2002).

67. "The loosening of social life" alludes to the Thaw, the period following Nikita Khrushchev's famous speech at the Twentieth Party Congress in 1956. Liberalization took place in many spheres of social life, including a lessening of restrictions on art, film, poetry, and theatrical works. Liberalization, however, did not apply to religious activities.

68. E. B.—That is, spontaneous, independent associations.

69. E. B.—Contemporary movements, which call themselves the Catacomb Church, do not have anything in common with the phenomenon described here.

70. E. B.—Pyotr Alekseevich Shipkov (1881–1959) was secretary of Patriarch Tikhon and priest from 1921 on in the Moscow Nikitskaia Church. Arrested in 1925 and 1928, he spent from 1928 to 1930 in Solovki, and from 1930 to 1934 in Turukhanskii krai; in 1934, he went "into the Catacomb Church," lived in Zagorsk, and worked as a bookkeeper. Arrested in 1943, from 1943 to 1950 (?), he was incarcerated in the Siblag [labor camp], and from 1950 (the date is uncertain), he lived in exile. After his release, he was restored to the priesthood, and in the last years of his life, he was elevated to archpriest, the head priest of a church in Borovsk.

71. E. B.—Fr. Ieraks (Bocharev, Ivan Matveevich, 1880–1959), priest in monastic orders. He was born in Voronezh guberniia, finished theological and musical school, and served as regent in the Zadonskii Monastery in Voronezh. In 1917–1918 (?), he became a monk of the Trinity-Sergiev Lavra, a priest in monastic orders. In the 1930s, he served in the Church of the Sacred Martyrs Cyril and John. Arrested on April 5–6, 1932, he was sent into exile in Kazakhstan. After that, he served and lived illegally in Losinka, in the home of his spiritual daughter V. A. Korneeva. He was arrested on November 6, 1943, in the case of the "Anti-Soviet Church Underground" (which included Bishop Afanasii Sakharov, Archpriest Pyotr Shipkov, the nun Kseniia Grishanova, and others), and received five years in an ITL [corrective labor camp] (first, in prison in the Liubianka, then in the Mariinskii labor camp). In the 1950s, he spent in an invalid home in Mordova, and from 1957 he lived in Vladimir, where he died.

72. E. B.—Vladimir V. Krivolutskii (1888–1956). In 1921–1922, he took courses in the Orthodox People's Academy and served in the Church of the Sacred Martyrs Cyril and John. In 1922, he was a deacon; in 1923, a priest; from 1924 to 1930, he also filled in for the head priest of the Znamenskaia Church in Seremet'evskii pereulok; he was in

opposition to Metropolitan Sergii. From 1930 to 1933, he was in exile in Pinega. From 1933 to 1946, he illegally served in Moscow and Egor'evsk. Arrested in 1946, he was sentenced to ten years in ITL. Because of illness, he was released in 1955.

73. E. B.—Aleksei Ivanovich Gabriianik (1895–1950), the husband of Anna, daughter of A. P. Golubtsov, a professor at the Moscow Ecclesiastical Academy, in 1925, he was consecrated to the priesthood by Patriarch Tikhon, served in a village, and then, until 1928, in the city of Sergiev Posad (Zagorsk); for his refusal to mention the governing power in prayer, he was suspended; after the suspension was quickly lifted, he was then sent to Moscow and, for a short time, served in the Church of the Sacred Martyrs Cyril and John, before being sent into exile for three years in Central Asia. After his exile, he lived in Voronezh, and in 1933, he received a term of three years in ITL (Temkinsk labor camp). In 1935, he was freed. In 1942–1946, by the blessing of Archimandrite Serafim (Batiukov), he lived in illegal status and served at home. In 1946, he was arrested (spent four years in the Vladimir prison), and after the conclusion of his term was deported to a settlement in Siberia. He died on the road to the prison in the city of Kirov.

74. E. B.—Dmitrii Ivanovich Kriuchkov (1874–1952), priest, spiritual son of the priest Vladimir Bogdanov. He served in the Church of the Holy Savva in Moscow. After the issuance of the July Declaration of 1927, he found himself in opposition to Metropolitan Sergii (Stragorodskii). In 1927, he was arrested and imprisoned. From 1928 to 1932, he served in the Church of the Sacred Martyrs Cyril and John. From 1946 on, he was in exile in the town of Abakan in the Krasnoiarsk region.

75. E. B.—Prelate Afanasii, Bishop of Kovrov (Sakharov, 1887–1962), canonized in 2000.

76. The published materials on Bishop Afanasii to which Men refers include Episkop Afanasii (Sakharov), "Mozhno li poseshchat' khramy Moskovskoi patriarkhii? Iz pis'ma k dukhovnoi docheri," *Vestnik russkogo studencheskogo khristianskogo dvizheniia* (*Vestnik RKhD*), no. 4 (106) (1972): 92–97; E. V. Apushkina, "Krestnyi put' preosviashchennogo Afanasiia Sakharova (1887–1962), *Vestnik RKhD*, no. 1 (107) (1973): 170–211.

77. E. B.—Subsequently, the last name of Fr. Serafim was pronounced as Bitiugov and Bitiukov, to which, from a consideration of secrecy, he did not oppose.

78. Fr. Aleksandr cites two Orthodox leaders who, in different ways, played a large role in the life of the Russian Orthodox Church in the twentieth century.

Sergei Nikolaevich Bulgakov (1871–1944) was born in Livny, a town in the Orel district of Russia. He attended the seminary in Orel, later became attracted to Marxism, and dedicated himself to studying and writing about political economy. Gradually, he moved from Marxism to Christianity, and after graduating from Moscow University's School of Law, he was ordained as a priest. His teaching and writing earned him a rapidly growing reputation in intellectual and church circles. In 1922, Lenin exiled him from Russia. After a short stay in Berlin, Bulgakov settled in Paris, where he founded the St. Sergii Institute, which became one of the leading Orthodox theological institutes in the world. Bulgakov is the subject of an immense number of studies; see, in particular, Catherine Evtukhov, *The Cross and the Sickle: Sergei Bulgakov and the Fate of Russian Religious Philosophy* (Ithaca, NY: Cornell University Press, 1997).

Born in Kerch, in the Crimea, *Archbishop Luk Voino-Iasenetskii* (Valentin Feliksovich Voino-Iasenetskii, 1877–1961) grew up in a family of modest means that moved to Kiev during his childhood. He had a strong sense of service to the poor and lived this out by studying medicine at the University of Kiev, specializing in surgery. He was one of Russia's first to perform surgery on the stomach, kidneys, and gall bladder. Some consider him the most accomplished Russian surgeon of the twentieth century. In addition to the practice of medicine, he also served the Church, and in 1921, in Tashkent, he was ordained as a deacon, shortly afterward as a priest, and in May 1923 consecrated as a bishop. A month later, he was arrested. Bishop Luk spent the next eleven years in imprisonment and exile. In 1937, he was again arrested. Freed after the war, he was appointed archbishop of Crimea. Bishop Luk's entire life was one of great suffering but also of major service, in his simultaneous practice of medicine and devotion to the Church. For an account of his life, see Metropolitan Nectarious of Argolis, "Saint Luke the Surgeon, Archbishop of Crimea (1877–1961)," https://pemptousia.com/2013/06/saint-luke-the-surgeon-archbishop-of-the-crimea.

79. The Sokol'niki (falconers) district is located in the northeast quadrant of Moscow and originally served as the tsar's hunting grounds. In the early 1900s, the area was the site of a large neighborhood garden, arboretum, and one of Moscow's major parks. Father John Kedrov served as head priest of the Church of the Resurrection of Christ in the district. Local people called this the Church of Kedrov, since he chaired the committee that oversaw the church's construction. Father John was the leader of the strong, unified Sokol'niki parish community. See Timothy J. Colton, *Moscow: Governing the Metropolis* (Cambridge, MA: Belknap Press, 1995), 26, 47, 55, 130, 264; "Church of the Resurrection of Christ in Sokolniki (Moscow)," http://www.voskresenie-sokolniki.ru.

80. E. B.—Fr. Dmitrii Delektorskii served in the Church of the Resurrection of Christ until it was closed. From there he was transferred to the Church of the Nativity of John the Baptist [on Presnia]), where he served until his death (1970). Being already a very old man, Fr. Dmitrii in gratitude remembered Fr. Sergii (Serafim), for he was certain that in the village where they appointed him, he would have been arrested or killed. (In the 1950s, according to the blessed nun Mariia, Aleksandr Men served in the church on Presnia).

81. E. B.—Diveevo—a women's monastery near Sarovskaia Pustyn', under the special care of Saint Serafim of Sarov.

82. The Iverskaia (Iveron) Mother of God is one of Moscow's most revered icons. The original is preserved in the Iveron Monastery on Mount Athos. According to Orthodox tradition, the icon was painted by the Apostle Luke, and it miraculously survived political disputes and extreme violence, eventually turning up on Mount Athos. There the icon was placed over the gates, and henceforth came to be known as the "Keeper of the Gate." In 1648, Patriarch Nikon commissioned a copy of the icon to be made. After its arrival in Moscow, the icon was installed in a special chapel built in the Kremlin's Resurrection Gates at the main entrance to Red Square. The icon was believed to have special wonder-working powers. A copy of the icon occupied a special place near the altar in the catacomb church in which Fr. Serafim served.

83. Bishop Afanasii (Sergei Grigorevich Sakharov, 1887–1962) grew up in the historical city of Vladimir to parents of modest means. Raised by his mother alone, following his father's death at an early age, Sergei Grigorevich developed a love for the Church. Although book learning did not come easily for him, he applied himself diligently and graduated from the Vladimir Theological Seminary and the Moscow Theological Academy. Appointed to a teaching position in the Vladimir Theological Seminary, Afanasii became known as an imaginative and talented teacher and discussion leader. Shortly after the revolution, the Church appointed him vicar of two

historic monasteries in the Vladimir diocese, Bogoliubov and the Nativity of Mary, Mother of God. He was then, in July 1921, elevated to bishop of Kovrov, also in the Vladimir diocese. Bishop Afanasii became one of the main opponents of the Renovation schism within the Church, which he viewed as apostasy. He was arrested in March 1922, the first of many years of imprisonment and exile. Tortured, weakened by hard labor, and assigned the most onerous jobs, he never lost his faith and all his life sang praises to God. Humble, compassionate toward the suffering, and extraordinarily resourceful, he lived a life of unceasing prayer. People were drawn to him—to his sympathy, gentleness, and love. Fr. Serafim and others in the catacomb church in Zagorsk considered him to be their bishop ("St. Afanasy (Athanasius) Sakharov, Bishop of Kovrov, Confessor and Hymnographer," http://orthochristian.com/98179.html; "Healing the Wound—A Timeless Letter from St. Afanasy (Sakharov)," http://www.pravoslavie.ru/98181.html).

84. E. B.—This refers to the Holy Righteous Archpriest Aleksei Mechev (1959–1923) and his son the Holy Martyr Archpriest Sergii Mechev (1892–1941), canonized in 2000.

85. E. B.—The venerable Fr. Nektarius (Tikhonov, 1853–1928), the last Optina elder, canonized in 2000.

86. E. B.—Vera Alekseevna Korneeva (1906–1999) came from an old nobility family. She spent her childhood on the estate of Prince Konstantin Romanov, the uncle of the tsar, as the close friend of his youngest daughter, Princess Vera (they were the same age). After the revolution, with her nun godmother, who was her aunt, Nataliia Leonidovna Ragozina (N. L. took the veil in 1919 from the last Optina elder Nektarius), she concealed priests, monks, and nuns from destroyed monasteries. In her home in Losinka, Father Ieraks (Bocharev) lived for eight years. In a room in the attic where he was hidden was constructed a secret church. In 1946, he was arrested, spent five years in an ITL and three years in exile in Kazakhstan; he was freed after the death of Stalin. In *The Gulag Archipelago*, A. Solzhenitsyn, who personally knew Vera Alekseevna, included her eyewitness account about life and confinement. It was published in full in *VRKhD* 3, no. 142 (1984): 209.

87. E. B.—The preface was written in the mid-1970s.

V. Ia. Vasilevskaia (1902–1975), Candidate of Pedagogical Sciences, worked in the Institute of Mental and Physical Disabilities; in addition to those mentioned above, to her belonged the work "N. I. Pirogov i voprosy zhizni" (*Sbornik psikhiatriia i aktual'nye problemy dukhovnoi zhizni* [Moscow: SF MVPKhSh, 1997]), and the manuscripts "Emotsional'naia zhizn' malen'kogo rebenka," and "Chto takoe Liturgiia?"

The translation of the book of Frantsisk Sal'skii, *Vvedenie v blagochestivuiu zhizn'* was published in Russia (Moscow: Stella Aeterna, 1999), without indicating the translator.

In an abbreviated form, the "Memoirs" were published in the collection *I bylo utro* (Moscow: Vita-Tsentr, 1992).

Part I. Fr. Serafim

1. E. B.—Before the dawn.

2. E. B.—Ivan Aleksandrovich Il'in (1883–1954), religious philosopher, jurist, and publicist. In 1922, he was sent abroad.

3. E. B.—Georgii Ivanovich Chelpanov (1862–1936), psychologist, philosopher, author of works on experimental psychology and philosophy.

4. Frs. Aleksei and Sergei Mechev were leaders of the St. Nicholas the Wonderworker Church on Maroseika Street in Moscow. Fr. Aleksei brought the traditions of the Optina elders, and the church attracted many students from Moscow University and members of the Russian intelligentsia, known as *maroseiki*. Frs. Aleksei and Sergei were arrested and then released in 1922, and Fr. Aleksei died the following year. Fr. Sergei was later arrested again and died in prison. On the *maroseika* community, see Pavel Aleksandrovich Florenskii, "Rassuzhdenie na sluchai konchiny ottsa Alekseia Mecheva," in *Sochineniia v chetyrekh tomakh*, comp. and ed. Igumen Andronikov (A. S. Trubachev), P. V. Florenskii, and M. S. Trubachev, 4 vols. (Moscow: "Mysl'," 1994), 2:591–600; Florenskii, "Otets Aleksei Mechev," in *Sochineniia v chetyrekh tomakh*, 2:621–27; and Sergei Sergeevich Bychkov, comp., *Maroseika: Zhizneopisanie ottsa Sergeiia Mecheva, pis'ma, propovedi, vospominaniia o nem* (Moscow: Martis, Sam, and Sam, 2001).

5. E. B.—Tonia Z.'s name is Antonina Zaitseva.

6. The revolution, Civil War, hunger, and disease ravaged the country (the death toll is estimated at ten million) and left large numbers of children orphaned and homeless (Orlando Figes, *A People's Tragedy: The Russian Revolution, 1891–1924* [New York: Penguin, 1996], 773–74).

7. As she recounted, Vera Vasilevskaia's trip to the Optina Pustyn' Monastery, as to many others, became a turning point in her spiritual life. For more on Optina Pustyn', see Editor's Introduction.

8. E. B.—Elena Semenovna Men, mother of Father Aleksandr Men. Lenocha is the diminutive name for Elena (Lena) and refers to Vera's cousin and close friend Elena Semenovna Men.

9. Lake Seliger, "clear lake," is in northern Russia between Moscow and St. Petersburg. Forests containing many mushroom and berries enclose this picturesque body of water, and all around the lake are ancient churches and monasteries.

10. Nilus-Stolobenskaia Pustyn' is a spiritual center on an island in the Lake Seliger region and is one of the most idyllic sites in Russia. It was named for St. Nilus, who settled here in 1528 (d. 1555). The monastery served as a prime destination for pilgrimages.

11. E. B.—At that time, a bacteriological station was located there.

12. The Symbol of Faith, commonly called the Nicene Creed, is sung during the Divine Liturgy and is among the most ancient prayers of the Orthodox Church.

13. The Great Martyr Barbara (Varvara) was an early Greek saint. The daughter of a pagan, she professed Christianity and was beheaded by the provincial prefect, who, returning home from the execution, died of a lightning strike and turned into ashes. The story of Barbara's martyrdom became popular in the Middle Ages.

14. A prayer to the Blessed Virgin Mary, "The Theotokos" (Mother of God).

15. "Old Testament Rites" denotes the practice of circumcising a male child on the eight day (see Leviticus 12:8). Fr. Serafim's reference is to Acts 16:3, in which Paul circumcised Timothy in order that Jews would not be offended.

16. Vera Vasilevskaia often called Elena Men "Sister."

17. Nicodemus, a Pharisee and Jewish leader, visited Jesus at night to talk with him about Jesus's teachings (see John 3:1–21). After the Crucifixion, he brought embalming spices to help Joseph of Arimathea prepare the body of Jesus for burial.

18. The Icon of the Three Holy Hierarchs represents the meeting of three of the Orthodox Church's greatest theologians: St. Basil the Great, St. John Chrysostom, and St. Gregory the Theologian.

19. *Solianka* is a traditional Russian spicy soup made with vegetables and meat or fish and garnished with sour cream.

20. E. B.—A settlement near Moscow on the Iaroslavl' railway line.

21. Kaliazin is a small town on the Volga River, between Moscow and St. Petersburg, noted for the bell tower of St. Nicholas Cathedral. When the nearby Uglich dam was constructed in 1939, the monastery was submerged, except for the bell tower, which is presently used as a lighthouse.

22. Bolshevo is a town in the Moscow region primarily known as a railroad station on the Iaroslavskaia line.

23. In many cultures, the nightingale represents a spiritual connection between the divine and the earthly. In Christian art, the nightingale also personifies saved souls.

24. E. B.—Tat'iana Ivanovna Kupriianova—the spiritual daughter of Fr. Sergii Mechev, the wife of the catacomb priest Boris Vasil'ev; she studied together with V. Ia. Vasilevskaia in the university.

25. Evgenii Abramovich Baratynskii (1800–1844), a leading young poet of his time, became a close friend of Alexander Pushkin, whose style his poetry closely resembled. His poetry is characterized by philosophical themes and metaphysical depth. M. I. Glinka put several of his poems to music.

26. The Roman Emperor Hadrian (117–138) promised riches and glory to Sophia's three daughters if each renounced her Christian faith. When the girls refused, he had them thrown into prison, tortured, and beheaded. Sophia and her daughters were given martyr's crowns. The Greek Orthodox Church commemorates the Holy Martyrs Faith, Hope, and Love on September 17. (See *The Great Collection of the Lives of the Saints*, vol. 1: *September*, trans. Fr. Thomas Marreta, from the Slavonic edition published by the Christian Print Shop of the Transfiguration Alms-House in Moscow in the year 1914, from the original compiled by St. Demetrius of Rostov [House Springs, MO: Chrysostom Press, 1995], 276–88.)

27. The Sacred Mystery refers to the Eucharist, a "holy act through which the Holy Spirit mysteriously and invisibly confers Grace upon human beings" (Archpriest Seraphim Slobodsky, *The Law of God* [Jordanville, NY: Printshop of St. Job of Pochaev, 1996], 471).

28. Founded in the fourteenth century, the Trinity-Sergiev Lavra later played a major part in the revival of monasticism in Russia and became one of Russia's most prominent spiritual centers. As Scott M. Kenworthy has admirably shown, the Trinity-Sergiev Lavra provided a connecting link between it, the people, and Russian history, which has shaped the consciousness of the Russian people (*The Heart of Russia: Trinity-Sergius, Monasticism, and Society after 1825* [New York: Oxford University Press, 2010]).

29. Located on Nevskii Prospect in St. Petersburg, the Kazan' Cathedral was one of the most important Orthodox cathedrals in the city. It held a copy of the Icon of Our Lady of Kazan', which represents Mary, Mother of God, known as the Holy Protector of Russia, as patroness of the city. Many churches throughout Russia display copies of the icon.

30. E. B.—The postcard reproduction is a picture of the artist J. R. Wehle, "Jesus among the Wheatfields" [or "Christ in the Grain Fields"].

31. The Tenderness Icon of the Mother of God provided inspiration to St. Serafim of Sarov during his entire life. When he was found dead on January 2, 1888, he was kneeling in prayer before it. The arms of the Mother of God are crossed in submission

to God and her eyes look downward in an expression of her humility. This icon is one of the few in Orthodoxy that depicts the Mother of God without the Christ Child.

32. E. B.—The spirit of delusion.

33. St. John the Theologian, who wrote the Gospel that bears his name, became one of the twelve disciples of Christ. He and the Apostle Peter are considered "pillars of the Church."

34. The Great Canon was composed by St. Andrew of Crete (b. 650), a bishop, theologian, and hymnographer. The Great Canon is sung during Lenten services.

35. The hymn "O Gladsome Light" is part of the Vespers of the Orthodox Church. Written in the late third or early fourth century A.D., it is the first known hymn in the Christian tradition.

36. Hunters' Row is a district located in the very center of Moscow.

37. The Liturgy of the Pre-Sanctified Gifts is a liturgical service of the Byzantine Rite performed during Great Lent. Communion is received and the Gifts, the body and blood of Christ, are consecrated in advance.

38. E. B.—Losinka is located on the Iaroslavl' railroad line. It is thus easily accessible to Moscow and Zagorsk.

39. The Holiday of the Annunciation is held on March 25, nine months before the birth of Jesus. On this day, the Archangel Gabriel appeared to the Virgin Mary and informed her that she was to be the Mother of God.

40. Elder Nektarius (1853–1928). Orphaned at a young age, Nikolai Tikhonov traveled to the Optina Pustyn' Monastery, where he entered the path of strict monasticism. When the Bolsheviks closed the Optina Monastery in 1923, they arrested Fr. Nektarius. After his release from prison, he received a constant stream of visitors seeking his counsel on how to live as religious believers in the new era. Fr. Nektarius died in 1928, the last surviving elder of the Optina Monastery in the Soviet era. See I. M. Kontsevich, *Elder Nektary of Optina* (Platina, CA: St. Herman of Alaska Brotherhood, 1998), and *Zhitiia prepodobnykh startsev Optinoi Pustyni* (Jordanville, NY: Holy Trinity Monastery, 1992), 325–57.

41. E. B.—Fr. Vladimir Krivolutskii.

42. E. B.—The passage refers to what is known as "The Protocols of the Elders of Zion," allegedly adopted at the Basel congress, which formulated a plan for the Jewish takeover of the world. As compiled, the "Protocols" were a falsification, composed by associates of the prerevolutionary secret police. The "Protocols" were included in a book by the church journalist Sergei Nilus, *Bliz' est' pri dveriakh* (The Antichrist is at the doors), Tsarskoe Selo, 1905. "The Protocols" were published in a particularly Orthodox format, with many references to the Sacred Fathers. The book gained a wide reputation (parts of it Hitler quoted in *Mein Kampf*). A Catholic priest established the real origins of "The Protocols" (see the almanac *Bridge* [New York, 1955], 155–88).

43. Vasilevskaia refers to a town southwest of Moscow, an administrative center and historic site. One of the most significant battles of the war of 1812 took place at Maloiaroslavets, where, on October 24, Marshal Mikhail Illarionovich Kutuzov confronted part of the army of the French commander Eugène de Beauharnais, Napoleon's stepson.

44. The Dormition Fast is celebrated in the Eastern Orthodox Church on August 15. It honors the ascension into heaven of St. Mary, Mother of Jesus. A fourteen-day period of fasting precedes the celebration.

45. "Joy of All Who Sorrow" refers to an icon of the Mother of God that is devoted to the sister of Patriarch Joachim (1674–1690). One morning, a voice came to her, instructing her to go to the Temple of the Transfiguration of My Son where she would find an icon called the "Joy of All Who Sorrow." The voice told her to ask the priest to celebrate a *moleben'* (the service of supplication for the well-being of the living) with the blessing of water, and then her incurable illness would be healed.

46. E. B.—Mariia Vital'evna Tepnina (1904–1992), a dentist, sometimes housed Fr. Vladimir Krivolutskii in her apartment. Arrested in October 1946, Tepnina spent five years in a corrective labor camp until July 1951 (village of Dolgii Most), and then, until September 1954, she spent three years "of permanent" exile (village of Pokateevo), in the Krasnoiarsk region. From the 1970s, until the end of her life, she worked in the Sretenskii Church of Novaia Derevnia [the church where Father Aleksandr Men served].

47. St. Serafim (b. 1758–1833) is one of the most revered saints in the Russian Orthodox Church. As a young man he went to the monastery at Sarov (north of Nizhnii Novgorod), where he became a priest. He was given permission to retire into the forest, and he lived as a hermit, engaging in continual prayer on a rock near his small hut. He attracted both the high- and the lowborn and eventually ended his silence, taking on the role of the traditional *starets* (elder). He was renowned for his practical advice, his clairvoyance, his insights into people's lives, and for relating to people as a loving father. See David Nicholl, "The *Starets*: Saint Seraphim." in *Triumphs of the Spirit in Russia* (London: Darton, Longman, and Todd, 1997), 11–66; and Michael Plekon, *Living Icons: Persons of Faith in the Eastern Church*, foreword by Lawrence S. Cunningham (Notre Dame: University of Notre Dame Press, 2002), 20–29.

48. Orthodox believers had long held that the bodies of saints were incorruptible. In the spring of 1919, the Bolsheviks exhumed the bodies of the most venerated saints in an effort to dispel what they considered to be popular superstition. Saints Sergii of Radonezh and Serafim of Sarov were two of the saints so targeted.

49. Nadezhda Konstantinovna Krupskaia (1869–1939) married Vladimir Lenin and went with him into exile. After the revolution, she remodeled the entire educational system, expanding the literacy rate and infusing Soviet education with Marxist-Leninist ideology. As vice-commissar of education, Krupskaia played a large role in the assault on the Russian Orthodox Church. See Victor Sebestyan, *Lenin: The Man, the Dictator, and the Master of Terror* (New York: Pantheon, 2017); and Robert H. McNeal, *Bride of the Revolution: Krupskaya and Lenin* (Ann Arbor: University of Michigan Press, 1972).

50. *Diveevskaia letopis'* refers to a book by Leonid Mikhailovich Chichagov (Fr. Serafim), *Letopis' Serafimo-diveevskogo monastyria*, 2nd ed. (1896, repr. St. Petersburg: M. M. Stasiulevich, 1903). The book describes the founding and development of the cloister and provides a biographical account of the life, ministry, and miracles of St. Serafim of Sarov.

51. E. B.—Kseniia Ivanovna Grishanova (in the monastery, Susana).

52. St. Nicholas's Day (December 6/19), a major religious holiday, is the feast day of St. Nicholas the Wonderworker. *Akathist* (*Akathistos*) is a hymn to the Savior recited in the Eastern Orthodox Church and devoted to a member of the Holy Trinity, a saint, or a holy event. Literally, the term means "not sitting," and it comes from the Byzantine tradition. The best known of the *Akathistoi* is the hymn to the Blessed Virgin.

In succession, parts of the hymn are sung every Friday of Great Lent, with the entire twenty-four stanzas of it sung on the final Friday of Lent. See John McGuckin, *The Orthodox Church: An Introduction to Its History, Doctrine, and Spiritual Culture* (Chichester: Wiley-Blackwell, 2011), 436.

53. Arzamas is a town east of Moscow, in the Nizhnii Novgorod region. It became a significant transportation and trading center, connecting Moscow with other Russian regions to the east.

54. On the Diveevo Monastery, see the Editor's Introduction.

55. Sovkhozy were heavily subsidized state farms that originated in the late 1920s as part of the collectivization of Soviet agriculture. As state-owned enterprises, they received a disproportionate share of equipment, although their total grain output did not match the output from the collective farms. Sovkhozy became main centers for agricultural experimentation. See R. W. Davies, *The Socialist Offensive: The Collectivization of Soviet Agriculture, 1929–1930* (Cambridge, MA: Harvard University Press, 1980), quotation from 109.

56. *Kanavka* literally means "little canal," and the reference is to the Holy Canal of the Theotokos at the Diveevo Monastery.

57. Simeon the New Theologian (d. 1036?) was a Byzantine monk, considered by some to be the "greatest of the Byzantine mystical writers." He based many of his teachings on the authority of the Desert Fathers. According to the Orthodox theologian Hilarion Alfeyev, he inspired controversy and may have been called "new theologian" to signify what was believed to be his break with Orthodox tradition. McGuckin calls his *Hymns of Divine Eros* "among the most rhapsodic of all Christian mystical celebrations of the love of God." See McGuckin, *Orthodox Church*, 17, 139, 140–41; Nikētas Stēthatos, *The Life of Symeon the New Theologian*, trans. Richard Greenfield, Dumbarten Oaks Medieval Library, no. 20 (Cambridge, MA: Harvard University Press, 2013); Hilarion (Alfeyev), Metropolitan of Volokolamsk, *St. Symeon the New Theologian and Orthodox Tradition* (New York: Oxford University Press, 2000).

58. Workers from the state farm at first assumed that Vera Vasilevskaia belonged to the administration and was engaged in computing and deducting expenses from their allotment of flour.

59. E. B.—Factory-industrial schools.

60. In the icon of the Holy Martyr Faith Sophia stands tall behind her three daughters Faith, Love, and Hope, who were executed for refusing to renounce their faith. Each holds a cross, signifying Jesus's words: "If any want to become my followers, let them deny themselves and take up their cross and follow me. For those who want to save their life will lose it, and those who lose their life for my sake will find it" (Matthew 16:24–25).

61. Kolkhozniks were members of a collective farm, a central part of Stalin's First Five-Year Plan. The human costs were enormous, both in terms of life and labor efficiency. See Alexander Gerschenkron, *Economic Backwardness in Historical Perspective* (Cambridge, MA: Belknap, 1962); Moshe Lewin, *Russian Peasants and Soviet Power: A Study of Collectivization*, trans. Irene Nove, with the assistance of John Biggarts, and with a preface by Alec Nove (London: George Allen and Unwin, 1968); and Arcadius Kahan, "The Collective Farm System: Some Aspects of Its Contribution to Soviet Economic Development," in *Agriculture in Economic Development*, ed. Carl Eicher and Lawrence Witt (New York: McGraw-Hill, 1964), 251–71.

62. The Kazan' Mother of God (Our Lady of Kazan') icon is one of the most venerated icons in the Russian Orthodox Church. The icon portrays Mary with her head inclined, her face looking at Christ. On her veil are star-shaped crosses, an ancient symbol of virginity. The soft play of light and shadow on her face "reflects the 'uncreated' luminosity of divine energy" (Alfredo Tradigo, *Icons and Saints of the Eastern Orthodox Church*, trans. Stephen Sartarelli [Los Angeles: J. Paul Getty Museum, 2004], 170–71).

63. Fedor Ivanovich Tiutchev (1805–1873) was a Russian poet whose philosophical poems reflected his love for his native country. He spent more than thirty years abroad as a diplomat, and his love poems are classics of Russian literature.

64. Aleksandr Aleksandrovich Blok (1880–1921) was the greatest Russian Symbolist poet, an original writer who celebrated freedom. His musical style, particularly in poems about St. Petersburg, depicted the mists and dreamlike qualities of the city. Blok's "The Rose and the Cross," while mostly conventional in subject matter, is of very high lyrical quality (D. S. Mirsky, *A History of Russian Literature*, ed. and abridged Francis J. Whitfield [New York: Knopf, 1960], 453–57, 461).

65. Nikolai Vasilievich Gogol (1809–1852) was one of Russia's great writers of the nineteenth century. Vasilevskaia refers to Gogol's book *Meditations on the Divine Liturgy*.

66. Vasilii Andreevich Zhukovskii (1783–1852) is acknowledged as having introduced to Russia the Romantic Movement in poetry. He became editor of the literary journal *The Herald of Europe* (Vestnik Evropy), and his reputation as a translator earned him a position on the staff of Field Marshal Kutuzov during the Napoleonic Wars. He later served as tutor to the future Tsar Alexander II. See "Vasily Zhukovsky Bio," https://mypoeticside.com/poets/vasily-zhukovsky-poems.

67. E. B.—Probably this is a reference to Natasha Sereda.

68. The reference to "social activity" is an allusion to the unpaid days of work expected of Soviet citizens on weekends as service to the state. Initially voluntary, these days became obligatory. Called *subbotniki*, they were meant to fulfill such menial tasks as cleaning the streets, repairing public conveniences, collecting materials for purposes of recycling, and removing rubble from housing construction.

69. Fr. Serafim was disappointed with Florenskii's work for the state. Pavel Aleksandrovich Florenskii (b. 1882) was one of Russia's greatest prophetic minds of the twentieth century. Born into a Russian family in Azerbaijan, he became a priest, philosopher, theologian, mathematician, and scientist. At the age of twenty-six, he published *The Pillar and Ground of Truth* (Stolp i utverzhenie istiny), an original and profoundly influential work that later religious figures found to be inspirational in their life's work and in understanding the relationship between science and religion. He was executed in 1937. In the late 1980s, Fr. Aleksandr Men gave a major public lecture on Pavel Florenskii, calling his teachings extremely important to rebuilding Russia's spiritual culture. See Pavel Florensky, *The Pillar and Ground of Truth: An Essay in Twelve Letters*, trans. Boris Jakim, with an introduction by Richard F. Gustafson (Princeton, NJ: Princeton University Press, 2004); Avril Pyman, *Pavel Florensky: A Quiet Genius. The Tragic and Extraordinary Life of Russia's Unknown da Vinci*, foreword by Geoffrey Hosking (New York: Continuum, 2010); and Protoierei Aleksandr Men', "Otets Pavel Florenskii," in *Russkaia religioznaia filosofiia: Lektsii*, ed. Marina Nasonova (Moscow: Khram sviatykh bessrebrenikov Kosmy i Damiana v Shubine, 2003), 198–223.

E. B.—During those years, as an engineer, Fr. Pavel Florenskii was a member of the Commission on Electrification.

70. The canon to Mary, Mother of God, "Distressed by Many Temptations" is a prayer of supplication, seeking refuge in the Holy Mother of God.

71. St. Sergii (b. 1314) was the son of a well-off boyar family that lived in the village of Radonezh, near Moscow. He took monastic vows, living for several years in the forest where he and his older brother had built a small chapel in honor of the Holy Trinity. Over time, he attracted others, and the area developed into the town of Sergiev Posad. St. Sergii played a significant role in Moscow's emergence from Tatar control and the unification of Russia. The great nineteenth-century historian V. O. Kliuchevskii attributed to St. Sergii the reawakening of Russia's moral consciousness. Monks considered the Trinity-Sergiev Lavra to be under the Mother of God's protection, and icon painters portrayed St. Sergii as having powers of intercession with God on behalf of Russia. In times of national danger, he represented the saint to whom Russians turned to for deliverance from peril. See David B. Miller, *Saint Sergius of Radonezh, His Trinity Monastery, and the Formation of the Russian Identity, 1392–1605* (DeKalb: Northern Illinois University Press, 2010); and Vasilii Osipovich Kliuchevskii, "Znachenie prep. Sergiia dlia russkogo naroda i gosudarstva," in *O nravstvennosti i russkoi kul'ture* (Moscow: Institut rossiiskoi istorii RAN, 1998), 92–108.

72. *Vzbrannaia Voevoda* is the *akathist* expressing gratitude to the "Victorious Leader," Mary, Mother of God, who is the "invincible possessor of all power." The *akathist* asks Her to "release us from all our troubles," and rejoice in the spirit that one is under the divine protection of the Mother of God, http://pravoslavie.ru/put/biblio/molitva/54.htm.

73. Vasilevskaia refers to her relative Lev Markovich Vasilevskii. Born into a Jewish family, he studied medicine and became an itinerant doctor in the zemstvo organizations. In addition to publishing his poetry, he wrote on the theater and translated plays from German. He published a collection of his poems in St. Petersburg in 1912, and it is likely that Vasilevskaia has this collection in mind.

74. Vasilevskaia refers to the historian Mikhail Osipovich Gershenzon and the landscape painter Isaac Il'ich Levitan. Gershenzon (1869–1925) could not at first attend a Russian university because of quotas on Jewish admissions, although he later gained entrance to Moscow University. A master prose stylist, his works on Russian cultural and intellectual history were widely read. He edited the famous anthology *Landmarks* (Vekhi), including writers who believed the spiritual life was the "only solid basis on which a society can be built." See Mikhail Gershenzon, "Preface to the First Edition," *Vekhi*, trans. and ed. Marshall S. Shatz and Judith E. Zimmerman, with a foreword by Marc Raeff (Armonk, NY: M. E. Sharpe, 1994), xxxvi–xxxviii; and Evgenii Borisovich Rashkovskii, "Istorik Mikhail Gershenzon," *Novyi mir*, no. 10 (2001): 128–38. Levitan (b. 1860) grew up in poverty and studied at the Moscow School of Painting, Sculpture, and Architecture. His paintings of forests, lakes, fields, and country roads depicted nature's tranquillity and power (James H. Billington, *The Icon and the Axe: An Interpretive History of Russian Culture* [New York: Vintage, 1970], 437; W. Bruce Lincoln, *Between Heaven and Hell: The Story of a Thousand Years of Artistic Life in Russia* [New York: Viking, 1998], 252–54).

75. The Entrance into the Temple of the Most Holy Mother of God is a feast day celebrating the story of Mary's parents, Saints Joachim and Anna taking her at the age

of three into the Temple and turning her over to the Heavenly Father. According to tradition, Mary was left there to be educated and prepared to be the Mother of God. The event foretold the promise of the birth of Christ and is celebrated on November 21 in the Orthodox Church. See Moscow Patriarchate, Patriarchal Parish in the USA, "The Entry into the Temple of the Most Holy Mother of God," http://3saints.com/entry-of-the-holy-theotokos-into-the-temple.html.

76. E. B.—Vera Maksimovna Sytina (1901–1988), wife of S. O. Fudel'.

77. E. B.—In the Monastery of Nikodim, Paraskeva Ivanovna Grishanova.

78. St. Spyridon the Wonderworker, bishop of Tremithus (270–348), is venerated in both the Eastern and Western Churches. Born in Cyprus, he was a poor shepherd who took monastic vows after the death of his wife. He became bishop of Tremithus, and at the Council of Nicea played a major part in the defeat of Arianism. As bishop, he continued to unite his pastoral duties with serving the poor. According to the Orthodox Church, he was given the gift of wonderworking, which enabled him to heal people. The Church celebrates St. Spyridon on December 12, https://oca.org/saints/lives/2000/12/12/103526-st-spyridon-the-wonderworker-and-bishop-of-tremithus.

79. The Great Canon "Helpmate and Protector, Be My Salvation" is sung on Tuesday during the First Week of Lent, following the singing of Psalm 69. The text is taken from Exodus 15: 2 and 1 and Psalm 117:14. The full text may be found at https://www.orthodox.net > greatlent > great-canon-tuesday.

80. *Kathisma*, literally a "sitting," is a monastic term signifying the division of the Psalter into twenty parts (*kathismata*), each of which can be read in one session in the liturgical service. The twenty *kathismata* are divided between Vespers and Matins, allowing all the Psalms to be read each week. In Great Lent, *kathismata* are read at other times during the day, so that the entire Psalter is read twice during the week. See Dimitri Conomos, "Kathisma," in *The Concise Encyclopedia of Orthodox Christianity*, ed. John Anthony McGuckin (Chichester: John Wiley and Sons, 2014), 292.

Part II. Fr. Pyotr Shipkov

1. E. B.—Vasilevskaia has in mind Archbishop Luke (Voino-Iasenetskii, canonized in 1905).

2. Tat'iana Ivanovna Kupriianova.

3. E. B.—Mother Superior Mariia for many years served as the spiritual mentor of many people, who came to her and lived with her (she died in Zagorsk at the age of eighty-one, in 1961).

4. E. B.—The man, the owner of the house in which Fr. Serafim and Fr. Pyotr served, was also arrested. Employees of State Security dug up the coffin with the archimandrite's body, carried it away, and opened and photographed it. Afterward, they sent the coffin to the cemetery and buried it in the earth. People close to Fr. Serafim tracked down the place of his burial and placed a cross over the grave. Many years later, on the closure of this cemetery, the body was transferred to another Zagorsk cemetery, where it presently rests. Mother Superior Mariia was buried in the same cemetery.

5. See note in Fr. Aleksandr Men's preface.

6. After the death of Patriarch Sergii in May 1944, the Russian Orthodox Church prepared to hold a new sobor and elect a new patriarch. In February 1945, in an elaborate ceremony, attended by Orthodox leaders from around the world, Aleksii,

metropolitan of Leningrad and Novgorod, was unanimously elected the thirteenth patriarch of Moscow and All Russia. He held the position until his death in April 1970.

7. E. B.—Fr. Serafim earlier said to his spiritual children: "While the sovereign Afanasii lives, you have your bishop."

8. See note in Fr. Aleksandr Men's preface.

9. Vera sometimes called Elena Semenovna Men (Lenochka), her relative and close friend whom she regarded as her sister, by the affectionate name of "Sister."

10. Aleksei Stepanovich Khomiakov (1804–1860) was one of Vasilevskaia's favorite poets. A historian, philosopher, publicist, artist, and co-founder of the Slavophiles, Khomiakov wrote poems illustrating the conflict between freedom and power and the individual against the crowd. A central theme of his writing concerned the representation of Christ in the Gospels as a victor who preserved human freedom. Fr. Aleksandr Men would later relate his strong biblical themes to present-day Russia (Aleksandr Men', *Bibliia i literatura: Lektsii*, ed. Marina Nasonova [Moscow: Khram sviatykh bessrebrenikov Kosmy i Damiana v Shubine, 2002], 135–44).

11. E. B.—God of compassion.

12. Borovsk is a town southwest of Moscow. It has historical significance as the site of a prominent wealthy monastery supported by Grand Prince Ivan III of Moscow in the fifteenth century.

13. Fr. Pyotr refers to Apollon Nikolaevich Maikov (1821–1897), an Imagist poet. The Imagists eschewed sentimentality and focused on realism and ideas. Dostoevsky particularly admired Maikov's poetry, became a lifelong friend, and enjoyed a lively correspondence with him. See Dmitrii Petrovich Mirsky, *A History of Russian Literature*, ed. Francis J. Whitfield (New York: Knopf, 1960), 205, 219–21; Victor Terras, *A History of Russian Literature* (New Haven: Yale University Press, 1991), 310, 314–15; and Mikhail Ivanovich Sukhomlinov, "Osobennnosti poeticheskogo tvorchestva: A. N. Maikov ob"iasnenyia im samom," *Russkaia starina*, 97, no. 3 (1899): 481–98.

14. Fr. Pyotr loved Ignatius of Antioch, also known as Ignatius Bogonosets (God-bearer), who lived around the turn of the first and second centuries and suffered greatly at the hands of the Roman Emperor Trajan. The martyrdom of Ignatius is the subject of a well-known icon that depicts Ignatius in bishop's robes, with a lion attacking him on both sides. At the top, the "Hand of God" reaches down to him from Heaven. St. Ignatius is said to have written seven letters to Christ's congregations while on a journey to Rome, and while the story may be apocryphal, these letters have had great significance in church tradition, providing support for a changing system of governance and elevating the bishop to a position of great authority as the central governing point. See McGuckin, *Orthodox Church*, 10–11, 243, 291.

15. Glinskaia Pustyn' is a monastery in the village of Sosnovka, a short distance from Russia's border with Ukraine. Like Optina Pustyn' to the north, Glinskaia Pustyn' became widely known as a center of spiritual enlightenment and operated largely outside the administrative hierarchy of the Orthodox Church, which gave its elders greater freedom to relate to people on a personal basis. Early in the twentieth century, the Holy Synod sent monks to Glinskaia or Optina to observe the practice of eldership. See Irina Paert, *Spiritual Elders: Charisma and Tradition in Russian Orthodoxy* (DeKalb: Northern Illinois University Press, 2010).

16. E. B.—Egorov was a well-known Moscow physician-cardiologist, a relative of Fr. Pyotr.

17. E. B.—Nina Vladimirovna Trapani (1912–1986), was born in Mytishcha in the Moscow region. In 1943, she was arrested in the case of "The Anti-Soviet Church Underground," in which Bishop Afanasii (Sakharov) was also arrested. In 1943, she was incarcerated in the Rybinsii (Volzhskii) labor camp. After she completed her term, the authorities exiled her to Kazakhstan. In 1954, the general amnesty freed her. From 1954 on, she lived in Mordovia (in the village of Bol′shie Berzniki), then in the city of Pot′ma, not far from the place where her spiritual father Ieraks (Bocharov) lived (in an invalid home for exiles). From 1957 to 1986, she lived in the city of Vladimir, working as a bookkeeper. She is the author of the memoir "Bishop Afanasii (Sakharov)," published in the collection *Molitva vsekh vas spaset* (Moscow: PSTBI, 2000). Her "Vospominanie ob ottse Pyotre Shipkove (1881–1959)," was published in *Vestnik russkogo khristianskogo dvizheniia*, 2nd series, no. 150 (1987): 256–77.

18. *Panikhida* is a special memorial service to commemorate the dead prior to burial. The service takes place either on Saturday morning, following the Divine Liturgy, or on the preceding evening after vespers. The priest offers prayers for the repose of the departed and may also prepare a liturgical meal of boiled wheat (*koliva*), which he blesses and sprinkles with holy water. Holding the service on Saturday is designed to parallel Christ's entombment on the same day of the week. See Jeffrey B. Pettis, "Psychosabbaton," in *Concise Encyclopedia of Orthodox Christianity*, 375–76.

19. In the early fourth century, St. Paphnutius (also Paphnutius the Confessor) served as bishop in the Upper Thebaid in Egypt. He was a disciple of St. Anthony the Great of Egypt, and spent several years with him in the desert. He played a leading role in defending the faith against the Arian heresy at the first General Council of the Church at Nicea. He is celebrated on September 11 (Rev. Alban Butler, "St. Paphnutius, Bishop and Confessor," *The Lives of the Saints*, vol. 9: *September*, https://www.bartleby.com/210/9/112.html).

Part III. My Journey

1. Elena Men included here a song from a collection compiled by Mikhail Ivanovich Popov (1742–1790), a Russian dramatist, poet, writer, and opera librettist.

2. E. B.—The Righteous St. John of Kronstadt (1829–1909), canonized in 1990.

3. Fr. John of Kronstadt (1829–1909) served as a missionary in eastern Siberia. As a priest, he ministered to the poorest sections of the city, particularly reaching out to children, and he gave away many of his possessions. His diary *My Life in Christ* is a classic work of Russian Orthodox devotional literature. His healing ministry attracted large crowds and he earned a reputation as a miracle worker. He would become one of the most beloved priests in the Russian Orthodox Church, although near the end of his life, he became attracted to right-wing ideologies. The Orthodox Church elevated him to sainthood in 1990. See Nadieszda Kizenko's excellent biography, *A Prodigal Saint: Father John of Kronstadt* (University Park: Pennsylvania State University Press, 2000).

4. St. Fabiola (d. 399 A.D.) is venerated in the Roman Catholic Church. After the death of her second husband, Fabiola appeared before the gates of the Lateran Basilica in Rome in penitential clothes and asked for public forgiveness of her sins. Given full communion by Pope Siricius, she bestowed her wealth on the poor and sick, built a hospital in Rome, and ministered to her patients herself. Moving to Bethlehem, she placed herself under the guidance of St. Jerome to study the Scriptures. She is one of

the early female practitioners of medical science (Marilyn Bailey Ogilvie, *Women in Science: Antiquity through the Nineteenth Century. A Biographical Dictionary with Annotated Bibliography* [Cambridge, MA: MIT Press, 1986], 83–84).

5. Before the revolution and for nearly a decade afterwards, books on early Christianity written by Western historians were easily obtainable. Frederic William Farrar (1831–1903), an English cleric and schoolteacher, wrote *The Early Days of Christianity* (Na rassvete khristianstva, 1882), which is likely F. V. F., *Skvoz mrak k svetu, ili, na rassvete khristianstva (povest' iz vremen Neronovskogo goneniia na khristian)*, originally published in Russian in 1897, reissued in 1995, in St. Petersburg by Satis Press.

6. E. B.—Vera Iakovlevna Vasilevskaia.

7. Men refers to the painting by Mikhail Vasilevich Nesterov (1862–1942) of St. Sergii of Radonezh, part of a series. Nesterov attempted to depict the religious ideal of Russia, which he closely connected to nature and the bond between human beings and animals, a companionship that "makes nature rejoice." (See Galina Churak, "An Artist's Journey," Current Exhibition, *Galereia*, no. 1 [38] [2013] https://www.tretyakovgallerymagazine.com).

8. The Petrovskie Gates, a historical landmark in central Moscow, formerly guarded the city from outside attack.

9. Kaulbach's *Madonna*, which Men placed above her bed, was possibly by the German painter Friedrich August von Kaulbach (1850–1920), whose religious paintings and portraits of the imperial family of Tsar Nicholas II were prominent in Russia. Ivan Nikolaevich Khramskoi (1837–1887), one of the leaders of the *Peredvizhniki* (Wanderers), belonged to a group of artists who turned away from the Imperial Academy of Arts, portraying life not in some idealized form but as it actually existed. Khramskoi's *Christ in the Wilderness* (1872) or *Christ in the Desert* was one of his most significant paintings. It portrayed Christ dressed in a dark wrap, sitting on a stone and absorbed in thought, against a barren, rocky background. Khramskoi displayed a human Christ who was introspective, worried about the humanity he had been sent to save. Khramskoi painted this work during a transitional period in his life when he, too, searched for direction (Nonna Aleksandrovna Iakovleva, *Ivan Nikolaevich Kramskoi, 1837–1887* [Leningrad: Khudozhnik RSFSR, 1990], 35–36).

10. In the twelfth century, Sretenka served as Moscow's main thoroughfare, the road to the city of Vladimir and other cities in the northeast. In 1395, as Mongol forces advanced on Moscow, the icon of the Vladimir Mother of God was brought to Sretenka Street, and the people of Moscow came there to pray for deliverance. The Mongol troops were turned away from the city.

11. Grand Duke Konstantin Konstantinovich Romanov (1858–1915), the grandson of Emperor Nicholas I, was a poet, dramatist, talented pianist, and president of the Russian Academy of Sciences. He developed a close friendship with Pyotr Tchaikovsky, and translated Schiller and Goethe. *The King of the Jews: A Sacred Drama* (1914) is a four-act play set in Bethlehem portraying the life of Jesus. Much of the play was written in verse and illustrated two kinds of power: that displayed by Caesar and that exemplified by Christ. K. R., *Tsar iudeiskii: Drama v chetyrekh deistviiakh i piati kartinakh* (St. Petersburg: Tip. Sel'skogo Vestnika, 1914); English translation: *The King of the Jews: A Sacred Drama*, trans. Victor Emile Marsden (New York: Funk and Wagnalls, 1914).

12. Men refers to a biography of St. Eustace (d. 118 A.D.), by Mikhail Ivanovich Khitrov (1851–1899), an archpriest and historian and one of the most popular writers of his time. His biography told the story of the great Christian martyr, originally a Roman pagan general who became a Christian after having a vision during a hunt, in which he saw a crucifix between the antlers of a stag. He and his family were burned alive for refusing to renounce their faith. As a Christian martyr, St. Eustace became a popular saint through the medieval period, and his story was a common subject in medieval religious art. He is commemorated on September 20, in both the Eastern Orthodox and the Roman Catholic Churches ("The Life and Passion of the Holy Greatmartyr Eustacius [Eustace] Placidas, and of His Wife and Children," http//www.pravoslavie.ru/74099.html; "Saint Eustace," http:projects.mcah.columbia.edu/treasures of heaven/saints/Eustace.php).

13. Born in St. Petersburg, Aleksei Konstantinovich Tolstoy (1817–1875) was the second cousin of Leo Tolstoy. A childhood friend of the future Russian tsar Alexander II, he became one of his personal aides-de-camp. He published a poem called "The Sinner," and another, "John of Damascus," both of which Elena Men admired. He challenged many prevailing political trends of his times. He is the author of three historical dramas that have defined his legacy in Russian literature: *The Death of Ivan the Terrible*, *Tsar Fedor Ioannovich*, and *Tsar Boris*.

14. Semen Iakovlevich Nadson (b. 1862) published his first poem in the journal *Svet* at the age of fifteen. Critics commented on his idealism, sincerity, and civic consciousness. His ideal was Christ: "My God is the God of sufferers, the God stained with blood, the God of humanity and brotherhood." Admirers of his poems often put them to music. Nadson died of tuberculosis at the age of twenty-four. See B. K., "Nadson, Semen Iakovlevich," in *Russkii biograficheskii slovar'*, vol. 11, ed. A. A. Polovtsev et al. (St. Petersburg: Tip. Glavnogo upravleniia udelov, 1914), 35–38.

15. Mikhail Iurevich Lermontov (1814–1841), author of the novel *A Hero of Our Time*, also wrote three plays and more than three hundred poems. He was praised as Pushkin's successor. Adventurous, passionate, and heroic, Lermontov tried to free himself from what he considered the stifling world of the government and the strictures of the political order. The poems Elena Men sang were Lermontov's. His "Prayer: In a Difficult Moment of Life" was a confession of sin and a plea for cleansing and forgiveness (W. Bruce Lincoln, *Between Heaven and Hell: The Story of a Thousand Years of Artistic Life in Russia* [New York: Viking Penguin, 1998], 138–40). Nikolai Mikhailovich Iazykov (1803–1846) wrote poetry that in his day rivaled Pushkin's in popularity. He participated in the literary salons of Moscow and attended gatherings of Slavophile circles in the city. During the last years of his life, Iazykov devoted his poetry to religious subjects. He believed the heart of the Slavophile philosophy lay in the Orthodox Church and its contributions to the development of Russian civilization. He became an ideological enemy of Pyotr Chaadaev, whose admiration of Catholicism Iazykov found offensive to Russia's national pride (Ian K. Lilly, "N. M. Iazykov as a Slavophile Poet," *Slavic Review* 31, no. 4 [December 1972]: 797–804).

16. The Ust'inskii Bridge in Moscow is located where the Yauza flows into the Moscow River. It is a well-known site where, in 1883, the first metal bridge in the city was constructed.

17. E. B.—The niece of P. A. Florenskii.

18. The dense Briansk forests are a vast nature reserve, one of the last remaining in European Russia and significant for protecting and maintaining the dark green broadleaf foliage. The woodland contains a large assortment of wildlife, with numerous brown bear, elk, red deer, lynx, wild boar, and the Northern eagle owl. See "Nerusso-Desnianskoe-Polesie, UNESCO-MAB Biosphere Reserves Directory," at http:www.unesco.org/mabdb/br/brdir/directory/biores.asp?mode=all&code=RUS+23.

19. Orekhovo-Zuev, the city of Vladimir Men's workplace, was located in a wooded region east of Moscow. In Zuevo, the Old Believer merchant-entrepreneur Savva Morozov established his first silk factory. A center of the textile industry, Orekhovo elected one of the first Bolsheviks in Russia. See Document 64, "Memorandum from G. G. Yagoda to Leading OGPU Officials for Increasing the Intervention of OGPU Central Organs in Dekulakivization," January 24, 1930, in *The War against the Peasantry, 1927–1930: The Tragedy of the Soviet Countryside*, ed. Lynne Viola, V. P. Danilov, N. A. Ivnitskii, and Denis Kozlov, trans. Steven Shabad (New Haven: Yale University Press, 2005), 237.

20. During the reign of Tsar Nicholas I (1825–1855), recruits coming from the lower orders of Russian society served a term of twenty-five years in the army.

21. Elena wished to hold the wedding on Beautiful Hill (*Krasnaia Gorka*) Day, or St. Thomas Sunday, the Sunday after Easter, coming after the long break connected to Lent. Small hills in Russian are popularly referred to as "red hills" or "beautiful hills." Traditionally, on Beautiful Hill Day, "spring is invited into the land." This day marked the beginning of a series of weddings. An old Russia proverb states that "Whoever marries on *Krasnaia Gorka* will never divorce" ("Red Hill Festival—Traditional Russian Krasnaya Gorka," https://color-mir.com/red-hill-festival-traditional-russian-krasnaya-gorka/).

22. Men's apartment was in central Moscow, in Kozhevniki, the old tannery district, twenty to thirty minutes on foot from the Kremlin.

23. Men's dacha was located at Tomilino, then a small settlement southeast of Moscow and easily reachable by railroad.

24. Simon the Canaanite, also known as Simon the Apostle or Simon the Zealot, lived in the first century A.D. and was one of the twelve apostles. After witnessing Jesus's first miracle of turning water into wine, he became a fervent follower of Christ, and according to tradition, proclaimed the Gospel of Christ widely, traveling from Britain to the Black Sea. The cave of Simon the Canaanite to which Elena Men referred is in Abkhazia, Georgia.

25. Tarasovka is a town on the Iaroslavskaia railroad line, between Moscow and Sergiev Posad. Ironically, it was in Tarasovka that Father Aleksandr Men would serve as a priest from 1964 to 1970, a significant period in the formation of his priesthood. See Wallace L. Daniel, *Russia's Uncommon Prophet: The Life and Times of Father Aleksandr Men* (DeKalb: Northern Illinois University Press, 2016), 107–15.

26. Losinka is the colloquial name for the Losinoostrovskii district of Moscow.

27. Men's reference here was to Leo Tolstoy, who had a low opinion of doctors and modern medicine.

28. The healthy child to whom Elena referred was her son Pavel (Pavlik), born in 1938, the younger brother of Aleksandr Men.

29. The Day of the Annunciation celebrates the angel Gabriel's visit to the Virgin Mary, in which he told her that she would be the Mother of Jesus Christ. The Church celebrates the Holy Feast of the Annunciation on March 25.

30. For the prayer "Victorious Leader," see Part 1.

31. E. B.—A village near Zagorsk.

32. For St. Nicholas's Day, see Part 1. Elena Men connects this date to December 19, because that date would be December 6 according to the Julian calendar.

33. Men's reference to the "other side of the line" was probably to the evacuation line in Zagorsk, established by the authorities during the Second World War.

34. E. B.—She has in mind M. V. Tepnina.

35. The troparion Elena Semenovna sings is related to the Icon of the Mother of God *Surety of Sinners*, against despondency, on which is the inscription, "I am the Surety of Sinners for My Son Who has entrusted Me to hear them, and those who bring Me the joy of hearing them will receive eternal joy through Me." In the troparion, as well as on the icon, the Mother of God extends her saving hand in help and in God's promise of forgiveness. See http://andronicus-athanasia.org/suretyofsinners.html.

36. E B.—Fr. Nikolai Golubtsov.

37. Father Nikolai Aleksandrovich Golubtsov (1900–1960) played a significant role in the Men family. A priest with wide-ranging intellectual views, he spent the first part of his professional career as a scientist. From his parish near the historic Danilov Monastery in Moscow, he reached out both to the poor and to members of the Russian intelligentsia, whom the Orthodox Church had mostly ignored. In his teaching and service to the Church, Golubtsov transcended educational and social boundaries, an example that deeply impressed the young Aleksandr Men and the members of his family. See I. K. Iazykova, "Dobryi pastyr'—Otets Nikolai Golubtsov," in *Tserkovnaia zhizn' XX veka: Protoierei Aleksandr Men' i ego dukhovnye nastavniki. Sbornik materialov Pervoi nauchnoi konferentsii "Menevskie chteniia" (9–11 sentiabria 2006 g.)*, ed. M. V. Grigorenko (Sergiev Posad: Izdanie prikhoda Sergievskoi tserkvi v Semkhoze, 2007), 139–48; and Daniel, *Russia's Uncommon Prophet*, 98–100.

38. The Pokrovskii Women's Monastery is one of Kiev's primary spiritual and architectural attractions. Aleksandra Petrovna Romanova founded the monastery in January 1889 and took monastic vows there under the name Anastasia. Her love for the poor and the suffering earned her the name of the Great Matryoshka (Mother), and people came in large numbers to the monastery to seek medical help and spiritual succor. Closed in 1923 and reopened in 1941, from 1945 to 1948 the monastery maintained a hospital for wounded soldiers. See http://www.sestry.ru/eng/content/bip/05/089.

Appendix. Childhood and Youth

1. Leonid Nikolaevich Andreev's play *Anathema*, written in 1909, portrayed the Devil standing at the gates of eternity. He pleaded for the silent guardian at the gates' entrance to allow him a look inside and observe the mysteries. Denied this opportunity, he returned to earth, vowing to corrupt the soul of a poor Jewish shopkeeper. See Lawrence Senelick, "Interpretations and Reinterpretations: Jews in Fashion at the Moscow Art Theater," in *Jews and Theater in an Intercultural Context*, ed. Edna Nahshon (Leiden: Brill, 2012), 219–42.

2. Chistye (Clean) Ponds is a large body of water located on the Boulevard Ring, in one of Moscow's prestigious neighborhoods.

3. St. Elijah's Day is the day of the Church's celebration of the prophet Elijah, on August 2.

4. Vasilevskaia's teacher had the class learn to make comparisons and to think more deeply by using Alexander Pushkin's novel in verse, *Eugene Onegin*.

5. Vasilevskaia recalled the changes made in Russian schools under the direction of Lev Aristidovich Kasso, who served as imperial minister of education from 1910 to 1914 and viewed Russian universities as hotbeds of revolutionary activity. He favored the expansion of technical institutes, often at the expense of Russia's most prestigious educational institutions, and ended the practice of having professors train and designate their successors, transferring this role to the Ministry of Education. By bringing the Russian professoriate more directly under the government's supervision, he intended to quell dissent in Russian universities, but his educational policies exacerbated it. Kasso's reforms reached down to the primary and secondary schools, seeking to curtail local autonomy, impose strict discipline, and return to traditional methods of education, all of which aimed at fostering greater government control. See Nikolai Vasil'evich Speranskii, *Krizis russkoi shkoly: Torzhestvo politicheskoi reaktsii. Krushenie universiteta* (Moscow: I. N. Kushnerev, 1914), 128–30; Alexander Vucinich, *Science in Russian Culture, 1861–1917* (Stanford, CA: Stanford University Press, 1970), 197–98, 216, 379; and Vladimir Nikolaevich Kokovtsev, *Out of My Past: The Memoirs of Count Kokovtsev, Minister of Finance, 1904–1914, Chairman of the Council of Ministers, 1911–1914*, ed. H. H. Fisher, trans. Laura Matveev (Stanford, CA: Stanford University Press, 1935), 350, 367, 446.

6. Vasilevskaia's scornful mention of the language of the "colorful, clumsy rattles" at the bazaar alludes to the rough, coarse speech of Vladimir Mitrofanovich Purishkevich (1870–1920), an ultranationalist, antisemitic, Bessarabian thug. Purishkevich served as a spokesperson for the Union of Russian People, a loose conglomeration of nobles, shopkeepers, and intellectuals attempting to rally support for the monarchy and the fatherland. Purishkevich was one of the main participants in the murder of Grigorii Rasputin. See Stephen Shenfield, *Russian Fascism: Tradition, Tendencies, and Movements* (Armonk, NY: M. E. Sharpe, 2001).

7. E. B.—The Roman World in Pictures.

8. The textbook Vasilevskaia has in mind was written by Robert Iur'evich Wipper (1859–1954), a historian who wrote many books on Russian ancient and medieval history. Easy to read, action-filled, and somewhat superficial in their presentation, his books were supported by both the tsarist and the Soviet establishments. Wipper's revised edition of *Ivan the Terrible* received glowing praise from Soviet reviewers and was translated into English for the benefit of foreign readers. In 1945, the Party awarded Wipper the Order of Lenin.

9. E. B.—A. S. Khomiakov.

10. S. N. instilled in Vasilevskaia knowledge of a wide range of historical and artistic figures. Vladimir Monomakh (1053–1125), the grand prince of Kievan Rus', founded the city of Vladimir, which eventually became the capital of Russia, prior to the "gathering of the Russian lands" by the city of Moscow. He wrote an *Instruction* to his children, which laid out a series of reforms calling for help to the poor, protection of orphans and widows, abolition of capital punishment, and prevention

of the powerful from oppressing the powerless; his *Instruction* helped alleviate social conflict in Kievan Rus'. Iuliana Lazarevskaia, also known as Iuliana of Murom (1533–1584), was the daughter of a nobleman and servitor of the tsar. She represents a "saintly precursor of many a long-suffering, kenotic character of modern Russian literature, whether female, like Dostoevsky's [Sonya] Marmeladova, or aristocratic, like Tolstoy's Father Sergius" (Julia Alissandratos, "New Approaches to the Problem of Identifying the Genre of the Life of Julijana Lazarevskaja," *Cyrillomethodianum* 7 [1983]: 242). This account of Iuliana Lazarevskaia is informed by Alissandratos, "New Approaches," 235–44; and T. A. Greenan, "Iulianiya Lazarevskaya," *Oxford Slavonic Papers* 15 [1982]: 28–45). In Greek mythology, the story of Niobe provides a warning to all mortals about the sin of pride and the consequences of comparing oneself to the gods. Philemon and Baucis were an elderly couple in Greek and Roman mythology who welcomed Zeus and Hermes, disguised as peasants, into their home; given one wish, they said they wanted to die together, and in death they were transformed into an intertwining oak and linden tree (*Ovid's Metamorphoses: Books 6–10*, ed., with introduction and commentary, William S. Anderson, Book 8 [Norman: University of Oklahoma Press, 1972], 98–101, 389–400; Thomas Bulfinch, *Bulfinch's Mythology: The Age of Fable, the Age of Mythology, and the Legends of Charlemagne* [New York: Thomas A. Crowell, 1970], 49–52).

11. Yasnaya Polyana (Bright Glade) refers to Tolstoy's ancestral home, to which he returned after his marriage to Countess Sophia Andreevna Behr. At Yasnaya Polyana, Tolstoy wrote *War and Peace* (1862–1869) and *Anna Karenina* (1873–1877). Here, too, he received many of Russia's leading cultural and artistic figures.

12. Vasilevskaia has in mind Arthur Drews (1865–1935), a prominent German philosopher and historian who wrote books on religion and the ancient world. His best-known work was *Die Christusmythe* (The Christ Myth [1905]). Embraced by Lenin, the book was translated into Russian. Christ as myth became a cardinal feature of Soviet teaching about religion that lasted well beyond the Second World War.

13. E. B.—"I have become all things to all people, that I might by all means save some" (I Corinthians 9:22).

Index

Page numbers in italics indicate a photograph.

Afanasii, Bishop (Sakharov), xxxvi–xxxviii, 87, 118, 180nn75–76, 181n83, 191n7, 192n17
Agafangel, Metropolitan, xxiii, 174n20
Aleksii, Patriarch, xxxvi, 87, 190n6
Alfeyev, Hilarion, 187n57
Amvrosii, Elder, xxvii, xxviii, 134
Anathema (Andreev), 138, 196n1
Andreev, Leonard, 138
"Anti-Soviet Church Underground," 179n71, 192n17
Apostle John, 25, 185n33
Apostle Paul, 9–10, 13, 19, 122, 163, 198n13
Apostle Peter, 71, 83, 168
arrests and imprisonment, xxii, xxxvi, xxxviii
    Afanasii, Bishop (Sakharov), 182n83
    Gabriianik, Aleksei Ivanovich, 180n73
    Ieraks, Fr. Ieromonakh, xxxix, 86, 179n71, 182n86
    Kriuchkov, Dmitrii Ivanovich, 180n74
    Krivolutskii, Vladimir V., 180n72
    Mechev, Fr. Aleksei, 183n4
    Mechev, Fr. Sergei, 183n4
    Pyotr, Fr. (Shipkov), xxxi, 86, 179n70
    Pyotr, Metropolitan, 178n60
    Serafim, Fr., xxvi, xxxvii
    Tikhon, Patriarch, xxi, xxxiv, 178n59
    Vasilevskaia, Volodia, 123
    Voino-Iasenetskii, Archbishop Luk, 181n78
Arzamas, 45–46, 187n53
Avgusta Germanovna (A.G.), 145, 154–55

Balaklava, 140
baptism
    at Baptist Church, 107
    Elena and Alik, 117
    Elena's promise, 103
    L'vovna, Inna, 103
    sign of the cross and, 14
    Vera's family members, 74, 83
    Vera's thoughts on, 1, 13
Baratynskii, Evgenii Abramovich, 19, 184n25
Batiukov, Sergei Mikhailovich. *See* Serafim, Fr.
Blok, Aleksandr Aleksandrovich, 60, 188n64
Bocharev, Ivan Matveevich. *See* Ieraks, Fr. Ieromonakh
Bogdanov, Vladimir, xxxvi
Bogonosets, Ignatius, 93–94, 191n14
Bolsheviks, xx–xxii, xxix, xxxiv, 158, 177nn56–57, 185n40, 186n48
Bolshevo, xxxix, 17, 38, 40, 120, 184n22
Bonaparte, Napoleon, xx
Borovsk, xxxix, 91–93, 97, 179n70, 191n12
Brianchaninov, Bishop Ignatius, 89
Briansk forests, 112, 195n18
Brothers Karamazov, The (Dostoevsky), xvi, xxviii, 108, 116
Bulgakov, Sergei Nikolaevich, 180n78

catacomb churches, xxii–xxiv, xxxiii, xxxvi–xxxvii, 30, 179n69
"catacombs" (*katakomby*), definition of, xxii
Chelpanov, Georgii Ivanovich, 2, 182n3
Chichagov, Leonid Mikhailovich, 186n50
Childhood Years of Mozart, The (Avenarius), 149
Chistye [Clean] Ponds, 141, 197n2
Chrysostom, John, 89, 91–92, 183n18
churches
    Annunciation Church, 127
    Church of Christ the Savior, 167
    Church of the Holy Savva, 180n74
    Church of the Martyr St. John the Warrior, 131

200 INDEX

churches (*continued*)
  Church of the Nativity of John the Baptist, 181n80
  Church of the Resurrection of Christ, xxxvii, 181nn79–80, 181n80
  Church of the Sacred Martyrs Cyril and John, xxvi, xxxvii–xxxviii, 23, 25, 179nn71–72, 180nn73–74
  Church of the Sacred Nicholas, 101
  Church of the Trinity in the Leaves, 108
  Kazan' Cathedral, 24, 184n29
  Moscow Nikitskaia Church, 179n70
  Mournful Mother of God Church, 131
  Nikolo-Khamovnicheskaia Church, 131
  St. Nicholas the Wonderworker Church, 183n4
  Znamenskaia Church, 179n72
Church Slavonic language, 107–8
churchwarden (*starosta*), 91, 97
Civil War, effect on children, 183n6
"Clergy and Faithful of the Patriarchate of Moscow, The," xxii, 178nn61–62
confessions, 33, 86–87
  See also Serafim, Fr.; Vasilevskaia, Vera Iakovlevna
Confessions, The (Augustine), 109
Country of the Long Night, The, 139
Crimea, 20, 44, 140, 181n78
Crucifixions and Crucifixes, 23–24, 51, 103, 117

Danilov Monastery, 173n14, 196n37
Dawn of Christianity, The (Farrar), 104
death and burial rites, *panikhida* for the departed, 99–100, 192n18
Delektorskii, Fr. Dmitrii, xxxvii, 181n80
Die Christusmythe (Drews), 198n12
Diveevo, 45–46, 51–54, 56, 175n28
Diveevo Chronicle (*Diveevskaia letopis'*) (Chichagov), 43, 186n50
Diveevo Monastery, xxvi, xxxviii, 47, 55, 77, 175n28, 181n81, 187n56
  underground springs, 48, 50–52
Dmitrii, Fr. (Kriuchkov), xxxvi, xxxvii, 86, 180n74
Don Carlos, 139
Dostoevsky, Fyodor, xxvii, xxviii, 7, 98, 108
Drews, Arthur, 198n12

Eckhart, Meister, 2
Egorov, Prof., 97–98, 191n16
"eternal memory," 63

Eucharist (Sacred Mystery), xxxiv, 23, xxxiv168, 184n27
Eugene Onegin (Pushkin), 146, 197n4

Fabiola, 104
Fabiola, St., 192n4
farms, state (*sovkhozy*), 47, 187n55
farms, collective (*kolkhozy*), 54, 187n61
Farrar, Frederic William, 104, 193n5
Filaret, Metropolitan, 175n26
Florenskii, Fr. Pavel Alexandrovich, 61, 188n69
food
  cottage cheese (*tvorog*), 129
  shchi (cabbage soup), 127
  solianka (spicy soup), 16, 184n19
Fudel', Iosif, 175n29
Fudel', Sergei Iosifovich, xxvi, 175n29
FZU schools, 50, 187n59

Gabriianik, Aleksei Ivanovich, xxxvi, 180n73
Germanovich, Viktor (V.G). *See* Rikman, Viktor Germanovich (V.G)
Gershenzon, Isaac Il'ich Levitan, 75, 189n74
Gershenzon, Mikhail Osipovich, 75, 189n74
Glinkovo, 65, 123
Glinskaia Pustyn', 93–94, 134–35, 191n15
Gogol, Nikolai Vasilievich, xxvii, 60, 188n65
Gospels
  Elena and, 79–80, 108, 112, 131
  Fr. Serafim and, 33, 74, 99
  Sergei Nikolaevich and, 159
  study of, 2
  Vera and, 6, 165, 167–68
Gospels, John, 28
Gospels, Luke, 80, 124–25
Gospels, Paul, 13
Great Canon of St. Andrew of Crete, 27, 185n34
Great Martyr Barbara, 9, 183n13
Grigorenko, Fr. Viktor, xxx
Grishanova, Kseniia Ivanovna (Susanna), 58, 77–80, 83, 86, 125–27, 186n51

Halfin, Igal, 177n53
Hellbeck, Jochen, 177n53
Higher Ecclesiastical Administration (VTsU), xxxiv
holidays and holy days
  All-Russian Saints Day, 64, 66
  Day of the Annunciation, 122, 196n29
  Day of the Holy Spirit, 98
  Day of the White Daisy, 150

INDEX 201

Dormition Fast, 37, 185n44
Easter, 15, 31, 34, 80, 129, 149
Entrance into the Church of the Most
  Holy Mother of God, 75, 189n75
Hanukkah, 139–40
Holiday of the Annunciation, 30, 185n39
Ignatius of Antioch, 93–94, 191n14
Jewish holidays, 139
Lent, 14, 34, 77–78, 113–14, 118, 129
Palm Sunday bazaar, 149
Passion Week, 30–31, 34
Passover, 14
St. Elijah's Day, 143, 197n3
St. Nicholas's Day, 46, 124, 186n52, 196n32
St. Thomas Sunday (*Krasnaia Gorka*), 113, 195n21
Yom Kippur, 140
Holy Canal of the Theotokos (*kanavka*), 47, 187n56
Hymns of Divine Eros (Simeon), 187n57

Iaroslavl', xxiii
Iazykov, Nikolai Mikhailovich, 109, 194n15
icons, xxv, xxxviii, 6, 43, 61, 186n49
  Holy Martyr Faith, 53, 55, 187n60
  Icon of the Three Hierarchs, 16, 183n18
  Joy of All Who Sorrow, 38
  Mother of God, 22–24, 55, 126, 181n82, 186n45, 188n62, 193n10
  Our Lady of Kazan', 184n29
  Serafim, St. of Sarov, 25, 54
  Sergii, St., 25
  Tenderness Icon, 25, 184n31
Ieraks, Fr. Ieromonakh (Bocharev), xxxvi, 32, 179n71
  church service in the forest, 37
  communion, 87
  Elena and, 30
  in Bolshevo, xxxix, 38
  in Maloiaroslavets, 36
  in Losinka, 120, 182n86
  Pavel's baptism, 40, 122
  Vera and, xxxi, 33
Ignatius of Antioch. *See* Bogonosets, Ignatius
Il'in, Ivan Aleksandrovich, 2–3, 182n2
Innokentii, Hegumen, 174n19
Institute of Mental and Physical Disabilities, 11, 81, 182n87
Iosif, Metropolitan (Petrovykh), xxiii–xxiv

Jewish population, WWII and, 71
Joachim, Patriarch, 186n45, 189n75
John, St. of Kronstadt, 103, 192nn2–3
Judaism, 17, 139–42
  See also Rebeka Abramovna

Kaliazin, 16–17, 184n21
Karpov, Georgii Georgievich, 179n66
Kasso, Lev Aristidovich, 148, 197n5
Katia, 12, 16–17, 118, 120, 122
Kaulbach, Friedrich August von, 108, 193n9
Kedrov, Fr. John (Ivan), xxxvii, 181n79
Kenworthy, Scott, 175n26, 184n28
Khar'kov, xxx, 103–4, 107–8, 160, 167
Khitrov, Mikhail Ivanovich, 194n12
Khomiakov, Aleksei Stepanovich, 90, 191n10
Khramskoi, Ivan Nikolaevich, 108, 193n9
Khrushchev, Nikita, xxxvi, 179n67
King of the Jews, The (Romanov), 109, 193n11
Kireevskii, Pyotr, xxvii
Kislovodsk, 167
Kliuchevskii, Vasily Osipovich, xxv, 66, 189n71
Korneeva, Vera Alekseevna, 179n71, 182n86
Krasnitskii, Vladimir Dmitrievich, xxi, 174n15
Kriuchkov, Dmitrii. *See* Dmitrii, Fr. (Kriuchkov)
Krivolutskii, Vladimir V., xxxvi, 179n72, 186n46
Krupskaia, Nadezhda Konstantinovna, 43, 186n49
Kseniia Ivanovna Grishanova (K.I.). *See* Mariia, Mother Superior
Kupriianova, Tat'iana Ivanovna (T.K.), 19, 82, 98, 184n24, 190n2

labor camps and prisons, xxxix, 186n46
  Mariinskii labor camp, 179n71
  Rybinsii (Volzhskii) labor camp, 192n17
  Siblag labor camp, 179n70
  Temkinsk labor camp, 180n73
Lake Seliger, 8–9, 183nn9–10
Lavra of St. Sergii. *See* Trinity-Sergiev Lavra
Lazarevskaia, Iuliana (Iuliana of Murom), 158, 198n10
Lenin, Vladimir Il'ich, xx, 180n78, 186n49
Lenochka. *See* Men, Elena Semenovna (Lenochka)
Leonid, elder (Nagolkin), xxvii
Lermontov, Mikhail Iurevich, 109, 194n15
"Liturgy of the Pre-Sanctified Gifts," 30, 185n37

INDEX

Living Church, xvi, xxi, xxxiv, 174n15, 177n57
Luke, Archbishop, 81, 190n1

Maikov, Apollon Nikolaevich, 191n13
Makarii, Fr., xxvii, 176n34
Maloiaroslavets, 36–37, 39, 185
Mariia, Mother Agafonika, 134
Mariia, Mother (Matrena Fedorovna, Diveevo nun), 49–54
Mariia, Mother Superior
  Alik and, xxvii
  Opina elders and, xxix
  spiritual mentor, 190n3
  spiritual questions to, 85–86
  Tonia and, 110
  Vera and, 83, 86, 126, 134
  visit by Polia, 45
Markova, Mariia, xxx
maroseiki (members of the Mechevs' parish community), 3, 183n4
Marxism, 158, 180n78, 186n49
Matrona Fedorovna, 49–54
Mechev, Archpriest Aleksei, xxxviii, 182n84, 183n4
Mechev, Archpriest Sergii, 182n84
Mechev, Fr. Aleksei, 3, 183n4
"Meditations on the Divine Liturgy," (Gogol), 60, 188n65
Mel'gunova, Agafiia Semenovna, 175n28
Men, Elena Semenovna (Lenochka)
  about, 183n8
  antireligious atmosphere, 110
  baptism of, 10, 103, 117
  Baptists and, 107–8
  called Sister by Vera, 10, 183n16, 191n9
  Christian leanings, 110, 114–15
  communion of, 118, 120
  dream of Fr. Serafim, 79–80
  early years, xxix–xxx
  education of, 105–6
  family of, xix
  family's response to Elena's Christianity, 107–8
  Fr. Nikolai Golubtsov and, 196nn36–37
  Fr. Pyotr and, 125, 128–29
  Fr. Serafim and, 116, 118, 120, 124
  in Glinkovo, 123, 196n31
  grandmother of, 101–3, 115
  health issues, 105, 120–21
  husband of, 62, 72
  Judaism of, 103
  Khar'kov Construction Technical College, 107
  Lenten customs, 114
  in Losinka, 30, 33, 39, 120
  marriage of, 7, 113–14
  Mental and Physical Disabilities' Section, 130–33
  in Moscow, 104, 107–8, 120, 130
  mother of, 101–2, 107
  new baby baptism, 10
  Optina Pystyn' Monastery travel, 112
  photograph of, *105–6, 111, 119*
  prayers to be said, 117–18
  pregnancy and birth, 115, 120–21
  religious education, 101–2
  Serafim, Fr. and, 31
  Soviet era life, xxxi–xxxii
  in Tarasovka, 16, 120, 195n25
  in Tomilino, 115, 118, 195n23
  Tonia and, 115–16
  trip to Moscow, 19
  tuberculosis and pregnancy, 36
  at Vera's baptism, 23
  Verochka and, 108, 115–16, 118, 128
  work of, 107–8, 110, *121,* 123
  in Zagorsk, 76, 126–28
  See also Men, Fr. Aleksandr (Alik); Vasilevskii, Iakov Veniaminovich
Men, Fr. Aleksandr (Alik)
  baptism, 10, 115–17
  birth of, 115
  in church, 39, 87
  communion of, 118
  confessions, 72–73
  conversion to Christianity, xvi
  Elena and, 39–40, 59, 115
  Elena's son, xix
  fear of war, 64
  on Fr. Serafim's death, 79–80, 125
  future career, 126
  grandmother and, 14, 121
  health issues, 33
  Lent and, 72
  Mother Superior Mariia and, xxvii, 86
  Optina Pystyn' influence, xxix
  Pavel Florenskii lecture, 188n69
  schooling, 122, 128, 131
  in Sverdlovsk, 72
  toboggan experience, 127
  with Uncle Iasha, 37
  Vera, 33, 62, 120
  in Zagorsk, 65
Men, Pavel Vol'fovich (Pavlik), xxx, 40, *93,* 104, 115, 121–22, 131, 195n28
Men, Vladimir Grigor'evich (Volodia), 62, 72, 112–14, 117, 120–24, *121,* 132

INDEX

Miller, David, 175n26
Miracle of the Pyramids of Ancient Countries, The, 149
"Moi put'" (My Journey)(Iakovlevskaia), xxxi
monasteries. *See* Danilov Monastery; Diveevo Monastery; Glinskaia Pustyn'; Optina Pystyn' Monastery; Pokrovskii Monastery; Sarovskaia Pustyn'; Trinity-Sergiev Lavra
Monomakh, Vladimir, 158, 197n10
Mordovian Autonomous Republic, 49–50
Morozov, Savva, 195n19
Moscow (Kozhevniki district), 114, 195n22
Moscow (Losinka district), 30–31, 33–34, 39, 120, 179, 182n86, 185n38, 195n26
Moscow (Sokol'niki district), xxxvii, 181, 181n79
Moscow (Ust'inskii Bridge), 110, 194n16

Nadezhda Nikolaevna, 87
Nadson, Semen Iakovlevich, 109, 194n14
Nastia, 45, 47, 49, 53
Nektarius, Optina Elder, xxvi, xxxviii, 33, 182n85, 185n40
Nesterov, Mikhail Vasilevich, 105, 193n7
New Testament, 85, 87, 101, 103
Nicodemus, 183n17
nightingale song, 18, 62, 184n23
Nikolaevan soldier, 113, 195n20
Nikon, Patriarch, 181n82
Nilus-Stolobenskaia Pustyn', 8, 183n10, 183n11
Niobe, story of, 198n10

Old Testament, 10, 101–2, 144, 165, 183n15
Olia (nanny), 122–23
On the Floating Pieces of Ice, 139
Optina Pystyn' Monastery
  Dostoevsky and, xxviii
  history of, xxvii, 176n34
  influence of elders, xxvi, xxix, xxxviii, 183n4
  Men visit, 112–13
  peacefulness of, 50
  Soviet closure, xxvii
  Soviets' closure of, 185n40
  trips by Vera and Elena, xvi
  Vasilevskaia visit, 7, 110, 183n7
Orbis Pictus Romanus, 153–54, 197n7
Orekhovo-Zuev, 112, 195n19
Osipova, Irina, xxiii–xxiv
Our World, 152

Paert, Irina, xxvii
Pankratov, Natasha and Serezha, 16

Paphnutius, St., 100, 192n19
Petrovskie Gates, 107–8, 193n8
pictures and paintings
  Blessing of the Children, The, 6
  Christ in the Wilderness (Khramskoi), 108
  destroyed church with mural, 127
  "Jesus among the Wheatfields," 24, 184n30
  Madonna (Kaulbach), 108
  Youth of St. Sergii, The (Nesterov), 105
  Pillar and Ground of Truth, The (Florenskii), 188n69
poetry
  "Carolers," 102
  "Christian [Woman]" (Nadson), 109
  Christian influence, 157
  "John of Damascus" (A.K. Tolstoy), 109
  "Palm Saturday" (*Verbnaia subbota*), 75
  "Reflections," 102
  religion and, 60
  "Sinner" (A.K. Tolstoy), 109
  "Song of Hiawatha," 128
  See also Blok, Aleksandr Aleksandrovich; Pushkin, Alexander; Rilke, Rainer Maria; Tiutchev, Fedor Ivanovich; Zhukovskii, Vasilii Andreevich
Pokrovskii Monastery, 134, 196n38
Polia, 45, 47
Popov, Mikhail Ivanovich, 102, 192n1
prayers
  akathist to St. Nicholas, 46, 76
  akathist to St. Serafim, 51
  Akathist to the Passion of Christ, 74
  Canon to the Mother of God "Distressed by Many Temptations," 62–63, 189n70
  hymns of all Twelve Holiday Feasts, 131
  Jesus prayer, 127
  "Lord and Master . . .," 29
  "Lord's Prayer," 10
  Mary, Mother of God, 76
  Savior, 76
  Symbol of Faith (Nicene Creed), 8–10, 23, 87, 183n12
  Theotokos "Surety of Sinners," 10, 131, 183n14, 196n35
  "Victorious Leader" (*Vzbrannaia Voevoda*), 67, 123, 189n72
  "Your Lamb Faith," 21
"Protocols of the Elders of Zion," 35, 185n42
Purishkevich, Vladimir Mitrofanovich, 149, 197n6
Pushkin, Alexander, 39, 146, 197n4

INDEX

Pyotr, Fr. (Shipkov)
  arrest of, xxxi, 86
  bookkeeper, 81
  burial services, 83–84, 92
  catacomb priest, xxxviii, 179n70
  church repair, 94
  communion, 87
  confessions, 91, 93–94
  Deus caritatis (God of compassion), 90, 191n11
  Easter service, 89
  Fr. Serafim and, 79–80
  health issues and death of, 91, 94
  letters from, 84–85, 88–90, 94–96
  liturgy and, 92–93
  Moscow region, xxxvi
  spiritual children of, 86
  spiritual father after Fr. Serafim, 81
  spiritual joy of, 90–93
  spiritual questions to, 85–86
  Vera and, 63, 83
Pyotr, Metropolitan (Polianskii)
  arrest of, 178n60
  cannonized, 178n62
  health issues and death of, 96–100

Quo Vadis (Senkevich), 103

Ragozina, Nataliia Leonidovna, 182n86
Rebeka Abramovna, 138–40
Renovationists
  council (sobor) of, 178n59
  coup against church leadership, xxi, xxii
  history of, 178nn58–59
  IPKh opposition, 174n22
  liquidated by Stalin, xxxvi
  political platform, xxxiv
  Renovationist Schism, xxiv, xxxiv, 177n57, 182n83
  Renovationists' declaration of loyalty, xxii
  response by church leaders, xxxv
  WWII and, 81
  See also Living Church
Rikman, Viktor Germanovich (V.G)
  death of, 171
  double life, 162
  on the eternal soul, 163–64
  health issues, 169
  Iasha and, 160, 169
  in Khar'kov, 168
  kindness of, 166
  music and, 165
  philosophy discussion, 165
  photograph of, *161*

prayers and religion of, 161–62, 165–66, 170
  schooling, 160, 162
  sinfulness, 162, 166
  travel of, 163
  Vera and, 163, 168
  youth and background, 160
Rilke, Rainer Maria, 49
Romanov, Konstantin Konstantinovich, 109, 182n86, 193n11
Russian Orthodox Church
  All-Russian Sobor (Council), xxxiii, 177n56
  anathema on Russian government, xxi
  associations (*avtokefalii*) of bishops, xxxvi, 179n68
  control by the state, 179n66
  elders in, xxvii–xxviii
  factions within, xxiii
  independent association (*avtokefalii*), xxxvi
  post-Civil War history, xx, xxxiv
  prerevolutionary years, xxxiii
  Sergianskaia line, 178n64
  See also Renovationists
Russian Orthodoxy, *starchestvo*, elder and acolyte, xvi
Russian Revolution, 138

saints
  exhumation of, 43, 186n48
  podvig (spiritual feat), xv
Sakharov, Sergei Grigorevich. *See* Afanasii, Bishop (Sakharov)
Sarov, xvi, 25, 43–46, 48–49, 51–53, 55, 60, 175n28, 187n58
Sarovskaia Pustyn', 44, 49, 52, 55
Savel'evna (nun), 126
School Comrades, 139
schools and schooling (Vera)
  changes in Russian education, 148, 197n5
  Easter holiday, 149
  French class, 145, 154–57
  German class, 146
  grammar school, 144–45, 148–49, 152–54, 160
  mathematics class, 151–52
  natural history class, 146–47
  Russian class, 146, 152, 157–58
  science class, 151
  singing class, 147–48
  state grammar school, 154
Senkevich, Genrik, 104
Serafim, Fr.
  Aleksei Ivanovich Gabriianik and, 180n73
  Archimandrite of Moscow region, xxxvi

INDEX

avoiding arrest, xxxviii
chrysanthemums and, 20
at Church of the Sacred Martyrs Cyril and John, xxxvii
coffin, treatment of, 190n4
confessions, 15–16, 25, 35
"consciousness of death," 58, 60
death of, 77–80, 124–25
early life, xxv–xxvi, xxxvii, 41
education and, 39
forget "Protocols of the Elders of Zion," 35–36
guidance of, 1
health issues, 72–73, 75–77
holiness or righteous, 24
house of, *11*
inquisitiveness of, 62
Katia and, 16–17, 117, 120, 122–23
letter to Natasha, 60–61
life of, xxxi
name and secrecy, 180n77
Optina Pustyn' guidance, xxxviii
parable of the mite, 19
photograph of, *xlii*
prayers for Vera's family, 69
religious calling, xxvi, xxxvii
resistance to Soviet government, xxvi
services in the catacombs, 28–30
spiritual children of, xxxviii, 16, 25, 30–31, 57–58, 63–65, 79
"suffering Russian power," 56
traditional eldership of, xxxviii
on value of work, 61
worker anecdote, 57
See also under Vasilevskaia, Vera Iakovlevna
Serafim, Fr., letters
accepting and understanding, 17
apostle Paul and flowers of the forests, 9
Christ as a Helmsman, 8
Christ Child in your heart, 8
Lenten letter, 14, 25–27
prayers over new baby, 10
written for Tonia, 7, 9
Serafim, St. of Sarov, xxvi, 25, 42–44, 51–54, 184n31, 186nn47–48, 186n50
Serafim Sarovskii. See Serafim, St. of Sarov
Sereda, Natasha, 60, 188n67
Sergei Nikolaevich (S.N.), 157–60, 197n10
Sergiev Posad. *See* Zagorsk (Sergiev Posad)
Sergii, Metropolitan (Stragorodskii), xxii–xxvi, xxxv–xxxvi, xxxviii, 174n19, 178nn60–61, 178nn64–66, 180n72, 180n74
Sergii, St. of Radonezh, xxiv–xxv, 23, 186n48, 189n71, 193n7
Shkarovskii, Mikhail, xxii, 174n17
Simeon the New Theologian, 48, 187n57
Simon the Canaanite, 195n24
Solianka Street, xxxvii
Solov'ev, Vladimir, xxvii–xxviii
songs
"Alleluia, O Give Thanks," 28
"The Angel," 109
"Baby Jesus Had a Garden," 104
"Christ Is Risen," 28, 33
"In a Difficult Minute of Life" (Lermontov), 109, 194n15
"Eule, Eule, Eule, was siehst du mich so an?" 146
"Helper and Protector," 99
"Helpmate and Protector, Be My Salvation," 78, 190n79
"Holy God," 28, 99
"Hop, hop, hop, Pferdchen lauf gallop," 146
"If I were a small brook," 145
"Lord, Have Mercy," 28
"My Soul Glorifies the Lord," 108
"Now Our Sea . . . Come to Ground" (Iazykov), 109
"O Gladsome Light," 28, 185n35
"Stille Nacht! Heilige Nacht," 148
"Ten Songs about a Little Boy," 40, 115
"Toreador, go more quickly into the corridor!" 153
Sophia, Mother, 21, 184n26, 187n60
Soviet Union
Christianity, danger of, xv–xvi
church valuables to government, xxi–xxii
Council for Russian Church Affairs, 179n66
Renovationist Schism, 174n19
Renovationists declaration of loyalty, xxii
value system, 177n53
See also Renovationists
spiritual crusade (*dukhovnyi krestovyi pokhod*), xxxv
Spyridon, St., 77, 190n78
Sretenka Street, 108, 193n10
Stalin, Joseph, xxxvi, 179nn65–66
Stalinist era, xxxi–xxxii
St. Eustace (Khitrov), 109, 194n12
Stolobenskii, Nilus, 9
Struve, Nikita, xxii, 174n19
Sverdlovsk, 72

INDEX

Symbol of Faith (Nicene Creed), 8–9, 183n12
(Sytina) Maksimovna, Vera, 76, 190n76

Tarasovka, 16, 120, 184n20, 195n25
Tat'iana. *See* Kupriianova, Tat'iana Ivanovna (T.K. or Tania)
Tchaikovsky, Pyotr, xxvii, 193n11
Temple of the Transfiguration of My Son, 186n45
Tepnina, Mariia Vital'evna (Marusa), 40, 46, 74, 128, 186n46, 196n34
Thaw, the, 179n67
theosophy, 61
Tikhon, Patriarch (Vasily Ivanovich Bellavin)
  Aleksei Ivanovich Gabriianik and, 180n73
  arrest of, xxi, xxxiv, 173n14, 178n59, 178n60
  death of, xxii
  elected patriarch, 177n56
  Fr. Pyotr and, 179n70
  Fr. Serafim and, xxvi
  Fr. Sergii and, xxxvii
  opposition to Metropolitan Sergii, xxxvi
  Renovationists and, 177n57
  spiritual crusade and, xxxv
  on Truth, xxxii
  on WWII, 65
Tikhonov, Nikolai. *See* Nektarius, Optina Elder
Tillich, Paul, xix
Tiutchev, Fedor Ivanovich, 18, 60, 188n63
Tolstoy, Aleksei Konstantinovich, 109, 194n13
Tolstoy, Leo, xxvii, 109, 120, 195n27, 198n11
Tolstoy, Lev Nikolaevich (L.N.), 158, 166
Tonechka or Tonia. *See* Zaitseva, Antonina
"To the Muse" (Blok), 60
Trapani, Nina Vladimirovna, 99, 192n17
Trinity-Sergiev Lavra, xv, xxiv, xxvi, xxxviii, 23, 77, 175n26, 179n71, 184n28, 189n71
True-Orthodox Christians (Istinnopravoslavnye khristiane, IPKh), xxiii, 174n22
Tsuperfein, Elena (Men). *See* Men, Elena Semenovna (Lenochka)
Tsuperfein, Leonid (Elena's brother), 103
Tsuperfein, Volodia (Elena's younger brother), 103
Turgenev, Ivan, xxvii

Uncle Iasha. *See* Vasilevskii, Iakov Veniaminovich (Iasha)
Uncle Volodia (uncle of Vera Vasilevskaia), 83

Vasil'evna, Mariia (M.V.), xv, 146–47, 149
Vasilevskaia, Vera Iakovlevna
  baptism of, 9–10, 17–23, 118, 120, 169–70
  brother (Veniamin), 18, 38, 44–45, 56, 67–69, 74–76, 82, 86, 164
  called Verochka by Elena, 193n6
  children and, 3–4
  conceal and deception, 28, 31, 36
  confessions, 21, 23, 33, 40, 55, 61, 63, 117
  considers monastery, 33
  conversion to Christianity, xix
  Crimean or Sarov trip, 44
  crosses, wooden and silver, 23
  death, questions about, 137–38, 141
  dissertation, 42, 85–86
  F.A. and, 37–38, 66
  forest and nature, 43–44
  Fr. Serafim and, 31
  godchildren, 40, 72
  Gospel reading, 6
  grandmother and, 14, 138–40, 142
  health issues, 34–35, 83, 94, 167
  icons and, 25, 144
  Ieraks, Fr. and, 33
  Lenochka and, 10, 12, 23, 33–34
  letter N.V. Trapani, 99–100
  life of, xxix, xxx, xxxix
  marriage question, 40–41
  mother and, 1–3, 77–78, 140, 143
  negatives of Orthodox Church, 17–18
  at Nilus-Stolobenskaia Pustyn', 8
  at Optina Pystyn', 7
  path of the Christian life, 56
  photograph with Elena, 105–6
  photograph with her father and Veniamin, 164
  photograph with Zina, 3
  poetry and, 59–60
  protection of children in WWII, 65–68
  representations of Mary and Savior, 24
  Serafim, Fr. and, 4, 12–13, 24, 28, 37, 55–76
  spiritual disposition of, 42
  travel to monasteries, xvii, 134
  travel with family, 140, 143
  university years, 2–3
  wish for a child, 8

work of, 41–42, 66, 81–82
writing her story, xxxi, xxxii
Zagorsk, travel to, 11–12, 29
See also Diveevo; Judaism; schools and schooling; Serafim, Fr., letters; Vasilevskii, Iakov Veniaminovich (Iasha)(Vera's papa); Zaitseva, Antonina (Tonia Z.)
Vasilevskii, Iakov Veniaminovich (Iasha) (Vera's papa)
death of, 128
health issues, 82–83, 167
malnutrition during WWII, 68
photograph with Vera, *164*
remarriage, 38
Uncle Iasha, 104, 114–15, 120, 128, 170
Vera and, 46
Vasilevskii, Lev Markovich, 75, 189n73
Vasilevskii, Veniamin (Venichka), 109, 112, 120, 124, 141–44, 156
Vasilii Nikolaevich (V.N.), 154
Verochka. *See* Vasilevskaia, Vera Iakovlevna
Viktor Ernestovich (V.E.), 151, 153
Viktor Germanovich (V.G.). *See* Rikman, Viktor Germanovich (V.G.)
Vladimir, Fr., 34, 76, 79, 185n41, 186n46
Ivanovich, Vladimir (V.I.), 150–51, 153
Voino-Iasenetskii, Archbishop Luk, 180n78
Vsekhsviatskii, Konstantin, xxxvi

War and Peace (Tolstoy), 193n7
Williams, Rowan, xxviii
World War I, 155–56, 158–59

World War II, xxxv–xxxvi, 64–72, 82, 87
evacuation line, 196n33
fear of Germans, 73–74, 76
food and hunger in, 128–30
Men family in, 103, 123–27
ration card, 73
Verochka and, 124

Yasnaya Polyana, 158, 198n11

Zagorsk (Sergiev Posad), xxiii–xxiv
Archimandrite Serafim's house, *11*, 33
catacomb church of, xxv
Elena travel to, 10, 19
Fr. Serafim in, xxxviii, 64
Optina Pystyn' influence, xxix
parable of the mite, 20
St. Sergii and, 65–66, 189n71
in WWII, 76
WWII and, 70–71
See also Mariia, Mother Superior
Zaitseva, Antonina (Tonia Z.), 183n5
baptism of Alik, 115–16
birthday trip to Moscow, 19
book in memory, 5–6
friendship of, 4–6
friendship of Elena, 108–10
Fr. Serafim and, 120
Zatvornik, Bishop Feofan, 89, 95
Zealous Defender, 55
Zhukovskii, Vasilii Andreevich, 60, 188n66
Zinaida Apollonovna (Z.A.), 152–53
Zosima, Elder, xxviii, xxxviii, 108, 116

www.ingramcontent.com/pod-product-compliance
Lightning Source LLC
Chambersburg PA
CBHW021854230426
43671CB00006B/388